S0-AXC-849

Robert J. Kreyche LOYOLA UNIVERSITY • CHICAGO

The Dryden Press PUBLISHERS • NEW YORK

LOGIC

FOR UNDERGRADUATES

Fifth Printing, December 1957

Manufactured in the United States of America

Preface

FEW BOOKS QUALIFY AS IDEAL TEXTS. But instructors and students alike are realistically and, at times, painfully aware of the need for good textbooks. The purpose in writing this book was to satisfy the need for a good textbook in logic—"good," that is, for undergraduates who have had no previous training in this subject. To this end the author has endeavored to write a text that is reasonably simple, clear, and concise.

To be reasonably simple, a book of this nature must make its appeal to beginning students, not to professional scholars. Indeed, every competent instructor will attest that those books which best serve his own interests as a scholar are not necessarily the best for his students. Since this book is for beginners, the author has tried to guard against a narrow specialization, on the one hand, and a mere popularization of the subject, on the other.

If a textbook is to be clear, it must be written in language that students can understand. The language of the scholastic manual, even if translated into English, is hardly a suitable medium of communication for today's students. Although the substance of this text is based on traditional logic, the method of presentation attempted is modern. Evidence of this is found in the relation of traditional types of arguments to the language of modern discourse and in the abundance of illustrative examples that are, for the most part, original. These features are evident in both the text and the exercises. The author has long been convinced that no past work in logic should be considered so authoritative that even the most commonplace examples must be repeated verbatim in all succeeding texts.

To achieve conciseness, the author has abstained from needless digressions and undue repetition. As a teacher he agrees with the maxim that repetition is the "mother of study"; but in textbooks a faulty application of this principle can lead to tedious and confusing extremes. If an explanation is sufficiently clear, there is no point in "rehashing" it until the reader is no longer certain of his ground.

With respect to content, the reader will, it is hoped, discover for himself the features that distinguish this work from related texts. Attention is drawn here to a few special points. The preliminary remarks *To the Student* are intended to bridge the gap between the student's "common sense" estimate of logic and the technical treatment that follows. The treatment of the categories in Chapter 2 and of the predicables in Chapter 3 is so presented that the student may see the bearing that categories and predicables have on the important matter of definition. The emphasis, in the later chapters, on the constructive side of logic is motivated by the fact that few books in logic devote as much as a single page to helping the student construct an argument of his own. Theoretically, the student can be acquainted with the entire theory of the syllogism and yet be incapable of drawing up systematically a single argument of his own. Finally, the treatment of induction, in Chapter 15, though brief, avoids any oversimplification of the contrast that exists between induction and deduction. The point of the interrelatedness of these two distinct methods of knowing is stressed.

In general, this text represents an endeavor to incorporate the best elements of material and formal logic. This is evident, for example, in Chapter 11 in the discussion of the fallacy of four terms and in Chapter 12 in the distinction that is made between probable and demonstrative reasoning. The author believes that any attempt to *separate* material and formal logic, especially for undergraduate study, is inadvisable. Consider, for example, the importance of helping students distinguish the different meanings that terms acquire in usage and the consequent necessity of defining terms within the course of an argument—points of emphasis that would be completely lacking in a "pure" logic of form, structure, and symbol. For reasons of this kind, it is perhaps even more unwise to go to the often nominalistic extreme of a purely formal logic than to risk losing sight of the distinction between logic as matter and logic as form.

Like many textbooks, this one has had, prior to its publication in book form, a rather long career in the form of notes and experimental editions. The original stimulus for the present work was the growing conviction at Loyola University, of Chicago, of the need for a new text in logic. The inspiration for this book came in its greatest measure from the Rev. J. V. Kelly, S.J., who, during the years immediately following World War II, was Chairman of the Department of Philosophy at Loyola. To Father Kelly, for his guidance and encouragement, the author owes his greatest debt of gratitude. No small amount of thanks is due also to the present Chairman of the Department of Philosophy at Loyola, the Rev. Jeremiah C. O'Callaghan, S.J., with whose encouragement the present manuscript began its career on home grounds. The author also offers very special thanks to Mr. Thomas Buckley, one of his confreres, many of whose enlightening suggestions have literally been incorporated into the text. Thanks are due also for the helpful comments of Mr. Nelson La Plante, another of the author's confreres, and to all of the author's former students, who have so generously submitted themselves to this experiment over the years. Finally, to the unremitting encouragement and invaluable secretarial services of his wife the author owes the practical realization of this work.

ROBERT J. KREYCHE, PH.D.

Loyola University,
Chicago
July 1954

Contents

Logic

FOR UNDERGRADUATES

To the Student

Is Logic a Cure-all?

What Is Scientific Knowledge?

Scientific Knowledge and Common Sense

Limitations of Common Sense

Psychological Factors

A Word of Advice to the Beginner

A Definition of Logic

LOGIC IS A SCIENCE WHICH is essentially intended for use. There are many reasons why college students should study logic, and it is, in part, our purpose here to indicate at least some of these reasons. The present course is based in large measure on the traditional, Aristotelian logic. There are, as a matter of fact, other methods of logical analysis than those which Aristotle devised. But few such systems of logic have proved to be as relevant and practically sound as that developed by the founder of logic himself.[1]

[1] Aristotle (384-322 B.C.) was the first to have constructed in a series of treatises (later entitled the *Organon*) a system of logical inquiry. The titles of his treatises are as follows: (1) *Categories,* (2) *On Interpretation,* (3) *Prior Analytics,* (4) *Posterior Analytics,* (5) *The Topics,* and (6) *On Sophistical Refutations.*

It may be argued that today people think differently from the way they did in the time of Aristotle. Whatever element of truth there may be in a suggestion of this sort, it would be a very serious mistake to imagine that the way Aristotle thought and the way men *should* think today have *nothing* in common. There are, after all, certain universal and objective standards of thought that are valid for all men at all times, regardless of race, nationality, or religion. It is precisely because Aristotle expressed these standards of thought probably better than anyone else that his logic is still being taught. As a matter of historical fact, Aristotle was a Greek philosopher who wrote his treatises in the fourth century B.C. Yet, even if he were an American philosopher writing in the twentieth century, his logic would deserve the same thoroughgoing study that it now receives in many colleges and universities. The logic of Aristotle, therefore, is recommended to undergraduates today, not because of its antiquity, but rather because of its proved and lasting merit.

In a system of logic such as the one we are about to study there is very little room for what is popularly called freedom of thought. Obviously, freedom of thought *in the true and proper sense* plays a vital role in the functioning of a democratic society. But there are certain domains in which the question of freedom simply does not arise. In mathematics, for example, one is not free to think that two and two equal five. It is an objective, mathematical truth that two and two equal four. This is a truth that one is called upon to learn, not to question or dispute. Much the same holds true of logic. Logic is a science that one must study, learn, and apply. Considered in this light, logic is a discipline which, though largely forgotten, provides a most powerful antidote for much of the loose, ineffectual, and—shall we say—circular thinking that so often prevails in our modern round-table discussions.

It is assumed that the reader of this text has had no previous training in logic. This introduction, therefore, will attempt to give him some idea of the nature, scope, and utility of the subject he is about to study by presenting a nontechnical analysis of certain problems which should provide a suitable background for the more technical study of logic in the chapters which follow.

IS LOGIC A CURE-ALL?

The science of logic is not, as many people—including students—often seem to think, a sort of panacea. Logic, it is true, is an instrument or a means which, when put to proper use, will help the user gain the oft-sought—but less often attained—*desideratum* of sound thinking. As such, logic clearly helps one to organize and give direction to one's thinking activity, but it does not on any count relieve one of the actual thinking. The knowledge of logic is not, in other words, a sort of substitute for thinking through a problem on its own merits.

A student of logic who remarked (somewhat regretfully) to his instructor that "logic does not solve all the problems of life" was puzzled to get the reply that it does not solve *any* of them. The intent of this remark was, of course, to call attention to the fact that every problem must be met on its own ground. The knowledge of logic will, indeed, help one to face a problem in a more orderly, systematic fashion and will, in many cases, make the solution of the problem less difficult and more certain, but logic, of and by itself, will not solve the problem.

The mere drawing of a blueprint gives no assurance that the house will be built. It would be even more ridiculous to suppose that the drawing of the blueprint can take the place of the actual building. Yet it would be the height of absurdity for anyone, in an attempt to build a house, to proceed without some sort of plan or direction. The same holds true in the important matter of thinking. If thinking is merely casual, it is apt to be erroneous; and it is this type of thinking that logic seeks to prevent. In this respect it is the purpose of logic to see to it that human thought, whatever the problem at hand, is not reduced to chance.

WHAT IS SCIENTIFIC KNOWLEDGE?

Since we have referred to logic as a science, we should say something here about the meaning of "science." Customarily science is defined in some such terms as an organized or systematized body of facts. This type of explanation is to a certain extent misleading, for it seems to imply that science is to be found only in a laboratory or a book. In other words, there is the possibility that science may be identified with the various sensible objects that are used for its communication or its development. To think of science in this way is to overlook the very important fact that *science is essentially of the intellect.* Books, charts, diagrams, laboratories, and microscopes are, of course, important and, for their own purposes, indispensable. Yet, none of these objects taken separately nor all of them together constitute the essence of science or of *a* science. The reason for this is a simple one: Science fundamentally is *knowledge,* and knowledge is to be found only in the mind of the person possessing it.

Any person, then, who has science has knowledge. Yet, to "have knowledge" (scientific or otherwise) means to have it as a *habit,* that is, as something which is ready for use. Thus, in order that a person may know something, it is not necessary for him to be thinking of what he knows at any given moment. A vacationing biologist, for instance, need not be thinking about biology. When it is said, therefore, that a person *knows* something, it is meant that he possesses a certain *habit* of knowledge that he may or may not be putting to actual use. So with respect to science, we may say that it is a habit—a habit of knowledge that can be put to use whenever the need for doing so arises.

There are, of course, many habits of knowing, and not all of them are sciences. Further, there are many habits of *scientific knowledge,* depending, in part, on the nature of the object that is known. Some scientific habits are of the purely speculative type in which we come to know something merely for the sake of "finding out." Other sciences are of a *practical nature,* that is, of the sort that we know "in order to put to use." As we shall presently see, logic is, in the main, a practical science, one that is designed for use.

Some sciences, then, are pure, or speculative; others are practical. All of them, however, are habits of a certain kind. Now, granted that a scientific habit implies, of necessity, a certain organization of material, it does not follow conversely that because one's knowledge of a certain group of data is systematized it is by that very token scientific. For example, a telephone directory is an assemblage of well-organized material, but the knowledge that it gives is not science.

To know scientifically, then, means far more than to have at one's disposal a group of facts, information, or data. A person who is in the habit of a certain science is one who knows how to judge and interpret facts in the light of a uniform set of principles. Merely to know facts is to know *that* certain things are as they are; but to know scientifically is (in a very strict sense) to know *why* things are so and not otherwise. In a word, *to know scientifically is to know of things through their principles and causes.* Thus, a person who knows logic not only knows that a certain type of inference is valid, but also knows in the light of the principles which govern his science *why* it is valid.

SCIENTIFIC KNOWLEDGE AND COMMON SENSE

The expression "common sense" is frequently used but seldom is it clearly defined. Everyone apparently knows what *he* means by "common sense," yet the school of common-sense philosophers is hardly in a position to present a unanimous platform of agreement.[2] This does not mean, of course, that we should abandon the attempt to define "common sense." According to one way of looking at it, the person of common sense is one who, when confronted with a practical problem or situation, has a knack for sizing it up with a minimum of deliberation, and, having done this, straightforwardly finds the appropriate means to its solution. Such a person, in all probability, will not be able to give a detailed analysis of the reasons that entered into his decision. Yet, he will be firmly convinced that to have thought or acted otherwise would have been a mistake.

The point we are concerned with here is that although scien-

[2] It is not the author's intention here to enter into a full-fledged analysis of the difficult problem of common sense. Obviously the term "common sense" has a variety of meanings. The purpose of the present discussion is, in the main, to stimulate the student to a critical and reflective awareness of the meaning of a term that is very often taken for granted.

tific knowledge *transcends* common sense (in any way you may choose to define the term), it is not intended to contradict it. Therefore, when we say that logic is a science, we do not imply that logic is something completely alien to common sense. Actually, if we understand common sense as implying an ability to form certain basic types of judgment, we should rather emphasize that logic uses common sense as its very foundation. Viewed in this light, the principles and rules of logical science are not greatly different from the dictates of common sense. In many instances, logic merely makes explicit what is only implicitly contained in the judgments of common sense. Further, it carries those same judgments to a higher level and in so doing gives them a wider range of application.

LIMITATIONS OF COMMON SENSE

Doubtless the most confirmed believer in the validity of common-sense solutions would, if he were in need of a medical operation, be quite unwilling to entrust himself to someone who had nothing else to rely on than common sense. Nevertheless, allowing for the unlikelihood of any emergency call for a logician, the need for correct thinking, as evidenced at times in even the most highly professional circles, is apparent.

One can readily grant, of course, that there is a certain "natural logic" attainable without any formal study of principles and rules. The logician is neither so presumptuous nor so naïve as to believe that he has a monopoly on the powers of human reasoning. Yet he is equally convinced, and justifiably so, that the fallacious reasoning of many an otherwise intelligent person could easily be forestalled by acquaintance with the elementary rules of logic. The fact of the matter is that there is no individual, whatever his native talent, for whom the study of logic does not have advantages.

Most people, however, including students, can make no claim to genius. They must simply make the best of what they have. Greatly to be pitied is the person who from discouragement, laziness, or (worst of all) overconfidence in his own ability is content to "let things ride." For example, many a student when registering for a course in English composition has wondered why he should take a course in a language that he has been using all his life. If the instructor who corrects the student's first composition could share this point of view, there might be some justification for the student's attitude. The facts usually reveal the need for a laborious analysis of the parts of speech in order that at the end of the course the student may express himself with some degree of clarity and precision.

What holds true of *language* holds equally true of *thought.* Definition, division, the complex variations of judgment and inference—none of these are such haphazard processes as can be learned by mere common-sense observation. The purpose of logic as a science is to guide one's intellect in the performance of these operations toward a secure attainment of truth, *especially in those matters where the attainment of truth is difficult and involved.*

The human intellect has many limitations, not the least of which is the difficulty of sustained attention, especially on an abstract point of argumentation. As witness to this fact, note that even a group of experts engaged in a discussion relevant to their own field have difficulty centering their discussion around a few essential points. The need for logical discipline is further evidenced in public addresses in which speakers cannot come to a conclusion, either because they became so involved in their proofs that they forgot what they were trying to prove or because they had nothing to prove in the first place.

For the intelligent handling of topics that transcend the level of conventional weather conversation, something more than common sense is required. What is necessary (among other things) is a basic understanding of logic. The understanding of logic, in its turn, can be effected only by the laborious work of learning new terms, making new distinctions, analyzing different types of argument, and, in general, becoming familiar with a whole new technical apparatus.

Note: As a practical means of convincing yourself of the need for studying logic, the following experiment is suggested. In the exercises of Chapters 11, 12, and 13 are numerous examples of syllogisms, some of which are valid, others invalid. Sample some of these exercises with a view toward determining whether the inference in question is valid or invalid. The difficulty of doing this by common sense alone is a lesson that should be of great value in convincing you of the real, practical need for the study of logic.

PSYCHOLOGICAL FACTORS

The student should be realist enough to understand that the causes of incorrect thinking frequently lie beyond the pale of logic. Although the remarks we are about to make do not comprise part of logic, they nevertheless have some bearing on the student's approach to the subject. The student should realize, therefore, that many people who could think correctly on, let us say, matters of religion, education, world problems, and the like fail to do so largely because of the presence of any number of factors that constitute a *psychological hindrance.* In general, these factors are conditioned partly by the temperament and disposition of the individual himself and partly by his environment.

There are many people who do not think or who think wrongly because they are *too lazy* to think correctly. Under any circumstances, careful, painstaking thought requires a considerable expenditure of *effort.* For those who have never formed the habit, thinking can, indeed, be a rather painful sort of activity. Whether their intellectual stupor is caused by an overdose of television, beer, or even work, there are some who maintain that the activity of human living can go along quite well without very much thinking —especially if there is enough money in the bank. Were it not for the fact that many people are of this sentiment, we should be wasting our time in answering this type of broadside objection.

It is true, of course, that through undue deliberation some individuals become so heavily involved in their *thoughts* that they do not know how to *act,* and the result of all this is procrastination. In *Hamlet,* Shakespeare has given us a classic picture of just such a person. Had Shakespeare, however, wished to depict the type of man who lives in this busy, twentieth century, he would very likely not have chosen Hamlet.

This last statement does not, of course, imply that the twentieth century is intellectually and culturally bankrupt, even if it has had its weaknesses. The truth of the matter is that there is a growing trend in a strong nucleus of individuals and social groups as well toward the recognition of values that transcend the level of progress conceived only in terms of bigger and better appliances, automobiles, and airplanes. This trend is especially manifest in the younger generation of our day. In this respect, too, the second half of the twentieth century gives much greater promise of an appreciation for the higher things of life than has been evidenced in some of its earlier decades.

On the part of many individuals, however, the trend is still not in the direction of "too much" thinking, at least in the sense of serious, reflective thought. If it is objected at this point that serious thinking is all well and good, but one must, after all, make a living, we need but recall Samuel Johnson's reply to a young man who maintained this idea: "Sir, I question the necessity." Dr. Johnson's reply was not the kindest remark he ever made but it was to the point, which is this: It is serious reflective thinking that gives human life its meaning. Thinking is not, of course, the whole of human life, though it is, or at least should be, an integral part of it. Without some measure of serious, reflectful thinking, the concept of human living is reduced to the concept of bare existence.

Besides those who fail to think either because of laziness or chronic fatigue, there are always those persons who think that they think. The classic enemy of this type of "thinking" is Socrates, who spent a good part of his life in exposing the pretensions of the sophists. Socrates, it will be recalled, was told by the Oracle at Delphi that he was the wisest man in the whole of Greece. Not believing the word of the Oracle himself, Socrates went about buttonholing everyone he could find for an interview in the hope of discovering someone who was truly wise. The result of all this questioning led Socrates to the conclusion that the Oracle was right after all, since he was the only man, at least, who knew that he did not know, whereas all of the others thought that they did.

Even today many persons (including university and college graduates) on the basis of a superficial knowledge of many subjects are prepared "at the drop of a hat" to talk authoritatively about anything one may choose to discuss. The prototype of this sort of person is Hippias the Polymath, who boasted that he could outwit anyone in a conversation, whether the topic be politics, art, philosophy, poetry, medicine, education, or wrestling. How many people there are who are given to this sham type of wisdom is open to question. It is rather significant, however, that even among those willing to admit their other limitations, very few, if any, are prepared to admit that they *do not know how to think.*

There are, of course, many who consider themselves skeptics, even though their skepticism is only a disguise for their ignorance. People of this sort are willing to admit that they do not know, yet an admission of this sort is most often coupled with the understanding that "nobody else knows either." This kind of attitude is perhaps just as much a hindrance to sound thinking as the other extreme of pretending to know everything. Most often too it stems from the same source, namely, laziness, in the sense at least of an unwillingness to probe beyond what is merely superficial. If, on the other hand, a person seeks to become a thoroughgoing skeptic, he will always be frustrated in his attempt to do so, that is, if he is consistent in his skepticism. If a person is to be consistent in his skepticism, he cannot even be sure of his own doubts, and the result is a complete mental paralysis. Gorgias of Leontini, in Sicily, made a noble attempt in this direction when he set forth his three propositions: (1) nothing exists; (2) if anything did exist, no one would know it; (3) even if a person did know, he would not be able to tell it to others.

Another group of persons who think, but think badly, consists of those who indulge in wishful thinking. Their so-called "opinions" are contingent in large measure upon their personal feelings, emotions, and prejudices. Everyone, of course, has a right to his own opinions, but *an opinion, to be worth anything as an opinion, must be based upon some solid reason or reasons for maintaining it.* Moreover, there is a great difference between something that is held as an opinion and something that is known to be a *fact.* A person may, of course, have an opinion as to the *interpretation* of a fact or group of facts; yet, the fact itself is something that he knows, and he knows it as an object of certain knowledge.

Clearly, the reader does not at this moment have an opinion about his reading of this text. He simply *is* reading it, and this he knows to be a fact. Suppose, on the other hand, that the reader is of the opinion that the Democrats will win the next election. Unless he knows for a certainty—and who does in matters of politics?—that the election is "in the bag," he should be prepared to revise his opinion, if necessary. In other words, an opinion is always in some danger of being contradicted. Further, anyone who truly holds an opinion (as thus understood) will grant that he may be in the wrong. *There can be no such thing as a closed opinion.* One may very well suspect, therefore, that what so often passes as opinion is in some form or another a prejudice. Here we should add that a prejudice is, quite literally, a judgment that has been formed beforehand, that is, before a consideration of the evidence. A prejudice is, in short, a *rash* judgment.

In our present discussion of the *psychology*—as opposed to the logic—of human thinking, we should also point out that *the way people think is most often determined by the manner in which they live, and not conversely.* Theoretically, man as a rational being should decide how he is *going to act* by the manner in which he *thinks* he should act. In practice, however, people most often act first and only later begin to "think up reasons" to defend their conduct. When people do this, they clearly are not reasoning; they are *rationalizing.*

This tendency toward rationalization is especially evident in the way many people think about what is right and what is wrong in matters pertaining to morality. They may even go so far as to say that "everything depends on how you look at it," failing completely to realize that the way *they* look at things is largely determined by the way they *want* to look at them. Thus, in matters that affect and should affect their lives, even those people who are otherwise very capable thinkers are liable to give a poor performance. In any case, it is not the business of a logician to tell people *how* to think about one kind of thing or another, but merely to point out certain inconsistencies in the way that they do.

In addition to the factors inherent in the attitudes of the individual, there are many external factors that are inimical to sound thinking. Here we can only point out that there is much in our contemporary civilization that anesthetizes the mind rather than provokes it to activity. For example, a person who works on a factory production line has, unfortunately, little time for any significant measure of serious thought and few occasions that require it. Such a person is limited in his work to the monotonous performance of routine mechanical operations, and when he is away from work, his thinking is determined to a large extent for him in the advertisements and news stories that constantly demand his attention in high-pressure circulars and sensational newspapers and magazines. Freedom of thought in the sense of its being put to use is, to an appalling degree, an illusion.

In all of these considerations as to the need for serious thought and the psychological causes that militate against it, one should, of course, maintain a sense of perspective. It is a mistake to view everything and everyone (oneself included) with unrelieved seriousness. Indeed, were it not for the fact that people at times enjoy being illogical *in jest,* they would probably miss out on a great deal of harmless fun and enjoyment. If, on the other hand, a person knowingly or otherwise transfers the illogicality of his witticisms to the more serious concerns of life, his fun will no longer be harmless either to himself or to others.

A WORD OF ADVICE TO THE BEGINNER

Although the science of logic dates to antiquity, it is something new to the student. Very few high schools provide instruction in logic, and whether more of them should do so is a matter of debate.

Unlike such subjects as history, English composition, and mathematics, logic is a subject for which the average undergraduate in college has had no advance preparation. Accordingly, the difficulty that the student initially experiences in his study of logic is due in no small measure to his total unfamiliarity with the subject matter. It should be some consolation, however, that there is nothing to *unlearn* or revise. Best of all, perhaps, there is little chance of thinking that this is "old stuff."

The only pitfall—if there is any—is one of impatience and discouragement. To guard against these, the student should be mindful of the following remarks of the well-known American psychologist William James:

> ...A great mistake of my past life, which has been prejudicial to my education, is an impatience of *results.* Inexperience of life is the cause of it, and I imagine it is generally an American characteristic....Results should not be too voluntarily aimed at or too busily thought of. They are *sure* to float up of their own accord, from a long enough daily work at a given matter....[3]

A DEFINITION OF LOGIC

Logic may be defined as *the science that directs our mental operations* in such a way that they may proceed with order, facility, and consistency toward the attainment of truth. The mental operations referred to in this definition are the three basic acts of the intellect, namely, *conception* (or simple apprehension), *judgment,* and *reasoning.* Each of these acts is distinct from the others, although in our actual thinking processes all of them are integrally united. Here the student will note with profit that the main outlines of his entire course in logic are constructed on the basis of these three acts.

Since conception, judgment, and reasoning will be examined

[3] From a letter to Thomas W. Ward, 1868, as reprinted in *The Philosophy of William James* (ed. by H. M. Kallen), New York: Random House, Modern Library Series, pp. 303-304.

in their proper place in the text itself, it is not necessary to study them now. In general, it should be noted (1) that the term "thinking" usually refers to any one of the operations just mentioned, even though in its most proper sense it refers mainly to reasoning; and (2) that the three of these acts together, that is, as covered by the rather loose and general term "thinking," constitute the *material object* of logic. In other words, they comprise the *matter* which logic studies. Thus, *thinking* (conception, judgment, and reasoning) is *that about which* the study of logic is concerned.

Important as it is to know the material object of any given science, it is even more important to have an exact knowledge of its *formal object.* A moment ago we indicated that the material object of a science is the very subject matter or content with which that science deals. Now, by *formal object* is meant simply the specific point of view that dominates a study of the material object. This notion should not be too difficult to grasp if we consider, for instance, that three people who look at the same automobile may each be regarding it from a different point of view. Thus, a mechanic is interested in the way the car performs; a designer, in its styling; an upholsterer, in its interior appointments.

Frequently it happens that the material object of two different sciences is in part the same. It is thus that logic and psychology are partly in agreement with each other, since the psychologist, like the logician, is also interested in the mental operations mentioned above. The question that arises is simply this: How do these sciences which partly overlap differ in their formal object? This is, indeed, an important question, since it is by reason of its formal object that one science is essentially distinct from another. We cannot hope to give here a complete answer to the question just raised; yet we should at least indicate that the psychologist in his study of our mental operations is *not* interested, as the logician is, in how we *should* think. What the psychologist wants to know is how we *actually do think.* Thus, the psychologist's problem is mainly a problem of *fact.* In other words, a psychologist is interested in conducting a theoretical and descriptive analysis of our mental operations, possibly with a view toward determining their nature.

Although the logician too must have some conception of the nature of our mental acts, his is not merely a theoretical interest. Since logic, as we have already remarked, is a *practical* discipline, the logician is mainly interested in *norms, standards,* or *criteria.* Just as the formal object of ethics is to determine (by human reason) the norms of moral behavior, the formal object of logic too is a matter of norms. The norms that the logician attempts to establish are simply the *norms of correct thinking*. It is necessary, therefore, for a logician to know the meaning and nature of a *concept* in order to prepare the way for correct definition and division. This applies also to *judgment.* The logician must have a knowledge of the nature and different kinds of judgment in order to know, among other things, what role judgment plays in the process of reasoning.

Finally, the logician must have some insight into the nature of the act of *reasoning itself* in order to direct and order the reasoning act in a manner that is logically consistent. In general, the formal object of logic is to direct and guide all of our mental operations in a manner that is orderly and consistent.

In order that the student may enlarge somewhat on the notion of logic which he has acquired up to this point, we shall examine in the remaining part of our introduction some of the implications of the last part of our definition of logic. He will note that according to the definition logic helps to make thinking *orderly, less difficult,* and *consistent.*

The logician is interested, first, in obtaining *order* in our thinking processes. *Order,* in its turn, can be defined as the proper disposition of parts in relation to a given whole or unit. Good order prevails when every part is in its correct place, fulfilling its proper function, for example, as the furniture in your living room. Disorder results when a part is missing, when a part is placed outside of the relation that it bears to a given whole, or when an attempt is made to unite two parts that do not belong to the same unit.

It is easy enough to illustrate these points if we confine our attention to physical objects. Thus, there is disorder in your living room if all of the furniture is missing, or if the television set is too near the lounge chair from which you are accustomed to view it, or if a pair of orange drapes are hung against a red wall. It is far more difficult, however, to specify in the same dramatic fashion a case of *disordered thinking,* even though the disorder be just as real in our minds as in our living rooms. In any event there are numerous evidences of disordered thinking, for which the following violations of the rules of division may serve as indicators:

1. A MISSING PART. Suppose one divides *government* according to *different levels of administration* thus:

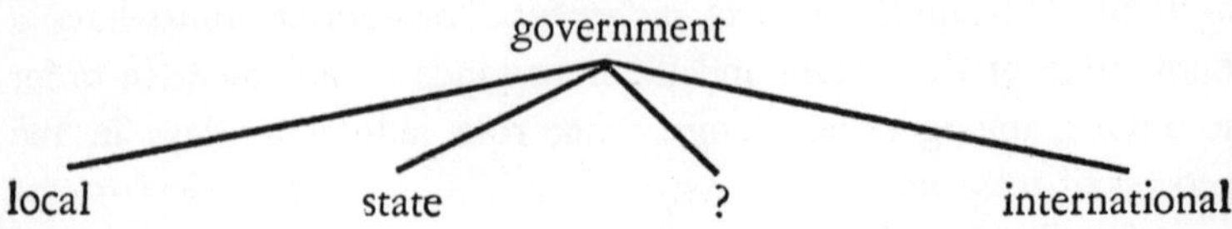

The omission here of "national" (government) involves a disorderly division and hence an illogical one.

2. A PART OUTSIDE OF ITS RELATION TO A GIVEN UNIT. If one were to include the United States as a coordinate member of the above division, this division would again lack the proper order. Thus:

3. TWO (OR MORE) PARTS NOT BELONGING TO THE SAME WHOLE OR UNIT. Although the following example is absurd, it will serve to illustrate our point:

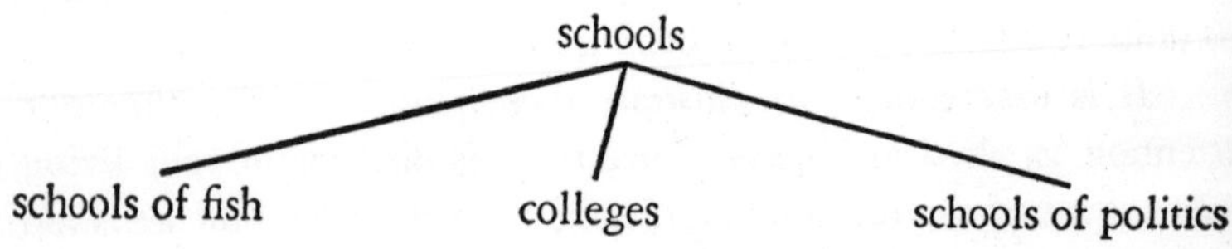

In our definition of logic we indicated that logic *facilitates* our thinking activity. Since this point is often subject to serious misunderstanding, we shall try to explain it. There are some people who mistakenly suppose that thinking, "once you know logic," is "as easy as falling off a log." This probably is the worst impression that one could have of the utility and scope of logic; it is even worse than the impression that logic is merely common sense. As a matter of fact, the student has already been warned of the danger of regarding logic as the solution for all his problems. Logic is no panacea, and the logician himself is the first to plead that point.

What we do have in mind when we say that logic "facilitates" our thinking is the fact, already set forth, that logic as a science is a *habit.* Now, one of the chief effects of any habit is a certain readiness of performance of those acts that are appropriate to the habit in question. What, then, are those acts that are appropriate to the *habit* of logic? Among other things, logic teaches us how to go about making good definitions and divisions and how not to make bad ones. Further, in familiarizing us with propositions, logic teaches us how to go about making proper implications and how to avoid those which are improper or wrong. Much of the same holds true of reasoning. Logic does not, of course, specifically tell us how to reason about politics, boxing, the movies. Yet it does tell us, if we are to reason correctly about these and about even more important matters, what general rules to observe and what general fallacies to avoid. In this way, and in no other, will a knowledge of logic help to make thinking easier.

When we say, therefore, that logic facilitates our thinking, we are merely applying the general truth of the popular axiom that the right way of doing things, once it is known, is a great deal easier than the wrong. Naturally, this does not imply that a baseball player will get a home run every time he swings his bat. What it does imply is that the prospective ball player, if he wants to get to first base, must at the very least learn how to hold his bat. The reason, therefore, why many people who sincerely try to think make a "mess" of it is simply that they do not know how. On the other hand, the reason why some people who know how to think do not actually do so is that they do not try. If, as a consequence, a person knows how to think and tries, none of his efforts will be wasted for lack of knowledge of the rules.

A mastery of logic, then, will ensure a certain measure of facility in the exercise of our mental operations, whether we are defining, dividing, implying, or reasoning. In order to acquire this mastery it is necessary for the student of logic to apply himself in a very special way with a view toward getting a genuine knowledge of the subject matter. If the student applies himself both diligently and intelligently, he should learn, among other things, how to reason not only correctly but proficiently. But the proficiency that logic as a habit produces can be maintained only through constant use. No habit can long endure unless it is regularly used. Even though the rules that originally instilled the habit are no longer committed to memory, the habit itself, *if put to use,* will persist.

Over and above the fact that logic makes our thinking more orderly and ready of performance, it also helps us to be consistent. As a matter of fact, consistency is so intimately bound up with logic that *to be logical* means, for the most part, to be consistent. Likewise to be illogical means, for the most part, to be inconsistent. In order, then, to get some notion of the meaning of logic, we must get some idea also of the meaning of the term "consistent."

A person is consistent, let us say, in his behavior toward his friends if he can be expected regularly to act in accordance with a few basic rules of good social conduct. There will be no sudden outbursts of temper, no unwarranted emotional displays, no sudden reversals of attitude. In much the same way, if a person is consistent in his reasoning, he will take care that each step in a given line of argument will follow naturally from the one that preceded it and that the whole process itself will be in accordance with the basic rules of correct thinking. Inconsistency, on the other hand, betrays itself when, for instance, someone unexpectedly draws a conclusion that is either completely unwarranted or is in some way or another beside the point. Any number of strange twists and turns characterize the thinking of persons who habitually take an argumentative "leap." In our later examination of fallacies we shall study some of the more flagrant types of inconsistencies.

In concluding this introduction let us briefly examine the very last part of our definition of logic. Logic, together with the order, facility, and consistency that it brings to bear on our thinking processes, is a pure means—*a means toward the attainment of truth.* Considered as a means or instrument, logic might conceivably be perverted to improper use. It may seem rather farfetched to imagine someone studying the science of reasoning with the avowed purpose of cultivating the shady "art" of deception. Yet, it would be a mistake to think that sophistry is purely an "art" of the past. In any event, the over-all intent of the study of logic is not victory in debate, but the discovery and communication of truth.

Truth, in general, is the *known conformity that exists between our judgments about things and the things themselves.* All our reasoning is for the purpose of arriving at *new* judgments that are *true.* As we shall see in Chapter 9, however, the correctness or validity of a reasoning process does not of itself guarantee the truth of a conclusion. To be true, a conclusion must be based upon *true premises.*

Even more urgent, then, than logic itself—that is, *formal* logic—is the need for a careful and critical examination of those judgments upon which, as premises, our reasoning process is based. Logic, of course, is to a certain extent an *aid* to critical thinking. At the same time, however, the right use of logic presupposes critical thinking. In any case, if the true purpose of logic is to be fulfilled, it is important to attend to the truth of our judgments. *Although the material truth of a judgment and the validity of a reasoning process are distinct from each other, they should never be separated in practice.*

I

The Concept

Characteristics of Our Sensible Experience
Origin of Concepts: Abstraction
Meaning of Conception, or Simple Apprehension
Meaning of Comprehension and Extension
Importance of Comprehension and Extension

INTRODUCTORY REMARKS. All human knowledge begins in the senses. It is through the external organs of sense that man, like the brute, makes his primary contact with the realm of external objects. In the earliest stages of childhood, in fact, knowledge is exclusively an affair of the senses. But human knowledge does not terminate in the senses, and as the child develops his distinctively human faculties, he acquires through his intellect a new kind of knowledge. This knowledge, though dependent upon sensation, goes beyond it. It involves, not only the seeing, touching, or tasting of different objects, but a mental grasp of them, an *understanding* (however inadequate) of their nature. When a child says for the first time "I see" in the sense of "I understand," he has passed beyond the stage of mere sense knowledge.

CHARACTERISTICS OF OUR SENSIBLE EXPERIENCE

The question that immediately arises is this: How do we as human beings come to an *understanding* of things? Or, in more technical terms, how do we account for the origin of our concepts? Do they arise in our sensible experience, and, if so, how?

To answer these questions we must first bring to light the nature of our sensible experience. Plainly enough, each of the senses has a special function to perform. It is the function of sight to perceive color, the function of hearing to perceive sound, and so on. Yet the data or impressions of sense, as reported through the external organs, are not of themselves sufficient to give us a *unified* impression of any given object—a piece of candy, for example. There must be, then, some centralizing agency of sense which coordinates these various impressions. This agency, which is a faculty of internal sensation, is known as common, central, or synthetic sense. The product of its coordinating, unifying activity is a single *sense image,* technically known as the *phantasm.* phantasm

The sense image or phantasm of a given object is not, however, the end-product of a person's understanding. That is to say, the phantasm is not to be confused with the concept itself. The difference between the phantasm and the concept will become evident from a careful inspection of the nature of each.

The elements, or *notes,* that compose the phantasm are no different in kind from the various sense impressions which make it up. Like the impressions that it embodies and unites, the phantasm is *concrete* and *particular.* The knowledge that I have of a book, let us say, as represented through the medium of a phantasm is an extremely limited sort of knowledge. From the standpoint of the phantasm alone, I do not even know that I am looking at a book. All that I perceive are the external, sensible characteristics of the extended object as it lies before me. I see its color; I feel its relative hardness or softness; I see on its cover certain markings which I do not know to be the letters of words. In short, I know nothing more about it than would a dog or a cat. Moreover, the sense image that I have of this individual book does not apply to another book whose external characteristics (such as color, size, and the like) are different. A phantasm, then, whether of a book or any other object, is *limited in its powers of representation to the individual object at hand.* It does not extend or apply to all the objects which I otherwise know to be of the same class.

ORIGIN OF CONCEPTS: ABSTRACTION

With these as the limitations, then, of my sensible knowledge of objects, another question arises: How do I get to know objects beyond their mere surface characteristics? Admitting that I do have *ideas* of these objects, are these ideas entirely unrelated to the order of my sensible experience? If a phantasm of a book is not an *idea* of a book, how do I get the idea?

Clearly, the idea, or, better, the *concept,* is not drawn from a vacuum. All our concepts are, as a matter of fact, based upon sensible experience. But how? To answer this question we must discuss the meaning of *abstraction.*

Abstraction is an activity of the intellect. By virtue of certain *active powers,* with which it is naturally endowed, the intellect focuses its attention upon the phantasm. In so doing the intellect reveals, or illuminates, the *intelligible* aspects, or notes, of the object in so far as they are implicitly contained or virtually present in the phantasm. To do this, the intellect disregards, as it were, the external, sensible, accidental features of the object in question. The chief concern of the intellect in viewing or contemplating the object through the medium of the phantasm is to learn something of the *essence* or *nature* of the object.

To clarify this last point, we must briefly explain that by the essence of an object we mean *that by reason of which a thing is what it is.* In other words, the essence is that which makes an object the kind of thing that it is. It is because of its essence that a thing belongs to one class or species of objects rather than to another. The essence man, for instance, is that which makes a man to be a man and not an animal or a plant. Thus, if one were to inquire as to the essence of man, it would be incorrect to identify this essence with some such characteristic as the color of the hair or the complexion of the skin. These latter characteristics are only accidents which vary from one individual to the next. Blond hair or a fair complexion does not make the man, for if such were the case, all men would have to be blond or all would have to have a fair complexion. The essence, then, is uniformly present in all members of a species and makes them what they are.

The point of this analysis is to show that the senses do not grasp the essence, but only the sensible, accidental characteristics of the object that they perceive. Only the intellect *by means of abstraction* can achieve some knowledge, however imperfect, of the essence. In view of this fact one can see the pointlessness of trying to perceive or imagine the essence of an object as though the essence were something sensible. It is ridiculous for anyone to imagine that he can get at the essence of an onion by peeling off layer after layer or to imagine that he can discover the essence of a desk by looking in one of its drawers.

Suppose, then, that we consider a book. We may not be able to say in so many words what makes it a book and not some other object. That is, we may not be able to *define* it. Yet, by means of abstraction we do know something about it beyond its color or size: we know that it is something to be read, for example. At the moment of writing this text, the author has no idea whether the finished book will be orange, green, blue, or some other color, nor does he know the thickness of the cover or the size of the type. But he does know that he is writing *a book,* that it is *a textbook,* that it is a textbook which *should be studied,* and that it should be studied by *college undergraduates* who are taking the *course in logic.* It is this kind of knowledge that the intellect seeks, knowledge which it acquires by abstraction.

When the intellect abstracts, therefore, it considers its object from a point of view not shared by the senses. Both the internal and external senses are incapable of "ferreting out" the essence, nature, meaning, or purpose of the object perceived. The reason is not that the object itself is unintelligible. Every object is, as a matter of fact, *intelligible;* it has the *capacity,* or *potency,* for becoming actually understood. However, the senses do not have the power to bring the intelligibility of the object out into the open; they do not have the active capacity to make *actual* the potency of the object to be understood. This is rather the work of the intellect, which accomplishes the task through its active powers of abstraction.[1]

Concept

The result of abstraction is the formation of an image that is intellectual and nonsensuous: namely, a *concept.* Like the phantasm, the concept is a representation of an object. Yet, it represents those notes (that is, aspects or elements) of an object which are intelligible and which escape our sensible knowledge. The concept reveals or manifests those essential characteristics that any object has in common with others of the same class. The concept of "book," therefore, is not, like a phantasm of an individual book, limited, let us say, to the one that lies on my desk. On the contrary, it represents first and foremost what is common to *all* books, and it applies to all the objects that belong to the class "book." For this reason, the concept—unlike the phantasm, which represents only particulars—is *universal.*

Any concept, then, such as "body," "organism," "plant," "animal," "man," is universal because it directly represents, not one individual or many individuals as such, but a certain essence or nature belonging to all individuals of a class. This essence, or nature, for which the concept stands, is, of course, realized *in* individuals. If it were not, we could not have abstracted it in the first place. But the main point is this: The concept itself, as it represents a certain essence or nature, is universal; for this reason it can be applied to all the individuals of a class. The various ways

[1] Whenever the intellect abstracts, it considers the object in one or more of its intelligible notes. This it does with regard mainly to a part or the whole of the *essence* of the object at hand. It must not be thought, however, that the work of intellectual abstraction is confined *solely* to a knowledge of the essence. Accidents, too, are intelligible. For instance, the intellect may confine its attention to one of the object's accidents, as when it considers the color of a watermelon, let us say. Therefore, although accidents are of themselves the direct object of sense perception, the intellect can still know *in its own way* the accidents as well as the essence.

in which a concept or a term can be applied will be discussed in the chapters that follow.

The following points of explanation are given partly to summarize what has been said thus far and partly to prevent misunderstanding in our study of the concept.

1. Intellectual abstraction does not involve positive denial of the sensible notes of an object. In abstracting an essence, the intellect simply withholds any explicit consideration of the sensible notes of the object. Thus, when a person thinks of an apple as *fruit,* he is not explicitly considering its redness.

2. The concept does not involve a replacement of the phantasm. When by means of a concept we come to some understanding (if only in an imperfect way) of what a thing is, a phantasm still remains. In fact, whenever we conceive of an object, we also have in our consciousness some kind of phantasm, however vague. When a person thinks, for instance, about "country," some kind of sense image (such as that of a geographical outline) will appear. *Note:* Apart from the question of pure or imageless thought, it is true that in our ordinary experience, at least, concepts are characterized by the presence in some degree of some kind of sense image or phantasm.

3. The presence of a sense image accompanying the thought of any given object does not in any way mean that the sense image *is* the concept. The dependency of concepts upon phantasms does not, in other words, imply the identity of the two. In fact, once we have a concept of a given object, the kind of phantasm which accompanies the concept is inconsequential. For example, once a person knows what "flag" is, it makes little difference whether he imagines an American, British, or Russian flag. The point is that he knows by means of his concept of "flag" the common nature of the object. He knows the object as a *class.*

That there is a sharp distinction between a concept and a mere sense image is further evidenced by the fact that two people may be thinking of the same thing even though they picture it differently in their imagination. If this were not the case, it is hard to see how two or more people engaged in a conversation could ever be sure that they were talking about the same thing. Further, the same person may at different times imagine an object in different ways, even though he thinks of it, or conceives it, in the *same* way.

4. To say that the concept is universal does not deny the capacity of the intellect for a knowledge of *singulars,* that is, individual things. Our discussion here, however, is to show that the intellect chiefly regards the essential characteristics in things.

5. The concept, like the phantasm, is a *representation.* We should never think of a concept as though it were a thing. On the contrary, the concept is simply a sign by means of which something is understood. *Note:* The meaning of a sign, that is, as referring to something beyond itself, will be discussed in the next chapter and applied to both terms and concepts.

MEANING OF CONCEPTION, OR SIMPLE APPREHENSION

The act or process by which the intellect forms a concept and hence comes to know what a thing is does not of itself involve the more complex act of judgment. The intellect, in forming a concept, simply apprehends something about the object that it contemplates. This act, known as *conception,* or *simple apprehension,* is defined as *an act whereby the intellect knows an object, but without either affirming or denying anything of it.*

Affirmation and denial are, as we shall see in Chapter 4, proper to the act of judgment, and conception, or simple apprehension, is preparatory to judgment. Moreover, once we have understood that simple apprehension results in concepts, not in sense images, it will be clear that when we *judge* (or, for that matter, *reason*), we do so through the medium of our *concepts of things,* that is, through our *intelligible* representations of them, and not through the medium of our sense images as such. It follows, then, that we judge and reason about things, not according to the way we *imagine* them (sensibly), but according to the way we *conceive* them (intelligibly).[2] For example, we may imagine a doctor as *one who goes about with a little black bag,* but we are aware that this sense image is not our *concept* of doctor. Accordingly, when we begin to judge or reason about "doctors," we judge and reason about them as *intelligibly conceived,* rather than as imagined.

An understanding of this important point should prove of considerable aid to the student in getting at a genuinely theoretical understanding of the real nature of judgment and reasoning. There is also a practical application of this for the student. He is in a better position to form *correct* definitions, divisions, and reasonings to the extent that in his concepts he does not rely too heavily on his sense images.

In concluding our analysis, it will be helpful for us to keep in mind the following terms and distinctions:

The Object

The object of knowledge, in general, is something which is known either as an individual thing (for example, Fido) or as a certain nature (for example, dog). The object of *sense* knowledge can only be something concrete, material, and extended. The object of *intellectual* knowledge can be concrete (chair) or abstract (beauty), actual or only possible.

The Faculty

A faculty of knowledge (for example, the intellect) is an *immediate* principle of operation whereby we come to know a given object. The *remote* principle of operation is the person doing the sensing, imagining, or thinking. In traditional terminology a faculty is often referred to as a "power."

[2] From one point of view, however, this is a question of "more or less." Many people are not trained to think "abstractly," and, failing to form proper "conceptions," they are very much inclined to judge and reason about things in a manner too closely associated with their sense impressions.

The Act

An act of knowledge is the operation involved in our coming to know an object. Each faculty exercises an act or acts appropriate to its nature. Although there are three fundamental acts which the intellect performs, our present concern is with the act of *simple apprehension,* as involving the use of abstraction and as resulting in a concept.

The Product

The product of each act of knowledge is the result or term (that is, terminus) of the act. The product of the first act of the mind is the *concept.*

MEANING OF COMPREHENSION AND EXTENSION

Once the student understands that a concept is an intellectual means of representation, he should have little difficulty in grasping what logicians refer to as its *comprehension* (intension, connotation). Every object has within itself certain distinguishable features or characteristics that are *capable of being understood.* These are the *notes of the object.* These same notes as *actually understood* are the *notes of the concept itself.* The *essential* notes, for instance, of the concept *plant* are substance, material, living, nonsentient. These are the notes of the concept "plant" which go to make up its *comprehension.* The comprehension of the concept, then, is simply *the embodiment of its essential notes.*

Comprehension must not be thought of as something really different from the concept itself. The comprehension of a concept *is* the very concept. It is the concept regarded simply from the standpoint of its *distinguishable contents or notes.*

In addition to its comprehension, that is, intension, or connotation, a concept has *extension,* or *denotation.* Extension is not the concept itself, but rather the objects to which the concept refers or applies. The extension of "plant," for instance, includes all the subclasses and individuals to which the concept applies. Clearly, *class concepts* are universal in that they can be applied to all members comprising their extension. When, however, in an act of judgment we actually put a concept to use, *we may or may not apply it in its full extension.* If we do apply it fully, the concept is said to be *distributed* or *universal;* if not, it is either *singular* or *particular.* This division will be explained in the next chapter.

IMPORTANCE OF COMPREHENSION AND EXTENSION

For the logician, the importance of distinguishing between the comprehension and the extension of a concept can hardly be overstressed. The failure to make this distinction or the attempt to understand the concept solely in terms of its extension has often led to a serious misunderstanding of the nature and validity of logic.

The significance of this distinction between comprehension and extension is emphasized by the fact that when we put our concepts to use in our judgments and reasonings, sometimes the comprehension, and sometimes the extension, predominates in our thinking. It is never a question of one *or* the other. The question is simply which point of view—comprehension or extension—*predominates.*

If we consider a certain object chiefly from the viewpoint of its comprehension, then the "object" that we are considering is a certain *nature.* Now, to consider a certain nature as such (whatever that nature may be) is to consider it, as we have already pointed out, *in abstraction from the individuals* that have that nature. Thus, when I judge that "A dog is a better pet than a cat," it is only *implicitly* that I may be thinking of *individual* dogs or cats. In other words, it is only by an implicit reference that I may be considering the *extension.*

On the other hand, if we consider only individuals, and not their nature as such, we are then employing a concept with primary reference to its extension. Suppose, for instance, that a person makes this judgment: "All of the boys in the Jones family are heavy eaters." He is not explicitly considering here the nature of "boy" or the nature of "family" as such. What he does have in mind are *all* of the boys who belong to *this* family. In this case, it is the extension of "boys" and "family" that predominates, even though some comprehension of their meaning is involved.

CONCLUDING REMARKS. In the next chapter we shall discuss the meaning of "term" and examine several of its divisions. Although terms are not to be identified with concepts, some of the things that can be said about terms can also be said of concepts, and vice versa. Terms are a means of expressing what our concepts represent, and it is as correct to speak of the comprehension and extension of a *term* as of a *concept.*

EXERCISES

1. What is man's original means of contact with the external world?

2. Is the human mind equipped with concepts at birth?

3. State in your own words the problem of the origin of concepts.

4. Are the external senses of themselves sufficient to give a unified impression of any given object?

5. What are the characteristics of a phantasm? of a phantasm you have of some newspaper, billboard, neon sign?

6. Is the phantasm of itself sufficient for one to know *what* each of these objects is? If not, give reasons.

7. What does the intellect do when it abstracts?

8. What does the concept reveal about an object? Explain.

9. What is meant by saying that the concept, unlike the phantasm, is universal?

10. Once we have a concept of a given object, does a sense image of it appear in our consciousness? Explain.

11. What reason or reasons can you give for showing that the phantasm is not the concept?

12. Are concepts *objects* of knowledge?

13. Carefully explain and illustrate the following statement:

When we judge or reason, we do so, not through the medium of sense images as such, but through the medium of our concepts.

14. Define and explain *simple apprehension.*

15. Contradistinguish (and exemplify the use of) each of the following terms: (a) object of knowledge; (b) faculty of knowledge; (c) act of knowledge; (d) product of an act of knowledge.

16. (a) What do you understand by the notes of a concept? (b) List one or more of the notes in your concept of "tree," "justice," "library." (If you can give a completely satisfactory list of the *essential* notes of these objects, observe that you are really *defining* them.)

17. (a) What is the comprehension of a concept? (b) Is the comprehension of a concept different from the concept itself? If not, is there any distinction at all?

18. (a) What is meant by the extension of a concept? (b) In what sense is a class concept—the concept of "organism," for example—said to be universal?

19. In putting a concept to use we sometimes have chiefly in mind its comprehension; at other times, its extension. Illustrate.

20. Do you think that a concept is the same as a term? If you cannot give a completely satisfactory answer to this question now, return to it after you have studied the next few pages.

2

Terms

Terms and Concepts as Signs

Distinction between Term and Word

Definition of Term

Terms and Concepts as Categories

Terms and Their Uses

INTRODUCTORY REMARKS. The logician's interest in terms centers around the role that they play as parts of a proposition or a syllogism. Most propositions (that is, categoricals and modals) are resolvable, from the standpoint of their matter or content, into two terms—a subject and a predicate. The subject term of a proposition is that about which the proposition gives information; the predicate term gives information about the subject. Hence, to predicate means to say something about a subject. Most propositions, then, are statements which embody a subject and a predicate term. In order that the proposition may have meaning, the terms themselves must express something that is intelligibly significant. A term, in order to be a term and thus function either as subject or predicate of a proposition, must *signify some object of thought* as attained or grasped in the first act of the mind, that is, in simple apprehension.

TERMS AND CONCEPTS AS SIGNS

In stating that it is the function of a term to *signify,* we mean that a term is a certain kind of *sign;* and a sign is *anything which points to something beyond itself.* In common with most types of signs, a term is something sensible, that is, *perceptible* by means of the senses. Thus, a term is something that we can *see, hear,* or even (if we used Braille) *feel.* As we read the letters of the word M-E-A-L, we not only understand the meaning of that word but see its letters. In fact, we could not *communicate* the meaning of this term unless we could make someone else *perceive* it.

Concepts and terms are both signs, but there are important points of difference. One is that concepts, unlike terms, are neither sensory nor sense-perceptible. We do not, after all, imagine a concept, far less see, hear, or feel it. Another difference is that terms are *conventional* signs, whereas concepts are *natural* signs. For example, the English term "father," signifying a male parent, is a conventional sign. It is natural, of course, for man to use terms, because, if he could not, it would be impossible for him to give adequate expression to his thoughts; and it is *natural* for man to want to do this. Nevertheless, the terms that he uses are not themselves natural signs. All terms are conventional signs, because their meaning is determined by usage. The very multiplicity of languages helps to show that terms are conventional rather than natural signs.

Although the concept is a natural sign, not every natural sign is a concept. There are many natural signs that are sensible—smoke as a sign of fire, for example. In any case, whether a natural sign is sensible or intellectual (a concept), it is not something that we arbitrarily construct for ourselves. This important point emphasizes the *necessary* character of our knowledge of things and the relatively arbitrary meaning of terms.

DISTINCTION BETWEEN TERM AND WORD

We may describe a term as a sensible, conventional sign which consists of a word or significant combination of words which may serve as subject or predicate of a proposition. Yet can *any* word function as a term? Clearly, certain words, mainly articles, prepositions, and conjunctions (*the, a, of, with, and, or,* and so on), cannot by themselves function as terms. The reason is plain: Words of this sort of and by themselves do not signify an object of thought. These words take on meaning only when used in conjunction with certain other words, such as "house," "tree," or "zoo." Words of this latter sort, which do have an independent meaning, can function by themselves as terms.

Terms are either simple (one significant word) or complex (a combination of words). Even if a term is complex (as most terms are in their usage), it may nevertheless signify a single object of thought, that is, an object conceived or grasped by the mind as a unit. These multiworded expressions are examples of complex terms signifying a single object:

The man who lives next door.
Whoever wins the next election.
The last person who entered this room last night.

DEFINITION OF TERM

With the above considerations in mind, we may define a term as *a word or combination of words which conventionally signifies an object of thought.* The student should carefully relate each part of this definition to the distinctions and explanations already set forth. Thus:

1. If a term is simple, it is a word that stands by itself; for example, man.
2. If a term is complex, it is a combination of words.
3. "Conventionally signifies" means that a term is a conventional sign as opposed to a natural sign.

4. "Object of thought" expresses *that which* the term signifies: something grasped by the mind in the act of simple apprehension.

TERMS AND CONCEPTS AS CATEGORIES

Now that we have seen what is meant by a term, we shall examine its various divisions. A division is always made from some point of view. Generally speaking, two such points of view are possible with respect to terms. A term may be considered solely from the point of view of *what it represents,* that is, independently of the way it is actually used in a proposition; or it may be considered from the point of view of its use. When we consider terms from the first point of view we are considering them as *categories.*

Before going on, the student should know *why* we study the categories in logic. A knowledge of the categories gives a person the theoretical satisfaction of knowing in advance what kind of predicates he can apply in a proposition in order to increase his knowledge of any given subject. Considered in this light, the categories are a list of possible predicate terms.[1] A knowledge of the categories also serves the practical advantage of knowing how to go about making good definitions. This will be developed in the next chapter.

Not every term or concept is a category. Actually, the categories are a list of only those terms and concepts that are *most general* in their signification. Take the term "red," for example. In one respect this is a general term, since it includes different shades of red. Yet, from another point of view, "red" belongs to the even more general "category" of "color." But since "category" as we understand it in logic is not *any* general term, but one so general that *it cannot be fitted into some other category,* there is an *ultimate* category to which both "red" and "color" belong. This category is

[1] There are a limited number of terms which cannot be fitted into a category: notably *being, one, true,* and *good.* Terms of this sort signify something that is realized in different ways in *all* of the categories. The study of these terms, however, and what they signify belongs, not to logic, but to metaphysics.

"quality." It is an *irreducible* category—the kind of category that we look for in logic.

Since terms and concepts (in their ordinary signification) refer to *things,* it is only reasonable that the categories of logic should be based on the order of things themselves. In deriving the categories, then, it is necessary to ask the question: What are the things to which terms and concepts refer?

Strictly speaking, there is only one kind of "thing," and that is *substance.* Examples are dog, plant, stone. Yet we also consider as real (though in a different sense of the term "real") *what belongs to* substance—size, shape, color, age, and so on. These latter characteristics are properly designated as *accidents.* The reality of an accident is to be "in" a substance, that is, as modifying or determining it in some way or another. An accident is not some *thing* which is real in its own right. Thus, the "reality" of "being old" is the reality of an accident belonging to a certain substance. Everything that exists, however, exists either as a substance or as an accident, and accidents do not exist by themselves.

Let us pause here and sum up what we have said thus far:

1. The categories of logic are a list of terms and concepts so general and universal that they cannot be reduced to some other category.
2. These terms and concepts are *based on* and *refer to* the order of things themselves.
3. The things, or aspects of things, to which the categories of logic refer are either substance or accident.

How many categories are there? The basic category is "substance." The other categories, of which there are nine, are decided by the different ways in which a substance is modified or determined by its accidents. The following is a list of the categories, together with examples of each.

1. *Substance*

This is the most basic of the ten categories, since "substance" refers to a *thing* in the proper sense of the word, that is, something which exists in itself and in its own right. The predicate term of each of the following propositions belongs to the category "substance":

The black bass is a *fish.*
This plant is a *rose.*
Savages are *men.*

Note: The category "substance" is regarded in logic as a *universal,* that is, as a universal nature that answers to the question of *what* a thing is.

2. *Quality*

The category "quality" is an accident that determines a substance with respect to its formal characteristics or attributes. This accident includes such varied phenomena as habits and dispositions, different types of capacity or the lack thereof, sense qualities, figure, and shape. For example:

This man *knows how to play the piano.*
Animals are *endowed with instinct.*
The meal was *delicious.*
Some buildings are *octagonal.*

3. *Quantity*

"Quantity" is a distinctive characteristic of corporeal substances; it is an accident by reason of which a corporeal substance is three-dimensional, having parts that exist outside of parts. Whenever we designate a corporeal substance with respect to such factors as its weight or size, we are referring to the accident "quantity." Thus:

This package weighs *five pounds.*
A yard is *three feet long.*
Some phenomena are *of microscopic dimensions.*

4. *Relation*

By reason of a certain reference that it bears to another, a substance is characterized by the accident "relation," as in the following:

This young man is a *father.*
You are my *superior.*
New York is *more heavily populated than Chicago.*

5. *Action*

"Action" is the accident whereby one substance is characterized as producing a certain effect upon another. For example:

Rover is *chasing a rabbit.*
My sister is *preparing the dinner.*
The policeman is *waving his club.*

6. *Passion*

The accident "passion" is the correlative of action. It connotes being acted upon, the receiving of an effect from another. Thus:

The public is *being victimized.*
The patient is *undergoing an operation.*
Your package is *being sent through the mail.*

7. *Time*

The accident "time" refers to the order of past, present, or future events. For example:

The meeting is *tomorrow.*
Today is *Wednesday.*
The child is *ten years old.*

8. Place

"Place" is the accident which determines a substance with respect to other surrounding bodies. For example:

My husband is *at home.*
The convention is *in Philadelphia.*
My trunk is *in the attic.*

9. Posture

The accident "posture" characterizes a substance with respect to the relative disposition of its parts in space. Thus:

The audience is *seated.*
The champion is *flat on his back.*
The heads of the students are *nodding.*

10. Habitus

Not to be confused with "habit," the accident "habitus" determines a substance with respect to apparel, costume, physical equipment. Thus:

The horse is *saddled.*
Mary is *attired in her evening gown.*
Our soldiers are *wearing bullet-proof armor.*

When placing a term in its proper category, the student should keep in mind the following considerations:

1. If it is possible to place a term within more than one category, ask the question: To which category *primarily* does the term refer?

2. If the term refers to only a *part* of a substance, place it reductively within the category "substance."

3. If the term refers to the *lack* of a certain quality, place it in the category "quality."

TERMS AND THEIR USES

There are many different ways in which terms are used in propositions; further, *how* a term is used most often determines its meaning. In the language of logic, the "supposition" of a term, that is, its meaning in context, frequently varies from one predication to the next. The following list of the way terms are used should be sufficient to guide the student in his subsequent study of inference. In general, for any inference to be valid the supposition of a term must be uniform.

The Univocal, Equivocal, and Analogous Use of Terms

THE UNIVOCAL USE OF TERMS. If the meaning of a term as applied to two or more objects is the same for each object, the term is being used in a *univocal* sense. To use Aristotle's example, the term "animal" (a sentient being) is univocally predicable of *man* and of *ox,* for if someone were to state in which sense each of them is "animal," the statement in the one case would be the same as that in the other (*Categories,* Ch. I, 1a, 8-12). Thus, the term "animal" has the same meaning with respect to both man and ox.

Of particular importance to logic is the fact that all class names are *univocally* predicable of the members which comprise their extension. Thus, the term "plant" as applied to different kinds of beings possessing vegetative life (tree, shrub, rose) is univocally predicable of them. Or again, if one applies the term "tree" to elm, oak, or maple, he is applying it in an identical, univocal sense. This is often said to be the "proper" use of a term.

THE EQUIVOCAL USE OF TERMS. The equivocal use of terms is, in effect, the ambiguous use of terms which are in themselves univocal. A term is used in an equivocal sense when it has totally unrelated meanings as applied to two or more objects. It is an accident of language that one and the same term can stand for two unrelated types of object. Thus, the term "ruler" might signify a measuring stick or, in an altogether different context, someone who governs a country. Most puns are based upon equivocation.

THE ANALOGOUS USE OF TERMS. Generally speaking, a term is used analogously when, as applied to two or more objects, it has different, *though not unrelated,* meanings. Thus, when a term is used analogously, it undergoes a partial shift of meaning, depending on the context. Note the difference of meaning in the underlined terms of the following:

Heavy taxes are a *burden.*
Carrying a load of groceries is a *burden.*

One of the most common instances of the analogous usage of terms is the metaphor. It is a curious fact, for instance, that men apply the names of many different animals, such as, "fox," "beaver," "lion," "tiger," "fish," to their fellow men, in accordance with the characteristics they wish to stress. However, not every instance of the analogous use of a term is metaphorical. There are different kinds of analogy, of which the metaphor is the most obvious.

Here are other examples in which a term is used analogously, though not metaphorically. The first is the term "judgment." It may be applied either to the *act of judgment* or to *a* judgment which results from the act. Again, note the difference of meaning in the use of the term "democrat" as it refers to a member of the *Democratic* party and to one who advocates *democracy* as a form of government. The two meanings given for each term are not, of course, unrelated; yet there is a difference of meaning. Nor is the use of the term in either case metaphorical.

Language is not so stable that a term will always have the same meaning, no matter what the context is in which it appears. Many people, however, for want of a certain discipline in distinguishing the different meanings that terms acquire in their usage, too often fail to look beyond the term itself, that is, to the object for which it stands.

The Collective and Divisive Use of Terms

COLLECTIVE USE OF TERMS. A term is taken collectively when the predication made applies to the subject *considered as a group or a unit* and not to the individuals that come under its extension. Take the proposition:

All the angles of a triangle are equivalent to two right angles.

Here the predication *equivalent to two right angles* is made in such a way as to apply to the subject taken only as a unit and not to the three angles taken separately.

DIVISIVE USE OF TERMS. A term is taken *divisively* when the predication made applies to each *individual* coming under the extension of the subject term.

The girls in our family have blond hair.
The members of our team are six feet tall.

In these examples the predicate is applied to *each* of the members falling under the extension of the subject.

Occasionally it is difficult to decide whether the subject is to be taken in a collective or a divisive sense. For example:

The audience applauded vigorously.

In an example of this sort one should take the statement in its *most obviously intended sense.* Although it may possibly be true that *each* and *every* member of the audience applauded vigorously, it is also a fact that, even if one or two members refrained, *the statement itself would remain true.* The most obviously intended sense of this proposition is a collective one.

Furthermore, although some terms are of their very nature collective, this fact need give us little cause for concern, since the question is simply that of their *logical use.* Take the term "organization," for example, in the following proposition:

All organizations have a chairman.

Even though the term itself is collective, it is here being used divisively, since the predicate is applied to each and every organization. Now, use the same term in another proposition:

Our organization has ample funds.

Quite evidently the predicate term in this example is being applied to the group as a group and not to the individual members of "our organization."

It is important for purposes of reasoning to distinguish between the collective and the divisive use of a term. Suppose that, in connection with our last example, I reason thus:

> Our organization has ample funds; since I am a member of it, I too have ample funds.

In this case, my reasoning would be invalid because I failed to distinguish between the collective and divisive use of a term.

The Extension of Terms

The extension of a term is the application of it in a given proposition to *all, some,* or *only one.*

UNIVERSAL TERMS. A *universal* or *distributed* term is one which, as used in a proposition, is applied (whether affirmatively or negatively) in its *complete* extension. It is *distributed* to all the members of a given class. For example:

> *All men* seek happiness.
> *No plant* is capable of locomotion.

The usual signs of universal extension are such words as the following:

all	whatever	no
each	whoever	none of
every	any	no one
everyone	anyone	nobody
everything	anything	nothing

PARTICULAR TERMS. A term has *particular* quantity or extension when it is applied to an indeterminate portion of a given class. For example:

> *Some* countries are ruled by dictators.
> *Certain* people do not exercise their right to vote.

If any one of the following or like signs of quantity is prefixed to a term, it should (for purposes of logical treatment) be regarded as particular:

a few	very many
almost all	most
many	practically all

SINGULAR TERMS. The extension of a term is *singular* if the term applies to only one specified object, whether that object be a person, place, thing, or event. For example:

Abraham Lincoln
Washington, D.C.
the largest telescope in the world
the discovery of America

Note: Because in conventional usage *particular* frequently has reference to *only one,* as in *this particular person, this particular event,* the student must not confuse *particular* and *singular* as these terms are used in logic.

SUMMARY. The following is a *general* outline of the contents of this chapter:

- I. Meaning of term
  - A. Terms as signs
  - B. Concepts as signs
  - C. Definition of term
- II. Terms and concepts as categories
  - A. Reasons for studying the categories
  - B. Meaning of category
  - C. The ten categories
- III. Use of terms
  - A. Univocal, equivocal, and analogous
  - B. Collective and divisive
  - C. Universal, particular, and singular

Note: To the extent that it is necessary, the *opposition* of terms will be treated informally in the discussion of obversion in Chapter 8.

EXERCISES

1. Why is a term called a *sign?* a *sensible* sign? a *conventional* sign?

2. Explain the difference between *terms* and *concepts* as signs.

3. Define *term.* Explain each part of the definition.

4. Explain the meaning of *category* as it is understood in logic.

5. What is the advantage for the logician of knowing the categories?

6. How is the category *substance* understood in logic?

7. List and briefly explain the other categories. Why are they called accidents?

8. Place each of the following *italicized* terms in its proper category:

   (a) The baby is *sleeping on his back.*
   (b) The weather is *unsettled.*
   (c) The picture is *on the floor.*
   (d) The patient is *encased in bandages.*
   (e) Some students are *superior to others.*
   (f) The dog is *limping.*
   (g) This steak *weighs a pound and a half.*
   (h) That bird is a *blue jay.*
   (i) The grass is *being cut.*
   (j) I met her *last night.*
   (k) My father is *simonizing the car.*
   (l) His hat was *soaked in the rain.*
   (m) Some pets are *canaries.*
   (n) This girl is *my sister.*
   (o) The camp is *in the mountains.*
   (p) Your skin is *sun-tanned.*
   (q) The fish are *biting.*
   (r) The election is *next month.*
   (s) The instructor is *looking for some chalk.*
   (t) Some of the students are *slouched in their chairs.*

9. Define the *univocal, equivocal,* and *analogous* use of terms.

10. Give an example of a term that is used analogously but not metaphorically.

11. Determine whether the following *italicized* terms are used univocally, equivocally, or analogously:

(a) *Knotty* pine; a *knotty* problem.
(b) Plato and Aristotle were *philosophers.*
(c) *Window* of an automobile; *window* of a house.
(d) *Running* for mayor; *running* a hundred yard dash.
(e) Poetry is *art;* music is *art.*
(f) Water is heavier than *air;* the *air* is fresh.
(g) To *air* one's opinions; to *air* the room.
(h) To *inherit* a fortune; to *inherit* the crown.
(i) Manufacturing *plant;* this tulip is a *plant.*
(j) A reddish *color;* Milwaukee has local *color.*
(k) John is a *kind* person. What *kind* of a person is he?
(l) *Paging* Mrs. Brown; *paging* through a book.
(m) *Hands* of a clock; *hands* of a human being.
(n) I can *digest* my food, but not my logic book.
(o) This package is *light;* this room is *light.*
(p) *Bark* of a tree; *bark* of a dog.

12. Determine *as best you can* whether the italicized terms of the following fish story have a univocal, equivocal, or analogous signification.

> Somebody ought to *tell* the fish that *swim* around this east coast *town* [Stuart, Florida] that the holiday *season* is over, so they can quit *celebrating*. . . . A few days ago the sailfish *fishermen* got *excited* when the news *popped* about their favorite gamefish "balling the bait." . . . *Ten,* fifteen, or more of these high *jumping gamesters* will surround a *school* of bait minnows, and drive them into a compact *ball.* Then in leisurely fashion, they play ring-around-the-rosy with the *poor* minnows. The *sails* just keep the little fish corralled by *circling* them, dashing into the *school* now and then to *seize* a few

for a quick snack. Since the sailfish started "balling the bait" a few days ago, the deep-sea fishermen have been *going around* starry eyed and *talking to themselves,* because when sailfish begin "balling" they're easy to catch.—Reprinted through the courtesy of *The Chicago Tribune,* from an article by Robert Becker, January 3, 1954.

Note: Discussion of the above examples should reveal some difference of opinion as to the use of certain terms.

13. Explain the difference between the *collective* use and the *divisive* use of a term.

14. Determine whether the following italicized terms are to be taken collectively or divisively:

(a) *The books in this room* are stacked ten feet high.
(b) *The apples in this bag* weigh four pounds.
(c) *Men* have free will.
(d) *All of our units* are well equipped.
(e) *The hairs of your head* are numbered.
(f) *These flowers* make a beautiful corsage.
(g) *The United Nations* is a world organization.
(h) *All men* have individual rights.
(i) *The actors of our organization* will make a fine cast.
(j) *The nation* has elected a new president.

15. What is the *extension* of a term?

16. Define *universal, particular,* and *singular,* giving the usual signs of quantity for each.

3

Definition and Division

Definition and the Predicables
Categories and Predicables
Analogous Meaning of "Species"
Kinds of Definition
Rules of Definition
Further Remarks on Definition
Division: Its Meaning and Importance
Physical vs. Logical Division
Essential vs. Accidental Division
Division vs. Enumeration
Rules of Division

INTRODUCTORY REMARKS. In the opening chapter we pointed out the salient points of difference between sensory perception and intellectual knowledge. The senses in their perception of an object are limited to a knowledge of its *external* characteristics, such as size, color, sound, and the like. They grasp the object without any formal knowledge of *what* it is. The intellect, on the other hand, endowed as it is with powers of apprehension superior to those of sense, penetrates beyond the externals of sense data and abstracts from the object those aspects or elements of it which in some way pertain to its essence.

It would be a mistake, however, to imagine that a concept does not admit of improvement. There is many an object which we know (of which we have a concept), but of which we should be unable to give a definition or division if asked to do so. For example, almost everyone knows what an airplane is. Yet, to explain by definition what an airplane is to someone who has no knowledge of it might prove extremely difficult. Moreover, in attempting such an explanation we may become aware of imperfections in our own idea. Again, if asked to explain to someone the different kinds of airplane (to give a division of them), we may become increasingly aware of the limitations of our own knowledge. In general, the purpose of definition and division, each in its own way, is to improve and perfect our conceptual knowledge of objects that are known only in a confused and imperfect way.

DEFINITION AND THE PREDICABLES

We define a given object by distinguishing within it those essential notes that make it the kind of thing it is *and no other.* Since every definition is expressed in the form of a proposition, the best way to understand definition itself is to examine the difference between those propositions that define their subjects and those that do not. To do this we must distinguish the five so-called *predicables,* that is, *different modes of predication.*

In Chapter 2 we stated that it is the function of the predicate term in a proposition to give information about the subject of which it is spoken. Not every proposition, however, is of equal value in the information that it gives about its subject. The reason for this is simple: Some predicates convey information about the essence of their subjects and others do not. Compare, for instance, the two following statements:

> Perjury is *something which few people commit.*
> Perjury is a *form of lying.*

The first statement gives no real clue to the true nature of perjury; whereas the second statement says something of its essence. *Every statement, then, either states something about the essence, or nature, of its subject or it does not.* If the predication is of the essence of the subject, it is a statement either of *the whole essence* or of *only a part.* "Man," for instance, is predic*able* of "John" as relating to his complete essence. Thus, when we say, "John is man," we actually predicate of "John" his complete essence or nature. To do this is to predicate of "John" the *species* to which he belongs. Species, then, is the first of the five predicables, that is, *different ways of saying something about a subject.*

If the predication of a subject relates to only *part* of its essence, there are two possibilities: The predicate states either that which the subject in its nature *has in common* with other species or that which *differentiates* it in its own species. Thus, to predicate "animal" of John is to predicate of him the *generic* part of the species to which he belongs, namely, that part which the species "man" holds in common with the species "brute." The predicate "animal," then, belongs to the predicable *genus.* If, on the other hand, we assign to "John" the predicate "rational," we are predicating of him that which essentially differentiates his species from all others. In this case, the predicable is very simply that of *difference.*

On the other hand, there are many statements in which the predicate term does not express the essence either in whole or in part. Here, again, there are two possibilities: The predicate expresses either something that is *characteristic* of a certain species, though not an essential part of it, or something that simply has *no connection* at all with the species. Thus, if we predicate of John "ability to laugh," we are expressing neither his species nor an essential part of it; yet we are expressing something *which belongs to the species as such,* because the ability to laugh is a characteristic of the species "man" *and of no other.* In this case, the predicable is *property.* Lastly, if we predicate of John "brown hair," we are expressing something that has no bearing on the species at all. "Brown hair" may just as well be predicated of a member of another species, for example, of a monkey. Predicates that are in no way characteristic of a species as such belong to the predicable *accident.*

There are, then, five predicables: species, genus, difference, property, accident. Two of these are the ingredients of definition taken in its strictest sense: *genus* and *difference.* Accordingly, to predicate "rational animal" of John is to give a *definition* of the species to which he belongs.

CATEGORIES AND PREDICABLES

Before concluding our discussion of the five different kinds of predicables, let us examine the precise meaning of the term "predicable," mainly in contradistinction to the *categories* studied in the last chapter.

We noted that the categories are a list of possible predicate terms considered solely from the standpoint of the natures, or essences, that they represent, in other words, considered independently of any subject to which they might actually be assigned. Thus, in order to place a term in its category, it is not necessary to consider *how* a term refers to a given subject. All that is necessary is to look to the term itself to see whether it stands for substance or one of the nine accidents. On this last point, even an accident is considered as standing for a certain nature, albeit an incomplete one.

Like the categories, the predicables too are a list of predicate terms, but regarded from the point of view of *how* they might be referred to a given subject. In other words, they are *the different ways or modes whereby it is possible to assign a predicate to a subject.* In order, then, to *specify* a term as one of the five predicables, it is not enough simply to consider the term by itself, since to do this would be to consider it as belonging to a certain *category.* On the contrary, *it is necessary to consider the subject* to see first whether the predicate in question is of the essence of the subject or not. The basic question, then, in determining a predicable is this: How does the predicate relate to the subject; that is, does it or does it not belong to the subject's essence?

ANALOGOUS MEANING OF THE TERM "SPECIES"

Very few objects are species in the strict sense in which, for example, man, brute, and plant are species. When zoologists distinguish different species of brutes, they use the term in a sense that is only analogous to that whereby man and brute themselves are characterized as species. Thus, the difference between one species of brute and another (for example, lion and tiger) is only accidental *in comparison with* the difference that exists between the species man and the species brute.

Shall we then limit the word "define" to a definition of only those things that are species in the strictest sense of the word, such as man, brute, plant? Clearly, if we did this, definition itself would be as rare as the species to be defined; and further, we should have to admit the validity of only one kind ("species," if you will) of definition—*a strict definition of the essence.* Yet the plain fact of the matter is that there *are* different kinds of definition, and it is necessary for the logician to take them into account. Therefore, if the student is led to understand that not every definition is a strict statement of the essence, he should have little difficulty in admitting as definitions (of one kind or another) the types we are now to distinguish.

KINDS OF DEFINITION

Nominal Definition

The function of definition, in general, is to *set limits to* the meaning of the object to be defined. In nominal definition the "object" to be defined is simply a *term.* Accordingly, to give a nominal definition is to *explicate in more simple language* the meaning of a relatively complex term. There are a number of ways in which a nominal definition may be given, such as explaining a term by its etymology; replacing it with a synonym; breaking it down (if a technical term) into its popular equivalent; translating it; and giving the meaning of a slang term. We have said that *to define* means to *set limits to* the object to be defined. This is itself an example of nominal definition, that is, one which gives the *root* meaning of the term. Some other examples are:

Pachyderm means a thick-skinned animal.
A *chiropodist* is a foot specialist.
Cul de sac means, literally, *bottom of the bag,* or, in common usage, *a blind alley.*
A *matriculation fee* is an entrance fee.

Note: It is sometimes difficult to decide whether a definition is nominal or real, since a nominal definition frequently gives some information about the thing itself, even though the *intent* of the definition may be merely to explain the term. However, in setting forth a nominal definition, it is customary to give some indication to this effect by the use of italic, quotation marks, or such words as "literally," "archaically," "in slang language," and the like.

Real Definition

ESSENTIAL DEFINITION. In general, a real definition is one that defines some *thing,* whether it be natural or an artificial product. Now, the first step in the making of an *essential definition* or of any *real* definition is to *place the subject one is defining in its proper category.* In Chapter 2 we explained how this should be done. Thus, if we wish to define man, we first place our subject in the category to which it belongs, namely, "substance." Note also the following examples:

Virtue belongs to the category *quality.*
Poundage belongs to the category *quantity.*
Motherhood belongs to the category *relation.*

To place the subject in its category is to state in a very general sense *what* the subject is, that is, to give its *remote genus.* Now, the *remote genus,* as opposed to the proximate genus, is the one farthest removed from the difference, that is, from the essential differentiating feature of the subject that is being defined. The *proximate genus,* on the other hand, is the one *immediately* determined by the difference or, as it is sometimes said, the one that immediately "lies above" the difference. Thus, the remote genus of both man and brute is *substance;* the proximate genus is *animal;* and the difference in the case of man is *rational* and in the case of brute *irrational.*

In the final wording of the definition itself it is incorrect simply to give the remote genus or, for that matter, one of the intermediate genera. These are only a help toward *selecting* the *proximate genus,* which will appear in the definition itself.

In the light of the above remarks it should be clear that an *essential definition* is a statement of the component parts of the essence of a subject, that is, the proximate genus and the (essential) difference. This is the ideal type of definition, because it states what a thing is in terms of its intrinsic nature or essence—its inmost constitution. The following are examples of essential definition:

> An organism is a living body.
> An animal is a sentient organism.

These are definitions of *natural* substances which are *species* in the strictest sense of the word.

Suppose, however, that we wished to define a "species" in its derived sense, for example, as referring to a zoological or a botanical species. In such a case it is best not even to attempt an essential definition but to make use of one of the other types. The reason for this is simply that in the case of derived species (for example, tiger, rose) we have no distinct knowledge of the essence. Further, in the case of *artificial products* (for example, automobile, building) it is futile to attempt an essential definition because an artificial product as such has no strict essence of its own, that is, in the same sense as does a natural substance. Thus, an artificial product is a joining together of many substances in a given manner for some specific purpose. Objects of this kind are most conveniently defined through their productive agents or the purpose for which they are constructed.

Finally, if the subject to be defined is not itself a substance but is one of the nine accidents, one should realize that the "essence" or "nature" of an accident is hardly the same as that of a substance. Nevertheless, a *quasi-essential* definition can be given. In so doing the category (one of the nine accidents) should first be determined and then narrowed down until a reasonably sound basis for a good definition is found. The following is an example:

Virtue is a good habit of the mind.

The remote genus or category of virtue is *quality*. Its *proximate genus* is *habit*. The difference is expressed by the words "good" and "of the mind." To say that virtue is a *good* habit is to differentiate it from vice. To say that it is "of the mind," that is, that it refers either to intellect or to will, is to distinguish virtue from some habit which may be found in another faculty, or "power."

DISTINCTIVE DEFINITION. To substitute for the difference one or more of the *properties* of the thing to be defined is to give a *distinctive definition*. For reasons of convenience, the term "property" may here be taken either in the strict sense (as already explained) or in the more commonly accepted meanings, as referring to any characteristic of an object which, though distinctive, may possibly be found in other species as well. Chemical properties, for instance, are properties taken in the looser meaning of the term. The following, then, are examples of distinctive definitions:

A body is a substance *having extension.*
Man is a *food-cooking* animal.
Mercury is a metallic element *remarkable for its fluidity at ordinary temperatures.*

CAUSAL DEFINITION. Strictly speaking, an essential definition is a causal definition by reason of its inclusion of the *intrinsic* causes (the essential component parts) of its object. Nevertheless, a causal definition is ordinarily understood to be one that explains its object by means of the object's *extrinsic*—that is, efficient or final—causes.

To *define by efficient cause* is to set forth an object in terms of the agent or agents (personal or impersonal) which produce it. The dictionary definition of an egg exemplifies this type of definition: "The reproductive body *produced by birds and many reptiles,* especially, in common usage, that of the domestic hen."

The final cause is the reason, end, or purpose for which an object (natural or artificial) exists. *Definition by final cause* is perhaps the commonest type of definition and, from a practical point of view, one of the most useful. The following is an example: "A seismograph is a scientific instrument *used for recording the motions of an earthquake.*"

Note: Frequently a single definition will combine various elements of the types we have distinguished, as is the case when a definition includes a statement both of the efficient and final causes.

Accidental Description

Accidental description is not really a form of definition; it is a device that is used for referring *denotatively* or "pointing" to a certain individual person, place, thing, or event. Since individuals as such cannot be defined, accidental description may be considered a substitute for definition. Its proper use lies in marking off one individual from all others by the use of a sufficient number of "telling" accidents. Thus:

> Washington, D.C., is the capital of the United States, located on the Potomac River, and bordered by the states of Maryland and Virginia.

RULES OF DEFINITION

In assessing a definition it is better to be neither unduly critical nor picayunish. Since nominal definition is not a strict type of definition, the general rules of definition should not be rigidly applied to it by way of criticism. Moreover, a person will frequently formulate a "working" definition, somewhat in the manner of a tentative hypothesis. In such a case it would be irrelevant to criticize the definition *as though* it were cast in its final form.

Necessary as it is to use good judgment in the application of the following rules, their fundamental importance can hardly be overstressed. These rules are indispensable means for detecting and avoiding the customary flaws of faulty definition.

Rule 1: The definition must be coextensive with the thing defined.

This first rule is the most basic test of the soundness of any definition. To define a thing, after all, is to delimit it in both its comprehension and its extension. To do this is to mark the thing off in such a way that what we say applies exclusively to this one thing alone. Not every statement, of course, in which the predicate is convertible with its subject is a definition of the subject. The point is, however, that *no statement in which the predicate is not convertible with its subject can be considered as a definition.* For this reason, a definition should be neither too broad nor too narrow. A definition is too broad if it can be applied to some subject other than the one of which it is predicated; it is too narrow if it over-restricts the scope of the subject defined. For example, if we say that "education is a *process of development,*" intending this to be a definition, our definition would be too broad, since the predicate term applies as well to many other things besides education. If, on the other hand, we were to give as a definition of science the statement that "science is the causal analysis of physical phenomena," our definition would clearly be too restrictive.

Once the student realizes the difficulty of constructing definitions that are neither too broad nor too narrow, he will appreciate the fact that definitions should not be given out as casually as they sometimes are—for example, in an examination paper. It is one thing to say something that truly pertains to a given subject, but quite another to *define* it.

Rule 2: The definition should be expressed in univocal terms, and, whenever possible, those terms should be kept simple.

This rule forbids the use of figurative language in the wording of a definition, as, for example, in "The eyes are the mirrors of the soul." Again, although no one would take seriously the definition of a politician as "a wholesaler dealer in public jobs," there is always the danger of constructing a definition by the use of analogy. Furthermore, it is incongruous to give a definition in which the language of the definition is more complex and involved than the thing being defined. For this reason, the terms of the definition (not necessarily monosyllabic in form) should be kept *relatively* simple. The classic example in violation of this type of definition is Samuel Johnson's (humorously intended?) definition of a "net" as ". . . a reticulated fabric, decussated at regular intervals, with interstices and intersections."

Without a doubt the greatest trial of any lexicographer's skill is to define a relatively simple and familiar object of human experience in a manner that is itself relatively simple and familiar. The student would therefore be wise to refrain from attempting to define objects that do not really stand in need of definition. Whatever the literary advantages of writing a 300-word composition about a door knob, whether by way of definition or description, such a procedure, from a logical standpoint, is clearly pointless.

Rule 3: The definition should not be circular.

One of the most flagrant violations of logical procedure is the *circular definition.* After all, the purpose of definition is to augment one's knowledge of a given subject and not, by means of mere verbalism, to bring it to a stalemate. For example, any attempt to define a unit of money in terms of its *monetary* equivalent—a dollar is a sum of two half-dollars—would be to define in circles. To avoid this in our example, it would be necessary to define a dollar in terms of its real and equivalent purchasing power.

The commonest instances of circular definition are those that employ terms that are merely synonymous. The use of synonyms is acceptable, of course, in a *nominal* definition, the purpose of which is simply to break down the meaning of a term. Yet, if we attempt to give a *real* definition of a "doctor," let us say, by stating that he is "a person who *practices the medical profession,"* we are defining in circles.

Rule 4: The definition should, whenever possible, be expressed in positive terms.

A definition is a statement of what a thing *is,* not of what it is *not.* Although certain objects are by their very nature negative in meaning (for example, "A bachelor is an unmarried man"), whenever possible the definition should be expressed affirmatively. Clearly, it is no definition of a lawyer to say that he is not a judge.

FURTHER REMARKS ON DEFINITION

For the purpose of avoiding confusion, the medieval scholastics agreed that in a disputation a nominal definition of the important terms of an argument should be a formal requirement. The average student today might consider the techniques of the scholastic disputation cumbersome and tedious. But the fact is that our own easygoing, informal mode of oral and written discussion too often leads to a *lack of precision* and a confusion of terminology. One of the obvious remedies for the comparative fruitlessness of many present-day discussions (not excluding those sponsored by radio and television) is a return to the use of the nominal definition.

In giving a definition, it is important to exercise the utmost care in the wording of it. This is a requirement, not only of sound logic, but of good grammar as well. One need not look too far to find so-called "definitions" like the following:

A democracy is *where* the people have a voice in government affairs.

Etiquette is *how* to behave nicely in other people's presence.

A university is *where* one gets a higher education.

To avoid such commonplace utterances, remember that a definition must always begin with a statement of the *proximate genus*.

Note too that a definition should be an objective statement of what a thing *is* and not a statement of how one reacts to or feels about the thing he is defining. Thus, although we might be amused at hearing a parking space described as an *unoccupied area on the other side of the street,* such a statement would be very confusing to a person who had no idea of a parking space.

DIVISION: ITS MEANING AND IMPORTANCE

Few students need to be convinced of the importance of division as a means of learning. Ordinarily, an instructor, in order to revive the lagging attention of his students, needs only to indicate to them that he is about to present an *outline* of their subject matter. Somehow students seem instinctively to realize that an outline (which is really a *division*) helps them more than anything else can to organize their knowledge. What can be more distressing to the student than to be confronted with a disorderly mass of unintegrated detail, and what more comforting than an outline which serves to integrate this mass of detail into an orderly arrangement of parts in their proper relation to the whole? Of course, the mere knowledge of the outline as such does not automatically relieve the student of the need to study detail. What it does is to help the user *to link the detail* to the constituent part of a given whole and *to know,* in turn, the meaning that each constituent part of the division bears in relation to its whole.

In view of the importance of division as a means of learning, let us devote some attention to the nature of division and the rules that govern it. In general, division is the resolution or analysis of a given whole, or unit, into its constituent parts. Let us divide "men," for example, into Europeans, Asiatics, Americans, Africans, and Australians. Obviously in this (as in every division) there is a whole which is to be divided (men) and there are parts into which it is divisible. Yet, neither the whole nor the parts are the most significant features of a division, since the two of them together constitute division in its purely *material* aspects. *Formally* considered, the division is its foundation or basis, which is *the very reason for the making of the division itself.* The basis of the division just given is that of men taken according to continental origin.

PHYSICAL VS. LOGICAL DIVISION

A *physical division* is the reduction of any natural or artificial unit into its actual (and really distinct) parts. To divide "engine," for instance, into pistons, bearings, fuel pump, carburetor, and so on, is to give a physical division of it. A *logical division,* as opposed to a physical division, is the resolution of a genus into its species or of a species into its subspecies. In order to differentiate physical and logical division, let us examine the following examples:

1. Government: divided into executive, legislative, and judicial.
2. Government: divided into democratic, monarchical, dictatorial, and so on.

Division 1 is a physical division, since the parts which it gives are the real and really distinct parts of *a* government—the so-called "branches" within a government. Division 2 is a logical division, that is, a division of the different *kinds* of government; it is the division of a generic concept into its specific determinants.

Both physical and logical division are important for purposes of establishing order in our thinking processes in that they are both a means of *analyzing* a given subject. One should not, therefore, think that "physical" division has no logical significance. With reference to the physical division of "government" above, it is a great help toward understanding the functions of *a* government if one knows its component physical parts.

In addition to the value that logical division proper has as division, it is an aid in the making of good definitions. This can be readily understood when we recall that a logical division is the resolution of a *genus* into its species. Thus, it is really by a series of logical divisions that we arrive at some of the definitions given in preceding sections of this chapter:

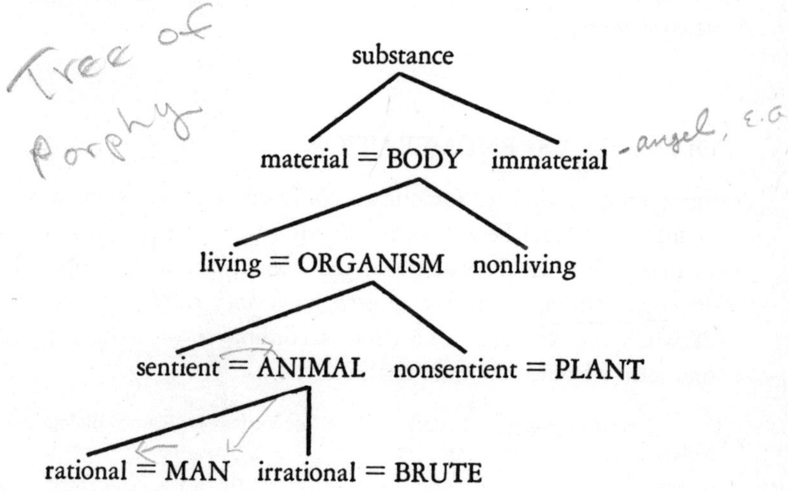

As a note of historical interest, it was Plato who first realized the utility of this type of division for the purpose of constructing definitions.[1]

ESSENTIAL VS. ACCIDENTAL DIVISION

If the parts of a logical division are divided from the whole by reason of the fact that each part is *essentially* distinct from the other, the division itself is an *essential division.* Thus, to divide the genus "animal" into the species "man" and "brute" is to construct an essential division, since man and brute are *essentially* distinct from each other, that is, distinct by reason of their essence or nature. Suppose, however, that a division is constructed on the basis of some difference that has no bearing on the nature of the subject; the division itself is an *accidental division,* as when "people" are divided according to whether they have blond, brown, black, or any other color hair.

Although essential and accidental division may both be regarded as forms of *logical* division, a division that is made by reason of the essence is logical division in its primary sense. Sometimes, too, a division is made on the basis of *properties.* This kind of division is also classified as *logical,* although again not in its strictest sense.

DIVISION VS. ENUMERATION

Since enumeration is sometimes confused with division, a word about it is in order here. *Enumeration* is *a mere listing of individuals,* as in naming the Presidents of the United States. As opposed to an enumeration, *a division as such gives only classes or subclasses,* as when one classifies Presidents according to whether they had one term of office or more than one term.

[1] Especially worthy of note in this connection is Plato's dialogue *The Sophist.*

RULES OF DIVISION

Although it is not always easy to ensure the practical application of the rules of division, the rules themselves are simple.

Rule 1: The parts of a division must (in their collective totality) be coextensive with the whole which they divide.

It is a violation of this rule to omit one or more of the parts of a whole or species of a genus. In the giving of a *dichotomous division* there is little, if any, danger of violating Rule 1, since the parts of a dichotomous division are formal contradictories, for example, textbooks divided into *bound* and *unbound*. The *negative* term in a division of this kind covers all the other members. In any but a dichotomous division, however, there is always the danger of an omission. To divide "transportation" into "air" and "land transportation" is to omit "transportation by sea."

Rule 2: The foundation of the division must be kept uniform throughout.

If a division is to be logical, it must be consistent. In order that a division may be consistent, all parts of that division must rest on a single foundation, or basis. Thus, it is a gross violation of the canons of consistency to divide climates into cold, warm, and *dry*. The sudden appearance of "dry climate" in this division implies a change in the basis of the division. Climates were first divided *according to their temperature;* then a "part" that pertains to *relative humidity* of a climate was inserted. The failure to apply Rule 2 results most often in a *cross-division,* that is, one in which the parts are not mutually exclusive. In the example just given, dry climate is not mutually exclusive of cold or warm climate.

Occasionally one or more parts of an attempted division are related only *analogously* (or *equivocally*) to the whole that they divide. Consider, for example, the division of *activity* into *physical* and *mental* activity. In a division such as this the whole or the genus that is divided bears no strictly uniform relation to its parts.

That is to say, neither of the parts or species of this division partakes in exactly the same sense of the common nature of the genus. Physical and mental activity are only analogously related to each other—not univocally. Since this division lacks a uniform basis, it violates Rule 2. In general, whenever there exists the danger of inserting as a part of a division a dividing member that really belongs to another division, it is advisable to make the foundation of one's division *explicit.*

CONCLUSION: CODIVISION AND SUBDIVISION. As we have just seen, it is a violation of Rule 2 to insert within *one and the same division* a part that really belongs to another division; that is to say, the basis of a division must be kept the same for each of its dividing members. There is no rule, however, that forbids the employment of two or more divisions for one and the same unit, or genus, provided that each separate division is constructed according to a different basis. There are many ways, for instance, in which it is possible to divide *science*: according to subject matter, according to method, according to recency of discovery, according to relative practical utility, and so on. All these divisions would be *codivisions* of *science,* but each would proceed (logically) according to its own basis. Codivision, then, is *the employment of more than one division (each according to a different basis) of one and the same logical unit.*

In contradistinction to codivision, *subdivision is the employ-*

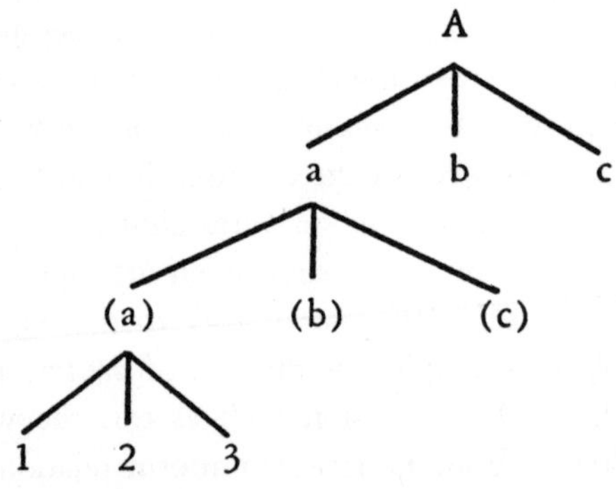

ment of another division which is subordinate to one of the leading, coordinate members of the original division. It is a process which, theoretically, at least, might be indefinitely carried on to other subordinate members, as in the accompanying diagram shown on page 66.

In making a subdivision care must be taken that no part which is a subordinate member of one division be linked as the coordinate member of another.

EXERCISES

1. What is the purpose of definition and division?
2. Derive the predicables, showing why there are five—and only five—kinds.
3. What is the importance of knowing the predicables as a preliminary step toward definition? Do they also have some significance for division?
4. Contradistinguish *category* and *predicable.*
5. Does the term *species* have more than one meaning? If so, what is the importance of distinguishing one meaning of the term from another?
6. Explain what you understand by *nominal* definition. What are some of the ways in which a nominal definition is given? Give three examples of your own.
7. How should one go about the making of a real definition?
8. What is an *essential* definition? Are most definitions of this kind? Explain.
9. What is a *distinctive* definition? Give three examples.
10. Distinguish the two types of causal definition, and give three examples of each.
11. Explain the statement: "Accidental description is a substitute for definition." Give an example.
12. What is the practical test for ensuring the application of the first rule of definition? What are the two ways in which Rule 1 may be violated? Give your own examples.

13. Give an example of violation of the second rule of definition.

14. What do you understand by a circular definition?

15. State the importance (a) of expressing a definition in positive terms; (b) of beginning a definition with the statement of the appropriate genus.

16. What is the importance of an outline?

17. Comment on the following statement: "The foundation of a division is the most important aspect of a division."

18. By the use of examples contradistinguish *physical* and *logical division.*

19. By the use of examples contradistinguish *essential* and *accidental division.*

20. By the use of examples contradistinguish *division* and *enumeration.*

21. State and explain the two rules of division.

22. Identify *as best you can* the type of definition illustrated by each of the following:

(a) A clock is a device used for indicating or telling time.

(b) Chloroform is a liquid made by treating acetone or alcohol with bleaching powder.

(c) "Effervescent" means "bubbling over."

(d) A juke box is a coin-operated phonograph permitting selection of the records to be played.

(e) A honeycomb is a structure consisting of adjoining hexagonal cells of wax made by bees.

(f) A tiger is a large feline mammal with transverse, wavy black and tawny stripes on the body.

(g) A saddle is a seat for a rider on an animal, bicycle, etc.

(h) A Mae West is an inflatable life-preserver vest for aviators who may fall into the sea.

(i) Time is the measure of the duration of an act, process, or the like.

(j) A plant is a nonsentient organism.

(k) "Philosophy" means "love of wisdom."

(l) Man is an animal endowed with the faculty of articulate speech.

(m) Lysol is a clear, brown, oily liquid used as a disinfectant and antiseptic.

(n) Sulfur is a nonmetallic element used in the manufacture of gunpowder, matches, and so on, in vulcanizing rubber, and in medicine.

(o) Arteriosclerosis is the hardening of the arteries of the human body.

(p) Barter is the interchange of one commodity for another.

(q) A catalyst is an agent which affects the velocity of a chemical reaction without appearing in the final product of the reaction.

(r) A wound is a physical injury characterized by breaking of the skin or other membrane.

23. Criticize the following as would-be definitions of their subjects and reconstruct your own definition of each:

(a) Security means contentment.

(b) Life is when you're still breathing.

(c) A separation is not a divorce.

(d) Personality is what it takes to have many friends.

(e) A circle is something which is round.

(f) Logic is the science of method.

(g) Education is a process involving the interchange of notes from teacher to student.

(h) Television is the graveyard of outdated movies.

(i) Mental cruelty is when you hurt the feelings of your partner in marriage.

(j) A treaty is a verbal agreement.

(k) An immigration official is a watchdog of aliens.

(l) A contract is something which is binding by law.

(m) The newspaper is the workingman's textbook.

(n) Life insurance is a means of post-mortem protection.

(o) A habit is a disposition which is not easily lost.

(p) A college degree is a testimony of academic achievement.

(q) Vice is a habit.

(r) Economic solvency is when you don't have any debts.

(s) A student is someone who studies.

(t) A teacher is a pedagogue.

(u) Happiness is the sunshine of the soul.

(v) Gambling is the sport of the devil.

(w) Character is what makes you a man.

(x) A secret is a form of pretense whereby nobody is supposed to know what everybody else knows.

(y) A high-school teacher is an educated policeman.

24. Explicate the *basis* of each of the following divisions:

(a) Science: inductive and deductive.

(b) History: ancient, medieval, modern.

(c) Toy: plastic, rubber, wooden, and so on.

(d) Terms: collective and divisive.

(e) People: sanguine, phlegmatic, choleric, melancholic.

25. Determine whether each of the following is a *physical* or a *logical* division:

(a) Election: local, state, national.

(b) Play: prologue, acts and scenes, epilogue.

(c) Library: offices, reading room, stacks.

(d) Literature: fiction and nonfiction.

(e) Homes: bungalows, cottages, ranch homes, and so on.

26. Carefully point out the defects in each of the following divisions:

(a) Libraries: school and public.

(b) Television programs: sports, entertainment, educational, variety, boxing, and musical.

(c) Words: nouns, verbs, adjectives, and swear words.

(d) Nonemployed persons: hoboes, housewives, and students.

(e) Musical instruments: violin, piano, voice.
(f) Speeches: political, conversational, oratorical.
(g) Taxes: federal, excise, and municipal.
(h) Ruler: president, king, yardstick.
(i) Mistakes: intentional, indeliberate, serious.
(j) Loans: short term and interest bearing.
(k) Paper: stationery, wrapping paper, newspaper.
(l) Bark: bark of a tree, bark of a dog.
(m) Life: life of an organism, life of the mind, life of a party.

4

Judgment and Proposition

The Nature of Judgment

Truth and Falsity

Proposition Defined

The Categorical Proposition: Matter and Form

INTRODUCTORY REMARKS. Through simple apprehension we come to know something about the essence, or nature, of an object. If the object that we know is conceived with sufficient distinctness and clarity, we can also define and divide it. As is evident, however, from our own experience, intellection does not terminate with the mere formation of concepts. Having formed a concept of any given object, we proceed forthwith to make certain judgments about it. Thus, a child who has attained a notion, or concept, of "train" goes on to *judge* that "this train is large," "gives out smoke," "is noisy," and "moves on tracks."

THE NATURE OF JUDGMENT

Concerning the nature of judgment the question that immediately presents itself is this: What does the intellect do when it judges? For the sake of clarity and convenience we shall restrict ourselves here to an analysis of judgment taken only in its primary and most basic sense—that is, the *categorical* judgment.

Every categorical judgment, then, consists of a *mental pronouncement* or *assertion* that involves two distinct objects of thought, that is, as grasped in simple apprehension. In order to form a judgment, we must first have *something about which* to judge, whether this "something" be actual (chair) or only in some sense possible (a chair operated by jet propulsion). Second, it is necessary that we have in mind some *attribute,* or *nature,* that we can assign as predicate to the subject about which we judge. A subject and a predicate are only the *prerequisites* of judgment. The judgment itself takes place when we *mentally* affirm or deny that this attribute belongs or does not belong to this subject. Thus, I am judging when I mentally assert of this chair that it "is" comfortable or that it "is not" adapted for purposes of study.

In striving to gain a precise understanding of the nature of judgment, the student must be careful not to imagine that judgment is a mere *association of images,* whether sensory or conceptual. To judge is not merely to place in juxtaposition two objects of thought, so that first one ("this play") is thought of and immediately thereafter the other ("hailed by the critics as a great success"). In judging, the intellect does not act as a slide projector, as it were, which involves the use of successive movements to create a unified effect. On the contrary, the intellect unites or disunites two objects of thought in a *single act,* and in the very instant in which two objects of thought are present in the mind, the intellect affirms or denies one of the other.

Keeping in mind the basic considerations just set forth, we may, accordingly, define a *categorical judgment* as *an act according to which the intellect asserts one object of thought to be identical or nonidentical with another.* The student should note first that judgment essentially is an *act of the intellect* as opposed to any act of *sensory* knowledge. This is the *proximate genus* of our definition which the act of judgment has *in common* with simple apprehension or reasoning.

From our discussion of the nature of judgment in the preceding paragraphs the second part of the definition should be fairly clear. With a view toward gaining a more precise understanding of it, however, we must explain that the term "object of thought" is a generic term that refers to anything that is grasped in simple apprehension. Accordingly, the question may now be raised: What are the "objects" that we grasp in simple apprehension and consequently employ in our judgments? To answer this question we must make the following distinctions:

1. Sometimes the object grasped is an *individual thing,* such as "this bone." If such is the case, the normal order of judgment requires that this type of object be employed as the *subject* of a judgment, as when one judges that "*this bone* is diseased." Thus, an individual thing (or a plurality of individuals) is normally that *about which* we judge as a *subject.*

2. Frequently the object that we employ in our judgments is some nature or attribute which is found *in* individual things, as "dog" (not this dog or that). If such is the case, we are thinking primarily of the nature itself, that is, of what is signified by the *comprehension* of a concept. Here we can return to an earlier example: "A dog is a better pet than a cat." In this example both the subject and the predicate are regarded from the point of view of the *nature as such* with only an indirect regard to the individuals, that is, individual dogs and cats. From the example just given it should be clear that when an object of thought refers primarily to the nature as such, it may then be employed either as *subject* or as *predicate* in a judgment.

Note: If the judgment that we make involves an "object of thought" in either of the senses just explained, then the concepts that it employs (and the terms that we use to express them) are said to have a "real" supposition. "Real" supposition means "referring either to individual things themselves or to some real nature that is found in individuals."

3. Finally the term "object of thought" may signify something *as existing only in the mind.* Note the following example: "Animal is a genus." As conceived in this judgment, "animal" *has no reference at all to individuals,* and the same can be said of

"genus." In the example both "animal" and "genus" are regarded only in their status as *logical* (that is, as opposed to *real*) entities. Therefore, when it is said that "animal *is* a genus," the "is" of this judgment has reference to something that is verified, not in things, but only in the order of concepts. When an object of thought is thus employed, it is employed *both as subject and as predicate* in a judgment. In this case the supposition is said to be *logical.*

By way of summary of the nature of judgment, it should be noted that the prerequisites of judgment, which involve two distinct objects of thought, comprise its *matter,* or *content.* The *form,* or the essence, of the judgment itself is the mental assertion of identity or nonidentity. It is precisely this assertion that makes a judgment what it is as distinct from simple apprehension and reasoning.

TRUTH AND FALSITY

Only to judgments and propositions are the terms *true* and *false* applied in their strict and proper sense. For example, one does not say that a sense impression is true or false. Consider the impression that a person receives of a rod that is partly immersed in water. Because of the double medium of air and water, the rod *appears* to be bent, and that is the way it *should* appear. Only if a person *judges,* on the basis of this appearance, that "this rod *is* bent" is there any falsity involved.

Is a *concept* true or false? Not in the strict sense, for either one has a concept of a given object, however imperfect it may be, or he has not. It is true, of course, that people speak of "false ideas," but it will be found upon analysis that what they mean is judgments—not ideas or concepts. Concepts may possibly be spoken of as *clear* or *confused, adequate* or *inadequate,* but not strictly as true or false.

People also speak of "false reasoning" or "false inference." Yet, strictly speaking, an act of reasoning is either *valid* or *invalid, correct* or *incorrect,* not true or false. What is probably meant by "false reasoning" is the kind that leads to, or is apt to lead to, a false *conclusion,* the conclusion itself being a *judgment.* In this case, the terms true or false are only *analogously* predicable of an act of inference.

It is beyond the scope of logic to determine the various means of *testing* the truth of judgments, that is, of establishing the various *criteria* of truth.[1] Yet, for purposes of logic, it is important to know that *a judgment is true* if it affirms of its subject an attribute that really belongs to it (for example, "Canada is a North American country") or if it denies of its subject an attribute that the subject does not possess (for example, "Detroit is not the capital of the United States").

On the other hand, *a judgment is false* if it affirms of its subject an attribute that does not belong to the subject (for example, "France is an Asiatic nation") or if it denies of its subject an attribute that the subject really possesses (for example, "Alabama is not a Southern state").

PROPOSITION DEFINED

We have seen in Chapter 2 that the function of a term is to signify some object of thought as grasped in simple apprehension. Correspondingly, a *proposition* may, for all practical intents, be regarded as the expression of an act of judgment. There are, of course, different kinds of judgments and different kinds of propositions, but for the moment we are concerned simply with the meaning of a proposition as such. What is a proposition? The answer to this question can be expressed very succinctly in the following statement:

A *proposition* is a sentence that expresses something that is *true* or *false.* This definition differentiates a proposition from every other kind of sentence, such as:

1. A sentence expressing a question. (Where are you going?)
2. A sentence expressing a prayer, wish, or hope. (If only I could remember what I said.)

[1] The examination of the criteria of truth belongs to the science of epistemology.

3. A sentence expressing an exhortation or a command. (Do this.)
4. A sentence expressing an exclamation. (Help!)

Every sentence, of course, has meaning, but only those sentences characterized as true or false are propositions.

Since in the remainder of this chapter and in the following chapter we shall concern ourselves exclusively with the *categorical* proposition, a brief explanation of the nature of this type of statement is in order here. A categorical proposition (as opposed to a modal or a hypothetical proposition) is one that simply asserts *as a matter of fact* that a certain predicate does or does not belong to a certain subject. Thus:

The doctor *is* in his office.
My house *is not* on fire.

THE CATEGORICAL PROPOSITION: ITS MATTER AND FORM

The *matter* of a categorical proposition consists of its subject and predicate terms, which we shall often refer to simply as the *S* and *P* terms. Its *form* is the *copula.* The function of the copula is to unite or disunite the two terms of the proposition. The copula of a categorical proposition is expressed by the verb *to be* in the present tense, indicative mood in the following forms:

am—am not
is—is not
are—are not

It is sufficient to indicate here that for purposes of logic it is often convenient to incorporate what is signified by the grammatical verb (if it is other than the verb *to be*) into the predicate term. To take a simple example:

My father smokes cigars.

This proposition may be expressed in logical form thus:

My father is a cigar smoker.

By way of conclusion we should note that the *sign of quantity* (*all, no, some*), which is prefixed to the subject term, has a bearing both on the matter and on the form of the proposition in which it is used.

SUMMARY. To sum up what we have said as to the matter and form of categorical judgments and propositions, note carefully the following chart:

	Matter	*Form*
Judgment	Two objects of thought	Mental assertion of identity or nonidentity
Proposition	Subject and predicate terms	Copula

EXERCISES

1. What are the prerequisites of judgment?
2. Refute the following statement: "Judgment is merely the association of images."
3. What is meant by saying that judgment is a single act?
4. Define *categorical judgment*. What is the *proximate genus?* the *difference?*
5. Distinguish the three basic meanings of the term *object of thought*.
6. (a) Give an example of a judgment that is said to have a *real* supposition. (b) Give an example of a judgment that is said to have a *logical* supposition.
7. Distinguish the matter and the form of a categorical judgment.
8. What do people mean when they speak of true and false *ideas?*

9. Explain the following statement: "Truth and falsity are only analogously predicated of an act of reasoning."

10. In what two ways can a categorical judgment be true? Illustrate.

11. In what two ways can a categorical judgment be false? Illustrate.

12. Give a general definition of *proposition.* Explain.

13. What is a *categorical* proposition?

14. Distinguish the matter and form of a categorical proposition.

15. Determine which of the following are propositions:
    - (a) Climb over the hill.
    - (b) Render unto Caesar the things that are Caesar's.
    - (c) How do you expect to learn?
    - (d) What a wonderful day!
    - (e) Many a man is the victim of his own fancy.
    - (f) Uneasy lies the head that wears the crown.
    - (g) Woodman, spare that tree.
    - (h) Please don't go away.
    - (i) India is part of Asia.

5

Categorical Propositions

QUANTITY • QUALITY • LOGICAL FORM

INTRODUCTORY REMARKS. Since all human knowledge that is true is embodied in the form of propositions, the analysis of propositions into their fundamental elements and types is an important part of logic. In this chapter our discussion will be restricted to an analysis of the most fundamental type—the *categorical* proposition. In Chapter 6, which follows, we shall consider at some length the more complex varieties of categoricals and other types, that is, modals and hypotheticals.

Note: In this chapter when reference is made simply to *prop-*

ositions, it should be understood that we are confining our attention to *categoricals.*

THE QUANTITY OF PROPOSITIONS

With regard to *inference,* one of the first things to note is the quantity or extension of those propositions that appear either as the premises or as the conclusion in an argument. As we shall see in a later chapter, much invalid reasoning is accepted as valid because of the failure to specify as *particular* a proposition that *poses* as a universal. Thus, whether an inference is *valid* or *invalid* depends most often upon the quantity of its propositions. It is mainly for this reason that the student of logic must have an exact knowledge of the means of deciding whether a proposition is *universal, particular,* or *singular.*

The basic rule for determining the quantity of a proposition is a very simple one:

> ***The quantity of a proposition as such is determined by the quantity of the subject term.*** Thus:

UNIVERSAL SUBJECT TERM: UNIVERSAL PROPOSITION

Every man is endowed with free will.
No historical event is without significance.

PARTICULAR SUBJECT TERM: PARTICULAR PROPOSITION

Some people are not interested in politics.
Certain events are easily forgotten.

SINGULAR SUBJECT TERM: SINGULAR PROPOSITION

New York is the largest city in the United States.
This man is guilty.

The student should recall here from our discussion of the quantity of terms certain typical words that are the usual signs of universal or particular quantity. Thus, such words as *each, all, whatever, no, none* are the signs of *universal* quantity; whereas words like *some, certain, most,* and so on are the usual signs of *particular* quantity.

As a further point to be noted, the logician needs to know that in logic *singular* propositions are treated as *universals.* One of the reasons for this is that the object signified by a singular term may be regarded fictitiously as a class by itself, that is, as taken in its complete extension. Thus, when we say that "John is at home," we mean "John" in the totality of his person. A singular proposition is not, of course, a *genuine* universal, since it stands for only one individual.

Every proposition, then, is to be taken either as *universal* or as *particular.* Now, in view of the fact that there are many propositions in which there is no indicated sign of quantity, there are several important considerations that we must here take up to supplement the rule we have stated above. Generally speaking, those propositions whose subject terms are not specified by a definite sign of quantity are called *indesignate:* for example, "Cars are expensive." Obviously, when confronted with a proposition of this sort, one must decide whether it is universal or particular. Note the following examples:

A cause is something that produces an effect.
Man is a moral creature.
Martyrs are sincere in the profession of their faith.
Good men are deserving of reward.
A happy child is a joy to behold.

The student will observe that in each of these propositions the predicate has some bearing—intrinsic or extrinsic—on the nature of the subject as such. Since this is so, such propositions are to be taken as *truly universal.* Thus, if a martyr is one who *by reason of his being a martyr* is sincere in the profession of his faith, then every instance of a martyr is an instance of a person of this sort.

The importance of the above consideration requires that it be fully understood. With respect to the subject terms of the above propositions, note that each of these terms primarily stands for a certain nature as such, and that it is in the light of this nature that the predicate is (truthfully) ascribed to its subject. Thus, when we judge that "a happy child is a joy to behold," we are thinking primarily, not of one or of an entire grouping of individuals as such, but of *what it is to be a happy child.* Our predicate may, of course, be assigned to the individuals, but it is not the individuals that we have in mind. Accordingly, it is preferable, though not necessary, in a judgment of this sort to employ as the grammatical subject a *singular* rather than a plural noun, as "child," not "children." No matter how this judgment is expressed, it is to be understood that *the subject is taken as a universal term.* For this reason, too, *the proposition itself is universal.*

In order, then, to supplement our previous rule—that the quantity of a proposition is decided by that of its subject—we shall now set forth another that is of equal, or even greater, importance. This rule is intended to apply to *indesignate* propositions of the sort that we have just been examining:

> ***Every proposition in which the predicate rightfully belongs to the nature of the subject as such is universal.***

Thus, if we say of "watch" that it is an "instrument for telling time," the predication is universal.

Note: No matter how the subject term is expressed,[1] if the requirements of the above rule are verified, the student should not hesitate to apply it. Each of the following propositions is truly universal:

The telephone is a means of communication.
Good books deserve to be read.
A square is a four-sided figure.
Charity begins at home.

Finally, there are many propositions whose subject term consists, not of a noun, but of an infinitive or a gerund. Thus:

To err is human.
Having one's face lifted is not a pleasant experience.

For very much the same reasons as given above, propositions of this sort are to be taken as *universal.*

[1] If the above rule is verified, it makes little difference whether the *S* term is expressed (a) by a grammatically singular or plural noun, (b) with or without an article (*the, a*), or (c) by a concrete or abstract term.

In concluding our study of the quantity of propositions we must note, finally, that there are many indesignate propositions which are *particular.* The following are examples:

Women are fickle.
Professors are eccentric.
Students get worried at exam time.
White collar workers are underpaid.

Note that none of the propositions above applies strictly to the nature of its subject *as such.* Thus, even if it is true that *many* or *most* students "get the jitters" at the time of their examinations, the predicate in question is not *universally* ascribable to its subject. Offhand, such propositions may *appear* to be universal, although they are not strictly intended as such; and even if they are so intended, they cannot stand up to the requirements of true universality. The reason for this is that propositions of this kind state something that is *accidentally* and *contingently* true in many, or even in most, instances, although not in *all without exception.* In general, an indesignate proposition that is understood to be true *usually, for the most part, as a general rule,* although not always and necessarily, should be regarded in logic as *particular.*

THE QUALITY OF PROPOSITIONS

Every proposition is either affirmative or negative, and this is what we mean by its *quality.* As a rule, the quality of a proposition is immediately evident. Thus, in an affirmative proposition we are *applying* or *assigning* a certain predicate to a subject; for example, "A miser *is* a lover of money." In a negative proposition we are *denying* a predicate of a subject: for example, "A communist *is not* a conservative." Yet, if there is room for doubt, the student should refer to the following rule:

The quality of a proposition is determined by the quality of its copula.

The practical import of this rule lies in the fact that, if a negation exists within one or both of the terms of a proposition, this negation does not affect the quality of the proposition as such. *Only if the negation is of the copula is the proposition itself negative.* Thus, in spite of any appearances to the contrary, each of the following propositions is affirmative:

> Not to be loved *is* to be lonely.
> Whoever is not with me *is* against me.
> Some not unfortunate people *are* inheritors of money.
> Some people who are not interested in performing their duties *are* avid defenders of their rights.

In each of the above examples the predicate is being applied to or assigned to the subject, even if the term itself is negative. Thus, the term "not to be loved" is to be considered *as a unit* to which the predicate term "to be lonely" is applied by way of affirmation ("is").

Certain propositions contain a double negation. It were better for the student at this point to disregard the aphorism that two negatives are the equivalent of an affirmative. This matter will be discussed under Obversion. For the present it is enough simply to apply the rule that the quality of a proposition is governed by its copula.

QUANTITY AND QUALITY COMBINED

Every proposition in its *quantity,* or *extension,* is either universal or particular; in its *quality* it is either affirmative or negative. By combining the results of both extension and quality, we get the four following basic types:

UNIVERSAL: AFFIRMATIVE AND NEGATIVE
PARTICULAR: AFFIRMATIVE AND NEGATIVE

Thus:

UNIVERSAL AFFIRMATIVE:	Every car has a motor.
UNIVERSAL NEGATIVE:	No ball is square.
PARTICULAR AFFIRMATIVE:	Some men are talented.
PARTICULAR NEGATIVE:	Some medicine is not effective.

As a matter of convenience, the logician uses the following symbols for each of the four types:

A Universal affirmative
E Universal negative
I Particular affirmative
O Particular negative

Regardless of the wording of their terms, the above-mentioned types are usually presented in the following way:

A Every *S* is *P*.
E No *S* is *P*.
I Some *S* is *P*.
O Some *S* is not *P*.

Note that in the *E* proposition, although the copula may *appear* to be affirmative ("No *S* is *P*"), it is really negative by virtue of the negative force of the word *no* or *none.* Thus, although the word "no" is prefixed to the subject term, it signifies not only universal quantity, but negative quality as well.

THE QUANTITY OF THE PREDICATE TERM

In every proposition we can distinguish three traits: the quantity of the subject term, the quantity of the proposition itself (as determined by the quantity of *S*), and the quantity of the predicate term.

Language does not permit us to affix a sign of quantity to the predicate term. For example, we never say, "All men are *some* mortals." However, we must not on that account adjudge that the predicate term does not have extension. Every predicate term does have quantity or extension (universal or particular), and it is just as important to know the quantity of the predicate as that of the subject. The rules for determining the quantity of the predicate are simple:

1) *The predicate term of an affirmative proposition* (A *or* I) *is always to be taken as particular* (*undistributed*).
2) *The predicate term of a negative proposition* (E *or* O) *is always to be taken as universal* (*distributed*).

The practical importance of these two rules in their bearing on the categorical syllogism cannot be overstressed.

The reason for the rules just given will become clear as we proceed to explain how in each of the four types of propositions *S* and *P* are related to each other *from the standpoint of their extension.* Here we should emphasize the point, however, that when two terms (*S* and *P*) agree with each other in whole or in part from the standpoint of *extension,* the reason is that these same terms agree also in their *meaning* (comprehension). Likewise, when two terms disagree in their extension, the reason, again, is that they disagree in meaning. Accordingly, although it is necessary and proper to examine the extensional relationship of terms in a proposition, it is important to keep uppermost in mind the fact that *the agreement or disagreement of two terms in their meaning or comprehension is even more fundamental.* If this fact is kept in mind, there is little danger of *overrating* the importance of the diagrams presented below, which are intended merely as graphic illustrations of the rules set forth in the preceding paragraph.

1. A *Proposition*

An *A* proposition affirms in effect that *every S* comprises *part* of the extension of *P.* For example:

Every textbook is intended for purposes of study.

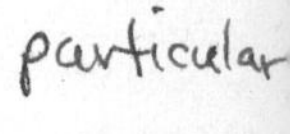

The intent of this statement is that a textbook *among other things* is intended to be studied. The predicate is applied to the subject, not in its (the predicate's) complete extension, but only in that *part* of it which relates to the subject. For this reason, then, the predicate is said to be *particular,* or *undistributed.*

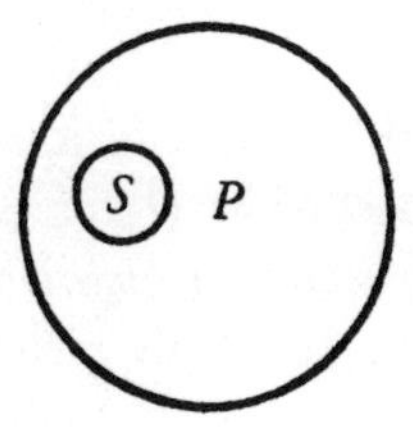

The most obvious exception to the above circular representation is the *A* proposition in which the predicate *defines* its subject: for example, "Every man is a rational animal." In a proposition of this sort the extension of *S* and *P* would coincide perfectly. For purposes of formal inference, however, even the predicate of this type of proposition is considered as particular (undistributed).

2. E *Proposition*

In an *E* proposition the subject term, taken in the totality of its extension, is excluded from the totality of the extension of *P*. For example:

> No true soldier is a coward.

No part of the extension of *S* (true soldier) comprises any part of the extension of *P* (coward). In other words, *P* (taken in its complete extension) is denied of *S* (taken in its complete extension). The predicate is, therefore, a *universal,* or *distributed,* term.

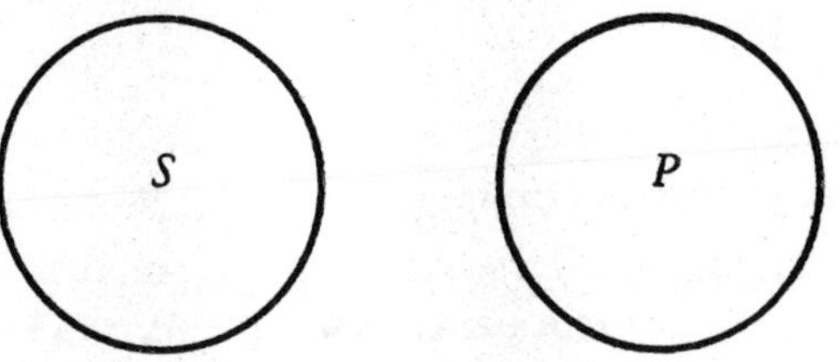

3. I *Proposition*

An *I* proposition affirms that an indeterminate portion of the extension of *S* comprises *part* of the extension of *P*. For example:

> Some coffee is imported.

Here, as in the *A* proposition, the predicate is affirmed of the subject but, again, in only *part* of its (the predicate's) extension. The predicate, therefore, is *particular,* or *undistributed.*

In this connection we need only mention a point that will be formally treated, under the square of opposition, in Chapter 7. The truth of an *I* proposition is not necessarily incompatible with the possible truth of its corresponding *A*. In stating the *I* proposition, "Some coffee is imported," we do not necessarily rule out the possibility that the *A* proposition, "All coffee is imported," is true. Nor do we, for that matter, *imply* the truth of the *O* proposition, "Some coffee is not imported."

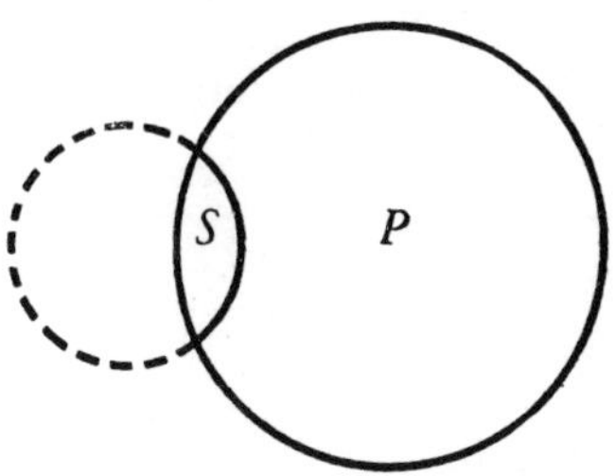

4. O *Proposition*

In an *O* proposition the predicate, as taken in its complete extension, is denied of the subject (some *S*). For example:

Some insects are not poisonous.

The *O* proposition states in effect that the predicate, in its complete extension, is to be excluded from a portion of *S*, namely, that portion of *S* which we are considering.

Here, too, it should be noted that the truth of an *O* proposition is not necessarily incompatible with the possible truth of its corresponding *E;* nor does it imply the truth of the *I* proposition.

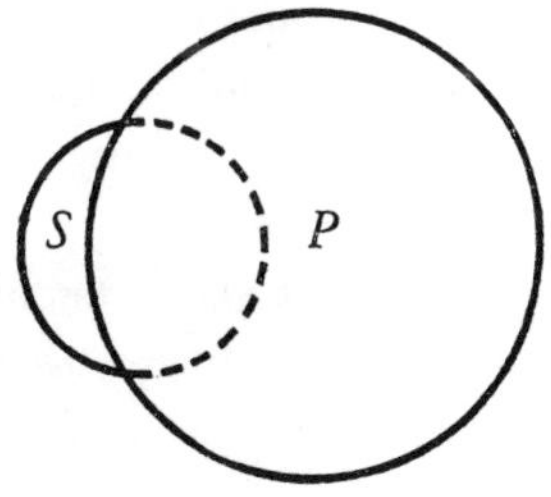

Since it is important that the logician know the quantity of both terms in a proposition as well as the quality of the copula, the following chart should prove helpful:

Type of Proposition	*Quantity of S*	*Quality of C*	*Quantity of P*
A	Universal	Affirmative	Particular
E	Universal	Negative	Universal
I	Particular	Affirmative	Particular
O	Particular	Negative	Universal

LOGICAL FORM

Since many propositions as given in their conventional form are rather loosely construed, it is often necessary to reformulate them in such a way as to clarify their basic logical structure. In general, to put a proposition into its logical form is to reconstruct it so that it conforms to one of the typical patterns: "Every *S* is *P*"; "No *S* is *P*"; and so on. Or, if no sign of quantity is required, as, for example, in singular propositions, it simply takes the form: "*S* is (or is not) *P*."

Although the need for logical form will become more apparent in subsequent chapters, it is well to indicate at this point that, independently of the utility of logical form for implication and syllogistic reasoning, the process is in itself an excellent means of determining the exact and explicit meaning of a proposition.

Because of the possibility that the *meaning* of a proposition may be confused with an *implication* (correct or incorrect) that is derivable from it, it is of prime importance to attend first to the exact, literal, and explicit meaning of any given statement before making any attempt at implication.

Often people upon hearing a given statement, but before ascertaining its meaning, immediately proceed to attach to it *their own* interpretation—an interpretation that is frequently remote from, if not altogether inconsistent with, the intended sense of the original statement.[2] In argumentation and discussion perhaps no complaint is more common than that of not being properly understood. Granted that many misunderstandings arise from inadequate expression, it is nevertheless true that most persons have a propensity for injecting their own interpretations and inferences into the statements of others before making a careful attempt to understand those statements. The best kind of listener, after all, is one who tries to be completely objective in an attempt to get at the intended meaning of a given statement.

Since it is the business of logic not only to teach the student to make implications and inferences that are correct, but—even more fundamentally than that—to help him get at the explicit *meaning* of a proposition, the discipline of placing propositions in their logical form should be considerably stressed. The immediate practical advantages of this exercise will be to help the student accustom himself *to give more exact expression* to the propositions that he himself maintains and *to clarify* for himself the statements of others.

HOW TO PUT A PROPOSITION IN ITS LOGICAL FORM

There is no single method of putting a proposition in its logical form. As a matter of fact, a considerable amount of latitude is permissible in the rearrangement of the words of a proposition. These verbal changes, however, must be rigorously consonant with the meaning of the original statement. The following suggestions should prove helpful:

1. *Look for the logical subject.* Wherever the need exists, the first thing to do is to determine the logical subject of a proposition, namely, that *about which* the predication is made. Once the subject term is decided upon, there is no further difficulty in setting forth the predicate. Note, then, the occasional need for the following:

[2] See page 266 for an example of the fallacy of "ignoring the issue."

Eliminate nonsignificant words. For example:

It is better to work than to starve.

In this example, the word "it" has no logical significance and should not be taken as the logical subject. In asking the question: What is the predication about? the student will have little difficulty in deciding upon the following as the logical form of the above proposition:

To work (*S*) is (*c*) better than to starve (*P*).

Transpose an inverted word order. For example:

Greatly to be admired is a person who is genuinely modest.

The logical structure of this proposition is more evident in the form:

A person who is genuinely modest (*S*) is (*c*) to be greatly admired (*P*).

Unite a term that is split. For example:

He jests at scars that never felt a wound.
He that never felt a wound (*S*) is (*c*) one who jests at scars (*P*).

2. *Determine (when necessary) the quantity of the subject term and the quality of the copula.* A number of suggestions have already been made along these lines. Here, however, it is necessary to deal in a special way with the difficulties attendant upon the correct formulation of *O* propositions. As we have seen, the correct logical form of an *O* proposition is

Some *S* is not *P*.

There are many ways, however, in which the *O* proposition as found in its nonlogical form can be an abundant source of confusion. In any case, every instructor in logic is agreed that it is a source of confusion to his students. Despite appearances to the contrary, each of the following is to be construed as an *O* proposition:

Not all examinations are easy.
Not every man is a genius.
Men are not all naïve.
All women are not fickle.
Every man is not a logician.

First of all, there is the possibility that a student may regard one or more of the above propositions as an *I.* Take the proposition, "Not all examinations are easy." Offhand, one may be tempted to think that this proposition *means that* "Some examinations are easy." Whether or not the truth of the *O* and *I* forms of the terms given here are compatible, we must first attend to the meaning of the statement *as given.* A careful inspection of our example reveals that in the proposition as stated one is not really affirming, but denying, *P* ("easy") of *S* ("examinations"). Thus, whether or not it is correct to imply that "Some examinations are easy," the *meaning* of the proposition as stated is really "Some examinations are not easy."

There is also the possibility that the student may regard one or more of the above propositions as an *E.* Judging by appearances, one might think that since "all" or "every" is universal, and since "not" signifies a negation, therefore, the proposition is a universal negative—an *E.* Yet, again, what does the proposition, "Every man is not a logician," for example, mean? Certainly it is not intended by way of universal denial, that is, "No man is a logician." All that it does mean is that "some are not." It is a mere accident of language that "every" in this context does not mean "every" but "some." This example is a rather forceful indication of the need for expressing certain propositions in a strictly logical form.

POPULAR SAYINGS AND AXIOMS

There are many popular sayings, mottoes, and axioms the meaning of which is not intended to be literal, but analogous. The following are typical examples:

What is sauce for the goose is sauce for the gander.
It is unwise to change horses in midstream.

Birds of a feather flock together.
A bird in the hand is worth two in the bush.
A rotten apple spoils the barrel.
A living dog is better than a dead king.

The first thing to note regarding these statements (as well as many more of this kind) is the fact that when people use them they obviously are not restricting their attention to "horses," "birds," "dogs," "rotten apples," or "dead kings." What they have in mind is something that terms of this sort signify only in an improper way, that is, "improper" from the point of view of logic. The supposition of the terms in such propositions is, in other words, analogous. In view of this fact it would be pointless to take such a statement *as it is given* and attempt to put it in its logical form.

As a matter of fact, it may be assumed that a proposition that is to be put in its logical form has a fairly *definite* meaning, even if that meaning is not perfectly expressed. Now it is true, of course, that the above propositions do have meanings and that the meaning of some of them at least is apparent. Take the proposition, "A living dog is better than a dead king." We may hazard a fairly safe guess that this proposition means: "Any living organism, however lowly, is preferable to one that is dead, regardless of the worth of the dead organism at the time it was alive." Yet, we cannot be sure that the person using this example *in context* is really talking about organisms. Conceivably this motto can have any number of meanings, depending on how it is *applied,* let us say, to a book or an automobile.[3] We can very easily imagine that a publisher might mean by this motto that a good-selling novel is of greater value to him than some classic volume that remains on the shelves. In a completely different context it might mean that a cheap model car that runs is more useful than an expensive car that does not.

The example in the preceding paragraph is a typical one, and what it reveals is the fact that the harder one tries to discover the "meaning" of statements of this sort, the more it becomes clear that they have *many* meanings. If such were not the case, sayings of this kind would not be so popular and so widely used as they actually

[3] Etienne Gilson in his *Being and Some Philosophers* uses this motto to illustrate the primacy of existence over essence.

are. In fact, they are frequently employed as a sort of "principle" that has dozens of different applications. Accordingly, although it is a very interesting and, up to a point, useful exercise to *interpret* propositions of this sort, to do so involves more than merely putting a proposition in its logical form.

Now the advantage of this type of statement is mainly the *rhetorical* advantage of expressing a judgment or opinion in a manner that is picturesque, forceful, and at least superficially convincing. It is a known fact that most often the person who wins the final "argument" in the course of an extended debate is the one who can effectively employ a saying of this kind against the abstract and detailed arguments of his opponent in a way that appeals to the imagination of his audience. Such axioms have a down-to-earth quality about them in the sense that their wording is based on the familiar objects of sense experience. We need only recall here the famous axiom of the inadvisability of changing horses in midstream.

In view of the insuperable difficulties of attempting to assign one—and only one—specific meaning to a popular motto or axiom of this sort, we can only advise the student at this point of the need to determine as exactly as he can the meaning each has in *context.* Finally, even though the meaning of a statement of this kind is clear in its context, the student must be on his guard against accepting it at its face value as an *argument.*[4]

SPECIAL TYPES OF PROPOSITIONS

Before we conclude this chapter, we must call attention to the fact that there are many propositions which, though categorical in the *generic* sense of the word, are not simply reducible to the form "*S* is (or is not) *P.*" Take as an example the following:

English is not spoken everywhere.

[4] The *argument from analogy* in the proper meaning of the term is one that is based on *literal* points of resemblance in the objects compared. It may be defined as an argument in which, on the basis of literal points of resemblance found to exist between two objects or classes of objects, an attempt is made to establish further points of resemblance. Such an argument does have *logical* significance. Suppose, however, that the two terms of the analogy are only metaphorically related. The "argument" from analogy in that case is purely *rhetorical and illustrative.* It is really no argument at all.

In attempting to put this proposition in its logical form, the meaning would be distorted if it were expressed thus:

Some English is not spoken(!).

At best, all that can be stated here is:

Somewhere English is not spoken.
(Somewhere *S* is not *P*.)

Propositions of this kind bear a close resemblance to the modals, which we shall treat in the next chapter, in that they do express a certain manner, or mode, of agreement between two terms. What characterizes these propositions, however, is the fact that *as part of their copula* they call special attention to a relationship of time, place, or some other circumstance. The following examples are typical:

Rosy cheeks *are not always* a sign of health.
Lying *is never* honorable.
Trains *are frequently* behind schedule.
The child *is nowhere* to be found.
Excusing oneself from class *is under certain circumstances* permissible.

In all examples of this type of proposition it should be noted that *P* is assigned to (or denied of) *S*, not simply, but according to some determinate means of qualification. It is impossible to present here a complete list of the words and phrases that signify this type of proposition. A sufficient number and variety will be given, however, to serve as a guide for the student in determining whether the proposition in which they appear is, generally speaking, an *A, E, I,* or *O* proposition:

A PROPOSITION

always, everywhere, anywhere, completely, wholly, entirely, in its completeness, in all cases, under all circumstances, in all respects, under all conditions, in all ways

E PROPOSITION

never, nowhere, in no part, in no case, under no circumstance, in no respect, under no condition, in no way

I PROPOSITION

sometimes, occasionally, often, at times, frequently, usually, somewhere, for the most part, partially, in some cases, under some circumstances, in some respects, under certain conditions, in some ways

O PROPOSITION

sometimes not, not always, frequently not, somewhere not, not everywhere, not completely, for the most part not, in some cases not

In setting forth the logical form of propositions that contain expressions of this sort, it is necessary to retain the word or phrase as given rather than to substitute for it the more simplified "Every (no, some) *S* is (or is not) *P*."

CONCLUDING REMARKS. Logical form, it should be remembered, is merely a means to an end. Its usefulness lies mainly in setting forth the thought structure of a statement whose original wording leaves something to be desired. The ideal of every student of logic should be the achievement in so far as possible of a clarity of expression that precludes the possibility of misunderstanding.

EXERCISES

1. What is the general rule for determining the quantity of a proposition?

2. (a) What is meant by an *indesignate proposition?* (b) How does one judge the quantity of this type?

3. What is the general rule for determining the quality of a proposition?

4. Give the two rules for determining the quantity of the predicate term.

5. (a) What is the extensional relationship of *S* and *P* in each of the four types of propositions (*A, E, I,* and *O*)? (b) Use the circular diagrams as a means of illustration.

6. Distinguish between *meaning* and *implication.* Do people confuse these terms?

7. Generally speaking, what is meant by putting a proposition in its *logical* form?

8. What are some of the typical nonlogical expressions of the *O* proposition?

9. Show that it is wrong to express an *E* proposition in the form "All *S* is not *P.*"

10. Can popular sayings and axioms be put in logical form? Discuss this point.

11. How does one decide upon the meaning of these sayings?

12. Give a few examples of your own, explaining what you understand by them.

13. There are certain *special types* of propositions that are not reducible to the form "*S* is (or is not) *P.*" Give examples of your own. Can you add to the list of words and phrases that signify this type of proposition a few of your own?

14. Identify each of the following as *A, E, I,* or *O* propositions, and when necessary place the proposition into its logical form:

(1) Prudence is a virtue.
(2) Not every cat is a suitable pet.
(3) Life is worth living.
(4) The possession of wealth is not without its advantages.
(5) Not to move forward is to fall behind.
(6) Charity covers a multitude of sins.
(7) Whoever is not with me is against me.
(8) Not all comedians are funny.
(9) There are certain inconsistencies in our foreign policy.
(10) Some people who are not wealthy create the impression that they are.
(11) Nothing is lost by taking time.

(12) There are some languages that take years to master.
(13) Unjust aggression is not something to be condoned.
(14) All mourners do not weep.
(15) A skillful operation is no guarantee that the patient will live.
(16) Certain historical events are unparalleled.
(17) All's well that ends well.
(18) Nothing is well that does not end well.
(19) All is not well that ends well.
(20) Not all campaign literature is educational.
(21) Baseball is a sport.
(22) Nothing that is material is indestructible.
(23) Everything of a spiritual nature is indestructible.
(24) Certain things are a matter of taste.
(25) Authority is not man-made.
(26) Not every contract that is legal is morally justifiable.
(27) All bureaucrats are not garbage collectors.
(28) There are many things that are invisible to the eye of the microscope.
(29) Most sins are not unforgivable.
(30) There is no temptation that is unconquerable.
(31) Pride is the root of all evil.
(32) Whatever is good is praiseworthy.
(33) An ingrained habit is not easy to uproot.
(34) Not to eat is to starve.
(35) To eat is not to starve.
(36) To love those you do not like is a distinctively Christian virtue.
(37) Certain people are in the habit of accusing others of the very faults that are their own.
(38) A mathematical point is an abstraction.
(39) All doctors are not research men.
(40) Whatever is not good is not deserving of praise.
(41) Writing a term paper is not an easy task.
(42) Most teachers are not wealthy men.

(43) Omniscience is not a human attribute.
(44) Americans are fond of sports.
(45) A wasted opportunity is a source of regret.
(46) Not everything that is memorized is learned.
(47) Beauty is not a product of manufacture.
(48) All idealists are not daydreamers.
(49) Man does not act without a motive.
(50) Electricity is a source of power.

15. Identify as *A, E, I,* or *O* propositions the following *special types* of propositions as discussed in this chapter:

(a) In no part of your term paper is there evidence of any original work.
(b) Gambling is not illegal in all its forms.
(c) Lying is never honorable.
(d) In some ways your appearance resembles that of your father.
(e) Students do not always write what they think.
(f) The past is never quite what you imagine it to be.
(g) In some ways this home is not designed for practical living.
(h) Under no circumstances will your schoolwork be interrupted.
(i) One should always respect his neighbor's rights.
(j) Somewhere there is peace.
(k) Hasty eating frequently causes indigestion.
(l) Examinations are sometimes hard to read.

6

Varieties of Propositions

Multiple Propositions
Half-truths
Kinds of Multiple Propositions
Modal Propositions
Hypothetical Propositions

INTRODUCTORY REMARKS. In this chapter our purpose is to analyze in some detail the different varieties of the three basic types of propositions—*categoricals, modals,* and *hypotheticals.* Such a study is important for a number of reasons. First, it should serve as an indispensable means for an exact determination of the *meanings* involved in statements of a more complex nature than those which we studied in the previous chapter. Second, the logician must know how to *contradict* any given proposition. This will be part of the burden of the chapter that follows this one. Yet, to know how to contradict a proposition one must be familiar with the *kind* of proposition that is involved. Finally, the present study is in part necessary as a preparation for an analysis of the different kinds of syllogisms, since the nature of a syllogism is determined by the kind of propositions that enter into its composition.

MULTIPLE PROPOSITIONS

In Chapter 2 we called attention to the fact that a term within a proposition may be either simple or complex. Thus, the subject and predicate terms of the following proposition, in spite of the difference in their length, are equally terms:

> Anyone who fails to learn from his past mistakes (*S*) is (*c*) a fool (*P*).

Note that if any proposition, regardless of the length of its terms, contains but one subject and one predicate, it is a *single* proposition. Our attention has thus far centered exclusively around *single categoricals.*

As opposed to the single categorical, a *multiple* proposition is *a sentence expressing more than one enunciation,* that is, object of assent or agreement. Such propositions contain more than one logical subject, predicate, or more than one of both. Thus:

> *Franklin Roosevelt* and *Harry Truman* were Democratic presidents.
> (More than one subject)

> Andrew Jackson was both *a military general* and *a president of the United States.*
> (More than one predicate)

> *Jackson* and *Grant* were both *generals* and *presidents.*
> (More than one subject and more than one predicate)

A casual inspection of the above examples will reveal that a multiple proposition is a means of expressing compactly in one sentence *more than one object of agreement.* Clearly, every such proposition is resolvable into the various single categoricals that it unites. Thus, the third example above breaks down into four single propositions:

> Jackson was a military general.
> Jackson was a president.
> Grant was a military general.
> Grant was a president.

A multiple proposition need not always be broken down into its simple elements, especially if its meaning is clear and its truth apparent. Yet, in actual practice there are many propositions—"package" statements—that should be broken down for the purpose of examining their meaning, their truth value, or both.

HALF-TRUTHS

In single propositions there can be no such thing as a half-truth, for every proposition that expresses only one enunciation must be either true or false. Nevertheless, the remark is often made that a given statement expresses a half-truth, the implication being that such a statement is partly true and partly false. Since a multiple proposition embodies more than one enunciation, it is unquestionably the source of the familiar half-truth. In such a case, the resolution of the proposition into its single components becomes necessary in order to determine which propositions, taken singly, are true and which are false.

Since, then, a multiple proposition expresses more than one object of agreement or disagreement, it should not be spoken of as true unless it is true in all its parts. In other words, *if a multiple proposition is false in any one of its parts, the proposition as such is false.*

Students will do well to apply this rule in the familiar true-false examinations. If any part of a true-or-false statement is false, it should accordingly be marked "false." For example: "Logic is the study of emotional reaction and reasoning."

Most professional writers or speakers are very careful to avoid presenting their readers or listeners with a deliberate falsehood. The student, however, must be constantly on guard against the "package" type of statement which contains a half-truth. Indeed, in critical thinking it is important to avoid being led into the admission of a multiple proposition in which a writer or speaker wittingly or unwittingly deceives the reader or listener. It is precisely when a falsehood is couched in a statement that is in every other respect true that the reader or listener is most likely to accept the falsehood.

KINDS OF MULTIPLE PROPOSITIONS

Since there are many ways in which two or more single propositions can be combined into a multiple statement, no attempt will be made here to give a complete or near-complete classification. Logicians, however, distinguish two fundamental types: those propositions that are *clearly* multiple in form, for example, "Donald *and* James are at home"; and those that are really multiple, although they have the *appearance* of a *single* proposition, for example, "Only you know the answer." The first type of proposition may be called an *overt,* or *evident,* multiple; that is, it is one whose multiple character is *readily discernible.* The second type is a *disguised* multiple and is spoken of simply as an *exponible* proposition.

Overt, or Evident, Multiples

COPULATIVE. A copulative proposition is one that unites or disunites its enunciations on a purely coordinate basis. The conjunctions most often used are such words as: *and, both—and, not only—but also, neither—nor.* For example:

Both Mary *and* Jane attended the party.
Neither the Chief Justice *nor* his associates are elected.
(Both parts negative)

ADVERSATIVE. An adversative proposition is a grammatically complex sentence in which the subordinate clause is set up *in opposition to* the enunciation expressed in the main clause. The enunciation expressed in the subordinate clause is usually indicated by such conjunctions as the following: *although, even though, even if, in spite of, but, despite, while, whereas.* For example:

Even though the sun is shining, it is raining.

RELATIVE (*Indicating Time*). In this type of proposition the subordinate clause introduces a time relation that has a bearing upon what is stated in the main clause. The usual signs are *before, during, after.* For example:

After submitting his examination, John realized some of the mistakes he had made.

CAUSAL. A causal proposition is one whose subordinate clause assigns the cause or reason for what is asserted in the main clause. The usual signs are *because, for, since.* For example:

Because some people fail to see the purpose of human existence, their lives are meaningless.

Since each of the types just described is an overt or evident multiple, the compound nature of such propositions is immediately apparent. As a rule, it is not necessary to resolve them into their component parts, except when it becomes necessary to examine them for their truth value.

Fundamentally, the truth of such propositions depends upon the truth of the separate enunciations that they contain. Yet over and above this, their truth—with the exception of the *copulative* proposition—depends also upon the connection or lack of connection that is asserted to exist or not to exist between the two clauses. Note, as an example:

Because Washington, D.C., is in the east, it is the capital of the United States.

Although both parts of this statement are *factually* true, the statement itself is false because it lacks the *causal* connection that it claims.

Exponibles or Disguised Multiples

EXCLUSIVE. Note the following example:

Nothing short of a sudden reversal of events will prevent the mayor from pursuing his present course of action.

A statement of this sort makes a double assertion—one of affirmation and another of denial. Thus:

A sudden revearsal of events will prevent the mayor. . . .

Nothing else (that is, no other circumstance or event) will prevent the mayor. . . .

Again:

Only humans wear shoes.

This resolves into the following:

(Some) humans wear shoes.
(No) one else (that is, no nonhuman) wears shoes.

In the above examples, a predicate is assigned to the subject *to the exclusion of all other subjects.*

The exclusive proposition may, of course, take the form: "*S* is only *P*." For example:

Certain things are only a means to an end.

Here the predicate is assigned to the subject *to the exclusion of all other predicates.*

Because of the boldness of the assertion involved in an exclusive proposition, considerable caution should be exercised in either using or accepting it. Further, to avoid ambiguity words like "only" or "alone" must be correctly placed. They should be placed before the word that they are intended to modify. This, of course, is a point of grammar, but it has a bearing on logic. Note, then, the difference of meaning in the following examples:

Only religion is tolerated in a dictatorship.
(Religion is tolerated; nothing else is.)
Religion is tolerated *only* in a dictatorship.
(Religion is tolerated in a dictatorship; it is tolerated nowhere else.)
Religion is *only* tolerated in a dictatorship.
(Religion is *tolerated* in a dictatorship; that is, it is *merely* tolerated, not encouraged or given active support.)

EXCEPTIVE. Closely related to the exclusive proposition is the exceptive. The difference between an exclusive and an exceptive proposition should become clear from an inspection of the examples below:

EXCLUSIVE:

Only the chairman was on time for the meeting.
(The chairman was on time. No one else—that is, no one not a chairman—was.)

EXCEPTIVE:

Everyone, except the chairman, was on time.
(The chairman was *not* on time. Everyone else—that is, anyone not a chairman—was.)

REDUPLICATIVE. In assigning a predicate to a given subject, it is often possible to consider that subject from more than one point of view. In general, it is the function of a reduplicative proposition to call specific attention to that aspect or formality of the subject in the light of which a certain predication is being made. Note the following example:

Every official *as such* is deserving of public respect.

The usual signs of a reduplicative proposition are the following: *as, as such, qua, inasmuch as.*

The example given above is a reduplicative proposition in the strict sense, for the words "as such" are a reinforcement of the subject term *as given.* Although the following proposition is not *strictly* "reduplicative," it may for all practical intents be assigned to this general category:

As a geographical neighbor of the United States Canada has a heavy traffic of American tourists.

The compactness of a reduplicative statement becomes evident when we attempt to resolve the above example into its component parts:

Canada is a geographical neighbor of the United States. She has a heavy traffic of American tourists. One of the reasons for this is the fact that she is a geographical neighbor.

The utility of a reduplicative proposition is evidenced, not only by its *compactness,* but also, and primarily, by its *precision.* In calling attention to that aspect of the subject which we are considering when we assign a predicate to it, we leave little, if any, room for being misunderstood. The reduplicative proposition is a *sine qua non* in the language of science. Certainly it should be put to more frequent use in the language of everyday life.

MODAL PROPOSITIONS

All the propositions dealt with thus far in this chapter have been of the sort that are ultimately reducible to the form: "S *is* (or *is not*) P." Besides categoricals, there is another type *which expresses a certain manner or mode of agreement or disagreement between two terms*—a mode of agreement that is not one of fact, but of *necessity, contingency, possibility, impossibility.* Compare the difference between the categorical proposition

Science has all the answers

and any one of the following four:

Science *must* have all the answers.
Science *need not* have all the answers.
Science *may* have all the answers.
Science *cannot* have all the answers.

Since the difference between a strictly categorical proposition and a modal, as well as the difference between one modal proposition and another, lies precisely in the manner of agreement or disagreement expressed, let us examine each of the four types.

Mode of Necessity

In maintaining a proposition whose mode is one of necessity, one not only *implies* that "S *is* P," but explicitly asserts that "S *must be* P." Take the following:

Every effect must have a cause.

When we make this assertion, we imply not only that every effect does, as a matter of *fact,* have a cause, but that every effect *necessarily* (that is, by a necessity of its very nature) has a cause. Thus, we rule out the very possibility of there being any effect without a cause. The mode of necessity is usually expressed in one of the following ways:

> S *must be* P.
> S *has to be* P.
> It *is necessary* that S be P.
> S *is of necessity* P.

Note: Here the italics indicate the *copula* of this type of proposition.

Because the words "must" and "has to" do not always express a strict, logical necessity, it is preferable at times to use the third and fourth forms. For example:

> Johnny *must be* a good boy at the party.

This statement, far from expressing logical necessity, merely indicates a firm hope that he will be or the conditioned assertion that, if he is not a good boy, something unpleasant may happen to him. Or again:

> One of these days it will *have* to rain (that is, if the crops are to grow, and so on).

Mode of Contingency

A contingent proposition is the simple denial of the mode of necessity. Thus:

> S *need not* be P.
> It *is not necessary* that S be P.

As a matter of practical import we should note here that the *denial of necessity* made in a contingent proposition *is not to be confused with a denial of fact.* Thus:

> A research scholar is not necessarily a good teacher.

Here the speaker is denying neither the possibility that a research scholar may become a good teacher nor the fact that some scholars are good teachers. What he is denying is the assumption that a research scholar *must* be a good teacher. Failure to make this elementary distinction gives rise to many misunderstandings.

Mode of Possibility

In contradiction to a categorical proposition, this third type of modal is one that does not express an outright agreement of two terms but affirms merely the *possibility* of such an agreement. Thus:

> S *can be* P.
> Men *can be* virtuous.

Clearly, this statement makes no factual implication; it merely affirms something as an open possibility.

Mode of Impossibility

This mode, which s clearly the contradictory of possibility, usually takes the form

> S *cannot be* P.
> It *is impossible* that S be P.

The assertion of impossibility involves—as the mode of possibility does not—the denial of the fact as well. For example:

> *No* man *can* understand everything.

This proposition implicitly involves the denial of the proposition that

> There is some man who understands everything.

It should be observed that any of the modals can be combined, together with categorical propositions, into the form of a *multiple*. For example:

> Although it is *possible* for a man to work eighteen hours a day, doing so *is not* advisable.

For purposes of implication and inference modal propositions are to be treated thus:

Mode of necessity: *A* proposition
Mode of contingency: *O* proposition
Mode of possibility: *I* proposition
Mode of impossibility: *E* proposition

HYPOTHETICAL PROPOSITIONS

"Hypothetical" usually means "conditional." It is customary, however, for logicians to use that term in the *generic* sense, that is, as including not only *conditional* propositions but also those which are *disjunctive* and *conjunctive.* These three basic types will be examined in the remainder of this chapter.

How a hypothetical proposition differs from those we have already examined will become clear from our study of each specific type and especially from the remarks we shall make in the next two paragraphs. Here we should note, however, that the copula of this type of proposition consists, not of a verb, but of the word or words used to unite or disunite the enunciations that it contains. For example: *if—then, either—or.*

Conditional Proposition

A conditional proposition usually takes the following form:

If A is B, *then* A is C.
If a man works, then he deserves the reward of his labor.

We distinguish as the two parts of a conditional proposition the *antecedent* and the *consequent.* The antecedent (familiarly known as the "if clause") expresses the condition whose fulfillment is necessary for the *consequent* to take place. The significance of a conditional proposition lies, not in the independent truth or falsity of the enunciations that it contains, but merely in the sequential dependence of the consequent upon the antecedent.

Earlier in the chapter we said that a multiple proposition is true if it is true in its separate parts. This principle simply does not apply to the conditional, nor is it, for that matter, permissible to resolve a conditional proposition into its separate parts. It must be left *as is,* and the same holds true for disjunctives and conjunctives. In order, then, for a conditional proposition to be true, it is necessary that the consequent follow *of necessity* from the antecedent. Hence, in *denying* the truth of a conditional, it is necessary only to point out that the consequent *does not necessarily follow* from the given antecedent. Take the following proposition:

If you are an American, you live in the United States.

Even though you are an American and even though you live in the United States, this proposition is false, because the consequent does not necessarily follow. There are some Americans who reside in a foreign country. Thus, although both enunciations *considered independently* are true, the proposition is false.

Consider, on the other hand, the proposition:

If man were all-knowing, he would be God.

Man is neither all-knowing nor is he God. Both enunciations separately considered are false, yet the proposition itself is true. In brief, a conditional proposition *prescinds from* the truth or falsity of its separate enunciations.

Although the "if" clause is the commonest means of introducing a conditional, it is far from being the only means. Note the following variations:

Provided that you study, you will learn.
Unless a man follow his conscience, he will suffer remorse.
Were you a brute, you would not have to study logic.
In the event that the child is lost, he will be hungry.
Assuming what you say to be true, I would have to admit I'm in the wrong.

Periodically it happens that a statement that is really categorical in nature takes on the form of a conditional. Note the use of the word "if" in the statement below:

If men quarrel, they don't always mean to.

The meaning of "if" in this statement is "even if" or "although."

Disjunctive Proposition

A disjunctive proposition is easily recognized by its copula,, that is, by the words *either—or*. For example:

A is either *B* or *C*.
The will is either free or determined.

As we shall see in a moment, there are two basic types of disjunctive propositions, though the following should serve as a general definition: A disjunctive proposition is one that alternatively combines two or more enunciations in a manner that states *indeterminately* that one of these enunciations is *true.*

In studying the above definition the student should carefully note that *the truth of a disjunctive is never dependent upon which enunciation specifically considered is true.* Thus, if it is said that "Either John or Bill will attend the party," the statement remains true no matter which one (Bill or John) goes to the party. For this reason we say that a disjunctive states *indeterminately* that one of its enunciations is true.

We must now distinguish the *two basic types* of disjunctives. Both, of course, are the *same* in *form,* inasmuch as they employ the same type of copula, namely, *either—or.* The difference, however, is in the *matter,* or the *meaning* of the statement, which most often must be gathered from the *context.*

PROPER OR PERFECT DISJUNCTIVE. A disjunctive proposition in its strictest sense states (indeterminately) that of the enunciations given *one is true* and the *other* (or others) must be *false.* The requirements of the above definition can be most readily recognized in a disjunctive statement that consists of two parts that are contradictory of each other. For example:

Every (individual) student is either a graduate or a non-graduate.

The meaning of this statement, like that of *any* disjunctive, is that *one* of its enunciations is true. What characterizes it, however, as a special type of disjunctive is the fact that *the other enunciation* (whichever it might be) is *false.*

Note also the following example:

> Washington died either before, during, or after the time of Napoleon Bonaparte.

This, of course, is a rather safe proposition, but it illustrates the point that *a strictly disjunctive statement may employ more than two enunciations.* Clearly, the sense of the above statement is that *if one enunciation is true, the others are false.*

In order that any proposition of this kind may be *true,* two requirements must be fulfilled. The enunciations given must be *complete,* and they must *mutually exclude* each other. Thus, *if* it is said, in the sense of a *strict* disjunctive, that "every American is either a Republican or a Democrat," the statement would be false, since an American citizen need not join or sympathize with any political party or may be a member of some third party. In either event, the alternatives given would be *incomplete.* Take also the following example: "Either you are a Democrat or you are not interested in the welfare of your country." With all respect to those who maintain this proposition, the alternatives that it gives are not *mutually exclusive.* One may very well be interested in his country's welfare without necessarily being a Democrat.

IMPROPER OR IMPERFECT DISJUNCTIVE. It would be a mistake to think that the proper disjunctive is the *only* kind. A disjunctive statement is most often made with no intention of giving a complete list of possibilities. Nor, for that matter, is it necessary that the enunciations exclude each other. Take the following as an example:

> Either Mary finds her subjects too time-consuming, or she does not care to study, or there are too many difficulties which prevent her from getting good marks.

If this proposition were examined in the light of the more stringent requirements for the truth of a proper disjunctive, it would obviously have to be adjudged false. On the other hand, if it were examined in the *context* in which it was spoken, it might very well prove to be *true.* The reason for this is that the sole requirement for the truth of an *improper* disjunctive is that *at least one* of its enunciations be true—the others *may* be true or false.

Accordingly, an *improper* disjunctive statement does not demand, as does a *strictly* disjunctive, that one of the given enunciations be true *and the others false.* It merely states that at least one of the alternatives is true. Thus, the only way to prove this type of proposition false is to show that *all* of its enunciations are false. The utility of this type of statement as a means of contradicting multiples will be explained in the next chapter.

Conjunctive Proposition

A conjunctive proposition is negative in form, and we may define it as a proposition that states that of two (or more) enunciations *both* (or all) *cannot be true.* Since the commonest type of conjunctive statement employs only two enunciations, we may restrict our attention to this form, as illustrated by the following example:

You cannot work and play at the same time.

A conjunctive proposition does not state, as does a disjunctive, that one enunciation is or must be true but merely that *both cannot be true.* This is an important point, for it is in this respect that disjunctive and conjunctive statements are essentially distinct from each other. Accordingly, a conjunctive proposition, unlike a disjunctive, permits the possibility that *both of its enunciations may be false.* All that a conjunctive proposition explicitly states is the impossibility of both enunciations being true at the same time and in the same respect. Thus, if it is said that "You cannot be both a European and an Asiatic," the truth of this statement does not depend upon your being one *or* the other, but rather upon the impossibility of being *both.*

SUMMARY. The following outline should help to summarize the content of this chapter:

- I. Categorical propositions
  - A. Single
  - B. Multiple
    - 1. Overt, or evident, multiples
      - a. Copulative
      - b. Adversative
      - c. Relative (indicating time)
      - d. Causal
    - 2. Exponibles (disguised multiples)
      - a. Exclusive
      - b. Exceptive
      - c. Reduplicative
- II. Modal propositions, expressing
  - A. Necessity
  - B. Contingency
  - C. Possibility
  - D. Impossibility
- III. Hypothetical propositions
  - A. Conditional
  - B. Disjunctive
    - 1. Proper (perfect)
    - 2. Improper (imperfect)
  - C. Conjunctive

EXERCISES

1. Define *multiple* proposition. Explain your definition.
2. Distinguish *overt,* or *evident, multiples* and *exponibles.*
3. From the standpoint of logic, what is signified by the expression *half-truth?*
4. What is the rule for determining the *truth* of multiple propositions?
5. Give your own examples of each of the types of overt or evident multiples discussed in the text.

6. Explain the difference between an *exclusive* proposition and an *exceptive* proposition.

7. (a) Define *reduplicative* proposition. (b) Give three examples. (c) Discuss the importance of this type of proposition.

8. What is the characteristic nature of a *modal* proposition?

9. (a) Give an example of each of the four types of modals. (b) Discuss some of the dangers of confusing a modal with a categorical proposition.

10. What are the parts of a *conditional* proposition?

11. What is necessary to ensure the *truth* of a conditional?

12. Is the truth of a conditional proposition, like that of a multiple, dependent upon the truth of its separate parts?

13. What are some of the ways of introducing the antecedent of a conditional other than by the word "if"?

14. Does the word "if" always signify a conditional proposition?

15. Give a *general* definition of *disjunctive* proposition.

16. (a) What is the intent of a disjunctive statement that is *proper* or perfect? (b) Give your own example. (c) What is required for a statement of this kind to be true?

17. (a) Distinguish an *improper* from a strictly disjunctive proposition. (b) Is the difference between the two evident from the form, that is, from the copula? (c) Give an example of an improper disjunctive. (d) What is necessary to make your statement true?

18. (a) Define *conjunctive* proposition. (b) Contradistinguish this type from the disjunctive. (c) Give your own example.

19. Determine the nature of each of the propositions listed below and assign the corresponding letter from the key:

a categorical single
b copulative
c adversative
d relative (time)
e causal
f exclusive
g exceptive
h reduplicative
i conditional
j disjunctive
k conjunctive
l modal: necessary
m modal: contingent
n modal: possible
o modal: impossible

(a) Were man a brute, he would not be morally responsible.

(b) All states, except a few in the South, voted Republican in the presidential election of 1952.

(c) Every *single* proposition is either true or false.

(d) Neither my parents nor my grandparents were born in Europe.

(e) Evil as such is never desirable.

(f) In spite of their being intelligent, there are some students whose marks are below average.

(g) Since I did not understand some of the questions, some of my answers were wrong.

(h) A criminal need not be a thief.

(i) Children can be well behaved.

(j) While he attended college, Bill was a sports enthusiast.

(k) Brutes cannot reason.

(l) You cannot watch television and read a book at the same time.

(m) Only the Russian delegation is obstructing the progress of the United Nations.

(n) Logic need not be difficult.

(o) A politician as such is not as a rule a disinterested person.

(p) If parents are at times impatient with their children, they still love them.

(q) To be interesting a book has to be readable.

(r) Every creature, except man, knows what is for its own good.

(s) Either you are a Parisian, or you don't know the joy of living.

(t) Everything that is moved must be moved by something else.

(u) Authority, inasmuch as it establishes order in society, is indispensable.

(v) None but a starving man would eat this meal.

(w) Anyone who is truly virtuous is happy.

(x) After leaving her place of work, my sister went shopping.

(y) History does not have to be dull.

20. *Resolve* propositions (b), (e), (m), (r), and (v) of the list above into their component parts.

7

The Square of Opposition

Meaning of Opposition

Rules of Opposition

Practical Observations

Opposition of Singulars

Opposition of Modals and of Special Types

Opposition of Multiples

Opposition of Hypotheticals

INTRODUCTORY REMARKS. Thus far we have confined our attention to an analysis of propositions considered in themselves, that is, in their purely isolated status *as* propositions. The only kind of relationship studied has been that which exists between the parts of a given proposition, so that we could determine its *meaning*. We are now about to examine some of the relationships that exist, not *within* the proposition itself, but *between one proposition and another*. In this chapter we shall discuss the type of relationship technically designated as *opposition*. In the first half of the chapter we shall restrict our consideration to the *opposition of single cat egoricals.* The remainder of the chapter will be a treatment of the opposition of the *other types,* which were studied in the preceding chapter.

MEANING OF OPPOSITION

In a discussion of opposition the first question that naturally arises is this: When are two propositions *opposed* to each other? To answer this question we should point out that we are confining our attention here to single categoricals which in comparison with each other have the same *subject and predicate terms.* Take, for example, the two following propositions:

S *P*
No *modern baby* is *undernourished.*

S *P*
Some *modern babies* are *undernourished.*

These propositions are, of course, different and "opposed" in their meaning; yet, the words they employ as terms are essentially the same. How, then, do such propositions *differ?* Briefly, they differ in their *quantity* or their *quality* or in *both respects.*

From the example given above, we get four combinations:

1. *Every* modern baby *is* undernourished. (*A proposition*)
2. *No* modern baby *is* undernourished. (*E proposition*)
3. *Some* modern babies *are* undernourished. (*I proposition*)
4. *Some* modern babies *are not* undernourished. (*O proposition*)

In relation to proposition 1, for instance, proposition 2 differs (or is opposed) in *quality* but not in quantity. Proposition 3 is opposed to proposition 1 in *quantity,* although not in quality. Proposition 4 is opposed to proposition 1 in *both quantity and quality.* The following, then, are the four different kinds of opposition:

Contrary opposition is that between two *universals* of different quality (*A* and *E*).

Subcontrary opposition is that between two *particulars* of different quality (*I* and *O*).

Subaltern opposition is that between *a universal and a particular* of the same *quality* (*A* and *I; E* and *O*).

Contradictory opposition is that between *a universal and a particular* of *different quality* (*A* and *O; E* and *I*).

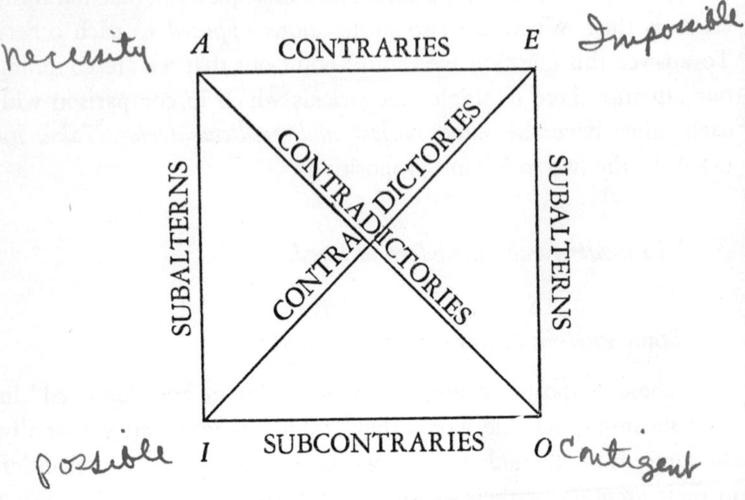

Here we should note that in popular usage an attempt is seldom made to distinguish *types* of opposition; one proposition is simply spoken of as the "opposite" of another. In the light of the distinctions just drawn, the student should accustom himself, therefore, to think of the term "opposition" as being only a *generic* term, which leaves unspecified the type or species of opposition that exists between two propositions.

Further, according to the popular meaning of the term, "opposed" propositions are of necessity *incompatible* in their truth, so that if one proposition is *true,* its "opposite" is to be considered *false.* Although it is true that this meaning of the term is verified in the case of both contrary and contradictory opposition, the same cannot be said of the opposition of subcontraries and subalterns. As we shall presently see, although two propositions may be "opposed" as subcontraries or as subalterns, it is possible for both of them to be true. Accordingly, the student should train himself to think of "opposition" in the purely technical sense of the term as we have defined it here.

In order to represent the different types of opposition, logicians make use of a traditional diagram referred to as the *square of opposition.*

As a preliminary exercise, refer to the accompanying diagram and determine which of the four types of opposition exists between each of the following sets:

All politicians are honest.
No politicians are honest.

Some housewives are good cooks.
Some housewives are not good cooks.

Some wars are futile.
Some wars are not futile.

No civilization is amoral.
Some civilization is not amoral.

Some harvests are plentiful.
All harvests are plentiful.

Some poetry is not sentimental.
All poetry is sentimental.

RULES OF OPPOSITION

If we *grant the truth or falsity of a given proposition,* it is possible in many cases to determine by pure logic the truth or falsity of another which is opposed to it in one of the four ways. Thus, the standard procedure in applying the square of opposition is to begin with a proposition that is *given as true or false* with a view toward determining whether its corresponding contradictory, contrary, subcontrary, or subaltern is true, false, or doubtful. Thus, if it is *true* that "*All* good men are virtuous," is the *contradictory* proposition, "*Some* good men are not virtuous," *true, false,* or *doubtful?*

Contradictory Opposition (A—O; E—I)

Contradictory propositions cannot both be true.

This rule supposes, just as does the *first* in each of the groups that follow, that the initial proposition is *given as true.* According to the rule just stated, if any proposition is *given as true,* its corresponding contradictory must be *false.* If, for example, an *I* proposition is true, then its *E* variant must be false.

(*I*) Some homes are expensive. (*given as true*)
(*E*) No home is expensive. (*false*)

Contradictory propositions cannot both be false.

This rule supposes, as does the *second* in each of the groups that follow, that the initial proposition is *given as false.* If any proposition is given as *false,* its corresponding contradictory must be *true.* Thus, if an *A* proposition is false, then its *O* variant is necessarily true.

(*A*) Every nuisance is a bore. (*given as false*)
(*O*) Some nuisances are not bores. (*true*)

The student will observe that the rules of contradictory opposition are the easiest to apply because there is no room here for doubt. Further, *contradictory opposition* is opposition in the *complete, unqualified sense of the term.*

Contrary Opposition (A—E)

Contrary propositions cannot both be true.

The initial proposition that is here given as true is an *A* or an *E,* and the question is simply this: If *A* is true, what can be implied of its *E* variant (that is, its contrary)? Is it true, false, or doubtful? Conversely, if *E* is true, what is to be said of its *A* variant? The rule states quite simply that contraries *cannot* both be true. It follows, then, that if one contrary is *given as true,* then its corresponding contrary must be *false.* Thus, if *A* is true, *E* must be false. For example:

(*A*) Every democracy respects human rights. (*given as true*)
(*E*) No democracy respects human rights. (*false*)

Conversely, if *E* is true, then *A* must be false:

(*E*) No child is a criminal. (*given as true*)
(*A*) Every child is a criminal. (*false*)

Contrary propositions can both be false.

According to the rule, contraries (*A* and *E* propositions) *can* both be false. Does this mean that if one contrary is *given as false* the other *must be* false? Clearly not, for if contraries *can* or *may* both be false, and one is *given as false,* the other is necessarily doubtful. Given as false the *E* proposition:

No man is a coward.

Its *A* variant is

Every man is a coward.

But this is *doubtful.* (Even though we may know this proposition to be false as a matter of fact, we cannot *imply* that it is.)

Subcontrary Opposition (I—O)

Subcontrary propositions can both be true.

We have seen that *contraries* cannot be true together. The rule is just the reverse for subcontraries: *both* can be true. By way of application it follows that, *given a subcontrary as true,* there is no implication as to the truth or falsity of its corresponding subcontrary. Since the rule states that subcontraries *can* be true together, and if, as a matter of fact, one of them *is* true, then the other may be true or false. Hence, it is doubtful. Given the truth of the *I* proposition:

Some candy is hard to chew.

Its *O* variant is *doubtful,* even though it may be true *as a matter of fact* that

Some candy is not hard to chew.

Again, given as true the *I* proposition:

Some logic texts deal with inference.

The *O* variant is doubtful on the basis of mere implication, even though in this case it is false *as a matter of fact* that

Some logic texts do not deal with inference.

In view of the common-sense supposition that the truth of an *I* proposition implies the truth of its *O* variant (and conversely), an explanation is in order here to account for the discrepancy between the point of view of logic and that of common sense. Why is it that common sense favors such an implication, whereas logic does not? Suppose, for instance, that someone makes the statement: "Some athletes are well built." Does it really follow *of necessity* on the strength of this statement that "Some are not"? According to the rule we have just set forth, no such implication is justified. From the point of view of common sense, however, it is.

The reason for this difference in point of view is rooted in the fact that common-sense judgments are purely *practical* as opposed to *scientific*. Now a purely practical judgment is one that seeks to settle a doubt (if doubt there be) on the basis of what is considered more or less *probable* or *likely*. Sometimes, too, an appeal is made to the "law of averages" or even to statistics. Applying this consideration to our present problem, we shall find that the common-sense implication from the truth of an *I* proposition to the truth of an *O* (and vice versa) amounts to this: If *I* is true, it is *likely* or *probable* that *O* also is true. In actual fact, it *usually* turns out that, according to the truth of the *matter*, both propositions are true. Such judgments, however, are far from infallible. Strictly speaking, there is room here for doubt, and this is precisely the point of view of logic. From a scientific point of view there is no theoretical (logical) necessity involved in judging that if "Some *S* is *P*," then "Some *S* is not *P*." Hence, there is no room for any *formal* implication.

On this last point the student must be fully aware that if *any* implication or inference is to be valid, it must *necessarily* follow—that is, according to a strict *logical* necessity—from what is laid down. If no such necessity is involved, there is simply no implication, and if any implication were drawn, it would be invalid.

Subcontrary propositions cannot both be false.

Whereas contraries may both be false, this condition does not apply to subcontraries. Given the falsity of any subcontrary, its corresponding subcontrary must be *true.* From the falsity of the *O* proposition, "Some men do not have emotions," we must imply the truth of its *I* variant. Or, given the falsity of the *I* proposition, "Some monkeys are human," the *O* variant is necessarily true.

Subaltern Opposition (A—I; E—O)

As a matter of correct terminology, in subaltern opposition the universal proposition is sometimes spoken of as the subalter*nant,* the particular, as the subalter*nate.* The two propositions when taken together are called *subalterns.*

If the universal is true, its subalternate (particular) is likewise true; if its subalternate (particular) is true, the universal is doubtful.

It is perfectly legitimate to pass from the truth of the universal to the truth of the particular, but not conversely. Hence, if an *A* proposition is true, its *I* variant is necessarily true. For example:

All snow is white.
Some snow is white. (*true*)

The truth of the particular is *contained* in the truth of the universal. It would be wrong, however, to imply the truth of the universal from the truth of the *I* proposition. For example:

Some convicts are innocent.
Every convict is innocent. (*doubtful*)

If the universal is false, its subalternate (particular) is doubtful; if its subalternate (particular) is false, the universal is false.

This rule, in effect, states that, if the universal is false, the particular may be either true or false; one does not know. If, on the other hand, the particular is false, it follows *for all the more reason* that the universal is false. If an *A* proposition is false, its *I* variant is *doubtful.* For example:

All weather is pleasant.
Some weather is pleasant. (*doubtful*)

If, however, an *I* proposition is false, then its *A* variant is certainly false. Thus:

Some dogs are centipedes.
All dogs are centipedes. (*false*)

The following chart is a summary of conclusions derivable from the square of opposition. The student should examine each conclusion of this chart and cite the appropriate rule that governs it. Then, he should close the text and reconstruct the chart on the basis of the rules just studied.

	A is	*E* is	*I* is	*O* is
If *A* is true	X	F*	T	F
If *E* is true	F	X	F	T
If *I* is true	D	F	X	D
If *O* is true	F	D	D	X
If *A* is false	X	D	D	T
If *E* is false	D	X	T	D
If *I* is false	F	T	X	T
If *O* is false	T	F	T	X

* Key: T (true); F (false); D (doubtful).

PRACTICAL OBSERVATIONS

Thus far we have centered our attention on the fourfold scheme of opposition as it relates to *single categoricals.* Presently, we shall continue our study of opposition as it pertains to the various other types of propositions discussed in the preceding chapter. At this stage of our study, however, we should give some indication of the utility of opposition as a means for correct, logical thinking.

The chief practical utility of the square of opposition is to enable the user to know how to *refute* a given proposition, for it is during *refutation* that the most flagrant blunders in a discussion or a debate are committed. If the student would avoid these blunders, he should note first that *the only propositions that are incompatible in their truth are contraries and contradictories.* This means that the only way to refute any proposition is to establish the truth of either its *contrary* or its *contradictory.* If this can be done, then, obviously the proposition of one's opponent is shown to be false.

In this connection it should be noted that one does *not* refute an *I* or an *O* proposition by setting up its subcontrary. This point would be too obvious to mention were it not for the fact that persons sometimes "argue" (much to their own distress and others' amusement) somewhat in the following fashion:

> You claim that some of the athletes on our team are *not* good sports. Well, it's my own contention that most of them *are,* and if you want me to prove it to you, I can.

It goes without saying that even if the person making the above statement *proves* his contention, in itself this is not enough to *disprove* the subcontrary statement against which he is arguing, for *subcontraries may both be true.*

A moment ago we said that the only way to refute a proposition is to establish either the contrary or the contradictory. We should now make it clear that, although it is possible to disprove a proposition by its *contrary,* doing so is neither necessary nor, as a rule, advisable. Clearly, *if* we can show that our proposition (which is the contrary of our opponent's) is *true,* then we have refuted our opponent's position, since *contraries cannot both be true.* The point of the present consideration, however, is to emphasize the equally important fact that *contraries can both be false.* Thus, there is the ever-present danger of opposing one false proposition with another that is also false. Let us suppose that a Communist is attempting to establish the following proposition:

> *All* economic activity should be in the hands of the government.

Not infrequently, in such a case an opponent may think it necessary to prove the *contrary*:

> *No* economic activity should be in the hands of the government.

If this second proposition could be *proved* to be true, it would obviously serve to refute in very strong terms the one to which it is opposed. In actual fact, however, the second proposition may well turn out to be as false as the original, since *contraries can both be false.* At least, one should be very certain of his ground before he attempts to refute one contrary by means of another, for most often "he who proves too much, proves nothing."

To sum up what we have said thus far: To attempt to refute one *subcontrary* proposition by means of another is no refutation at all, because subcontraries can both be true. To attempt to refute one *contrary* by means of another is to resort to a risky means of refutation, because contraries can both be false.

In line with these considerations, then, it should be noted as a cardinal rule of logic that the only thing required to refute *any* proposition is to establish the truth of its *contradictory.* Thus, all that is necessary to refute the proposition, "*All* economic activity should be in the hands of the government," is to establish the following (contradictory): "*Some* economic activity should *not* be in the hands of the government."

Under *most* circumstances the only sane, practical way to refute a proposition is to establish its contradictory. Under *all* circumstances this is all that is necessary.

OPPOSITION OF SINGULARS

A singular proposition *as such* is not susceptible to the fourfold scheme of opposition, admitting, as it does, only of a simple denial. This holds true both of concrete and so-called abstract singulars, as is evident from the examples below:

John is at home.
John is *not* at home.

The weather is disagreeable.
The weather is *not* disagreeable.

What is true of singular propositions is equally true of those propositions whose subject term is an infinitive or a gerund. These too admit only of a simple denial:

To exist is to live.
To exist is *not* to live.

Eating soup without wearing a bib is a hazardous experience.
It is *not* a hazardous experience.

OPPOSITION OF MODALS AND OF SPECIAL TYPES

In the preceding chapter four types of modals were examined. The method of treatment for these propositions according to the square of opposition is shown in the chart on the following page. In modals, as in all other types of opposition, the same sets of rules apply as those which we have already set forth for the opposition of single categoricals. Consequently, once the student knows how to locate each of the four types of modals as given in the chart, there

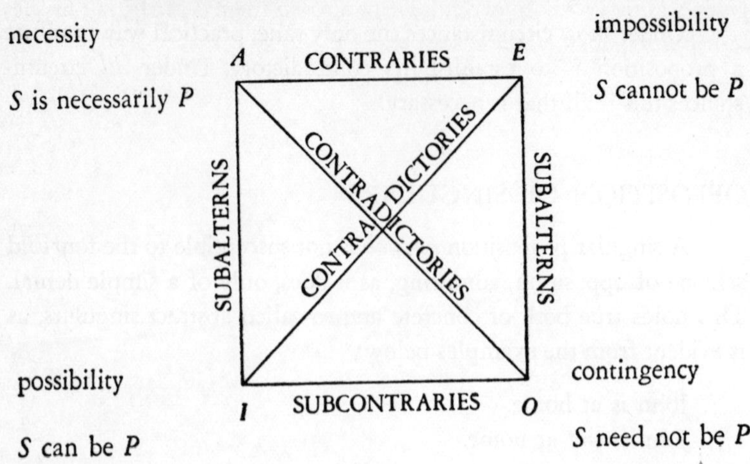

should be little difficulty in applying the rules. Consider, for example, the following statement as *true*:

Learning *need not* be an unpleasant experience.

This is a *contingent* proposition. Handling it as an *O* proposition, one gets the following results:

(*A*) Learning *is necessarily* an unpleasant experience. (*false*)
(*E*) Learning *cannot* be an unpleasant experience. (*doubtful*)
(*I*) Learning *can* be an unpleasant experience. (*doubtful*)

This is an example of a proposition that is treated *simply* according to its mode. Occasionally a proposition will combine one of the usual signs of quantity (that is, "dictum") and mode. The following example is treated both according to the usual sign of quantity (every, no, some) and according to mode:

(*A*) *Everyone must* make mistakes. (*given as true*)
(*E*) *No one can* make mistakes. (*false*)
(*I*) *Someone can* make mistakes. (*true*)
(*O*) *Someone need not* make mistakes. (*false*)

Beyond the indications we have just given, it is well to note also that a *singular* proposition of whatever type, if its copula is given in one of the four modes, can also be treated according to the fourfold scheme of opposition; thus:

(*A*) Mexico *must* have revolutions. (*given as false*)
(*E*) Mexico *cannot* have revolutions. (*doubtful*)
(*I*) Mexico *can* have revolutions. (*doubtful*)
(*O*) Mexico *need* not have revolutions. (*true*)

Or take a case of an abstract singular:

(*E*) The American suburb *cannot be* self-sufficient. (*given as false*)
(*A*) The American suburb *must be* self-sufficient. (*doubtful*)
(*I*) The American suburb *can be* self-sufficient. (*true*)
(*O*) The American suburb *need not* be self-sufficient. (*doubtful*)

Finally, in connection with the study of modals, we must call attention to the opposition of the special types discussed at the end of Chapter 5. These are the propositions that are not simply reducible either to a strict type of categorical or to a strict type of modal: for example, "Boys *are sometimes* mischievous." For purposes of opposition propositions of this kind must be treated as a class by themselves. The method of handling them according to the square is indicated in the following chart:

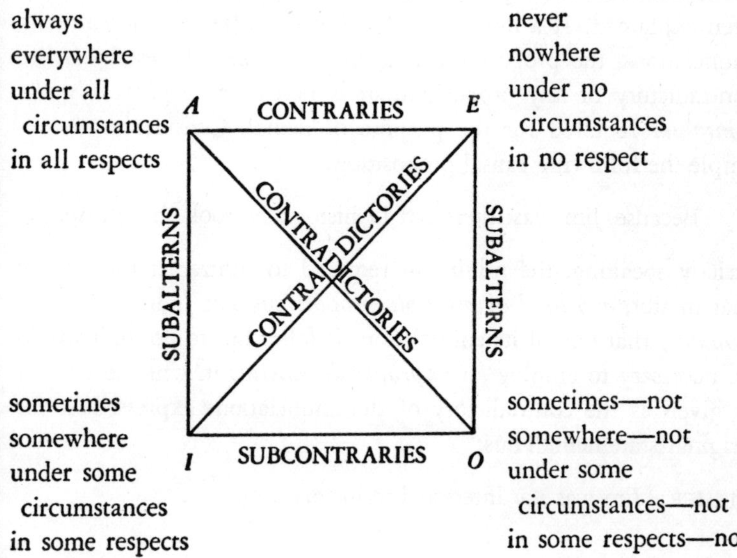

Let us suppose the following proposition to be *true*:

Lying is *never* permissible.

If this is considered an *E* proposition, the following results are obtainable:

(*A*) Lying is *always* permissible. (*false*)
(*I*) Lying is *sometimes* permissible. (*false*)
(*O*) *Sometimes* lying is *not* permissible. (*true*)

Note: Any *singular* proposition containing a word or phrase of the type just illustrated can be treated in the same way according to the fourfold scheme of opposition.

OPPOSITION OF MULTIPLES

It is possible to draw up a complete scheme of opposition for multiple propositions. For our purposes, however, it is best to regard only their simple denial as *practicable*. Hence, we shall content ourselves here with only a few hints as to the means of establishing the *contradictory* of any such proposition. To this end, the student should keep in mind two basic points that have already been explained: If a multiple proposition is *false in any one* of its enunciations, the proposition as it stands is *false*. To establish the contradictory of any proposition, it is necessary to *give only the minimum* required for the purpose of denial. Consider as an example the following causal proposition:

Because Jim was interested in history, he took the course.

Strictly speaking, the minimum required to contradict this or, for that matter, *any kind of multiple proposition* is to indicate *indeterminately* that one of its enunciations is false. But to do so, it would be necessary to employ an *improper disjunctive* in which each part is given as the contradictory of the enunciations expressed in the original statement. Thus:

EITHER: Jim was *not* interested in history.

OR: He did *not* take the course.

OR: He did *not* take it for the reason given.

The student will recall at this point that the sense of an *improper* disjunctive is that *at least one part of it is true.* In opposing this type of statement to a multiple proposition, the speaker means to indicate, then, that at least one part of his statement is true and *that the original proposition is therefore false.*

A careful examination of each type of multiple discussed in Chapter 5 will show that it is possible to contradict *all* of them by means of an improper disjunctive each separate part of which is the contradictory of each enunciation of the original proposition.

It should be noted that in ordinary discourse the improper disjunctive is only rarely used as a means of contradicting a multiple proposition. The more usual method of contradicting a multiple is to deny *specifically* (not *indeterminately* as the disjunctive does) that part of the original proposition which one considers false. With reference to the example just used the denial might simply be, "Jim did not take the course." It is also quite customary in ordinary discourse to include in a statement of denial an admission that one part or more of the original proposition is or may be true. For example:

> Admitting (it to be true) that Jim is (or may be) interested in history, he did not take the course.

The following type of statement is also given in conjunction with a denial:

> Whether or not (that is, apart from the question of whether) Jim is interested in history, he did not take the course.

Whatever means the student may employ in order to contradict a multiple proposition, he should guard against giving *as the contradictory* some statement that is *to the contrary* of the proposition to which he stands opposed. In general, it should be remembered that to give the contrary of any given statement is to go as far as possible in the direction of the other extreme. For example:

John was the only student in his class to fail.

We should be giving the *contrary* of the above if we were to say:

Everyone *except* John failed,

or, by a change in the *matter,*

John was the only student in his class to *pass.*

The exact *contradictory* of the original statement would be

Either John did not fail or he was not the only one to fail,

or

Either John did not fail or there was someone besides John who did.

OPPOSITION OF HYPOTHETICALS

Although it is possible to treat a *conditional* proposition according to a complete scheme of opposition, we need concern ourselves here only with the means of giving its contradictory. We have already indicated in a general way that one *denies* a conditional simply by pointing out that the consequent *does not necessarily follow* from its given antecedent. This type of denial is *formally* effected by means of an *adversative* proposition. For example:

If a person is poor, he must be virtuous.
Even though (that is, although) a person be poor, he *need not be* virtuous. (*denial*)

In this denial one part of the statement admits the antecedent as a possibility; the other *denies the necessity* of the consequent.

Consider another example:

If you are intelligent, you *cannot be* prejudiced.
Although you may be intelligent, you *can* be prejudiced. (*denial*)

With respect to the *proper disjunctive* we have already noted that it may be false either because the enunciations given are not complete or because they are not mutually exclusive. Note the following statement:

You are either a scholar or an ignorant person.
(*enunciations incomplete*)

The denial of the above statement may simply be expressed thus:

I *need be neither* (a scholar nor an ignorant person).

To take another example:

You are either a scientist or a philosopher.
(*enunciations not mutually exclusive*)

To show that the enunciations of the above statement do not exclude each other, the following denial is sufficient:

I *may be both* (a scientist and a philosopher).

Note: Since the intent of an *improper disjunctive* is that at least *one* of its enunciations be true, the only *practicable* way in which to deny it is to show that *all* the enunciations given are false.

Finally, the denial of a *conjunctive* proposition consists merely in showing that the alternatives given *can* both be true:

One cannot be a teacher and a research scholar at the same time.
One *can be* both. (*denial*)

CONCLUDING REMARKS. It is not necessary or practicable for an elementary text in logic to present all of the possible variations derivable from the square of opposition. The most important ones have been indicated. The student need only remember that whatever the type of proposition handled, it is always according to the same set of rules.

The following is a summary of opposition as we have studied it in this chapter, that is, with respect to the various types of propositions:

1. Single categoricals
2. Singulars

3. Modals and special types
4. Multiples
5. Hypotheticals
    a. Conditionals
    b. Disjunctives
    c. Conjunctives

EXERCISES

1. Define each of the four types of categorical opposition.

2. Cite the appropriate rules for each of these four types.

3. According to one of the rules, the truth of the universal subalternant cannot be implied from the truth of the particular subalternate. Do you think this rule is frequently violated in practice? If so, exemplify.

4. (a) Discuss some of the mistakes that are commonly made with regard to the "logic of refutation." (b) In what way or ways should your knowledge of opposition help you to avoid these mistakes?

5. Decide whether the following statements are correct or incorrect:

(a) Given an *O* proposition as false, its *A* variant is doubtful.

(b) Given an *O* proposition as true, its *I* variant is false.

(c) Given an *E* proposition as false, its *A* variant is doubtful.

(d) Given an *I* proposition as true, its *A* variant is doubtful.

(e) In stating that "Some politicians are local officials," I imply of necessity that "Some are not."

(f) In order to disprove the proposition, "Every American is a Communist," I *must* establish the proposition, "No American is a Communist."

(g) The contradictory of the proposition, "All men are not happy" is "All men are happy."

6. With respect to the examples given below, determine in

each case whether the corresponding variants (*A, E, I,* or *O*) are true, false, or doubtful.

(a) Given as *false*: "Some trees do not have branches."

(b) Given as *true*: "Many a drug is harmful."

(c) Given as *false*: "No holy person is happy."

7. (a) Given as *false*: "No monkey lives in a cage." Is the following proposition true, false, or doubtful? "All monkeys do not live in cages."

(b) Given as *true*: "Every examination isn't difficult." Is the following proposition true, false, or doubtful? "Some examinations are difficult."

8. To what extent do you think people are justified in thinking that "Because some *S* is *P*, some *S* is not *P*"? Why is such an implication *invalid* from the standpoint of logic?

9. How does one oppose a *singular* proposition?

10. Give your own example of a *contingently modal* proposition that is false. What implications can you derive from it?

11. With respect to the examples given below, determine in each case whether the corresponding variants (*A, E, I,* or *O*) are true, false, or doubtful:

(a) Given as *true*: "An organism must have life."

(b) Given as *false*: "Miracles can't happen."

(c) Given as *false*: "A scientist must be a genius."

12. With respect to the examples given below, determine in each case whether the corresponding variants (*A, E, I,* or *O*) are true, false, or doubtful:

(a) Given as *true*: "Professors are sometimes punctual."

(b) Given as *false*: "Students always say what they mean."

13. What is the most logically correct means of refuting a multiple proposition? Exemplify.

14. What is the correct procedure for refuting a conditional? Exemplify.

15. (a) What are the two means of refuting a *proper disjunctive?* (b) What is necessary to refute an *improper disjunctive?* (c) Give a *conjunctive proposition* and refute it.

16. What proposition do you think *must* be established to refute each of the following:

(a) Only fish can swim.
(b) Politicians never live up to their campaign promises.
(c) Men are in no respect more clever than the brutes.
(d) What you say is for the most part true.
(e) Nothing of what you told me is false.
(f) If a person is dishonest, he must be a liar.
(g) Man is either a brute or a god.
(h) You cannot talk and chew your food at the same time.
(i) A criminal as a criminal is sometimes a good person.
(j) Unless a person studies logic, he cannot reason correctly.
(k) If you have read tonight's newspaper, you must have seen the weather report.
(l) New York and Chicago are both eastern cities.
(m) All sins are forgivable.
(n) All students, except the *A* students, must take the final examination.
(o) *Some* people *can* give what they do not have.

8

Eductions

Obversion

Conversion

Methods of Material Implication

INTRODUCTORY REMARKS. In order to understand the principal purpose of obversion and conversion, it will be helpful at this point to examine the etymological significance of the term *implication.* As we have already noted, every proposition has a certain *meaning;* that is, it has a meaning that is explicit, even though it may be knowable only from the context in which it is found. Yet, over and above this explicit meaning, every proposition "implies" something. Now, the "implied" meaning of a proposition is one that is literally "folded under" or "folded within" the explicitly intended sense of the original statement. In a manner of speaking, then, to study a proposition for its "implications" is to "turn it inside out." This is done partly for the purpose of gaining a more complete understanding of the statement as given in its original form.

Obversion and conversion are methods of implication that are commonly spoken of as *eductions,* that is, methods of "drawing out" the implied meanings of a given proposition. Clearly, "eduction" is not "deduction" for the simple reason that in eduction we are not examining a *new* truth but merely the *same* truth from a different point of view. Accordingly, we may define an *eduction* as *a process of making explicit in a second proposition a meaning that is virtually contained in the original from which it is derived.*

Although obversion and conversion are somewhat limited from the standpoint of their immediate practical value, a study of these forms of eduction should prepare the student for a ready understanding of inference in its strict and proper sense.

OBVERSION

The purpose of obversion is to effect, by means of a second proposition, a change in the *quality* of the original upon which it is based. The second proposition must, of course, be consistent in meaning with the original. The original statement is called the *obvertend;* the derived statement, the *obverse.* Thus:

OBVERTEND: All of his arguments are refutable.
OBVERSE: None of his arguments is irrefutable.

Here the student should recall that under square of opposition he was studying propositions that were *different* and *opposed* in their meaning, although they had the same subject and predicate terms. By way of contrast, the very purpose of obversion (as well as that of conversion) is to set forth a second proposition that is essentially *alike* in its meaning. With respect to obversion, then, if the obvertend is true, the obverse is *necessarily true.*

To say, then, that "All of his arguments are refutable" is to say in affirmative form essentially the same thing as that which can be expressed negatively thus: "None of his arguments is irrefutable."

Rules of Obversion

Rule 1: Negate the copula.

To negate the copula means simply to make an affirmative copula negative (change *is* to *is not*) and a negative copula affirmative (change *is not* to *is*). Recall here that in an *E* proposition (No *S* is *P*), the copula, although *apparently* affirmative, is really negative by virtue of the word "No." Hence, in obverting an *A* proposition to an *E*, the copula is automatically negated by the use of such words as "no," "none," "nobody."

Rule 2: Contradict the predicate term.

The contradictory of any given term is its simple denial. Very often a prefix or a suffix is used as a means of contradicting a term, for example, *in-*, *im-*, *ir-*, *-less,* and so on. A great deal of care should be exercised, however, in determining whether prefixes and suffixes—especially prefixes—really involve a denial. Note the following list of terms:

adequate—*in*adequate	valuable—*in*valuable
mortal—*im*mortal	tense—*in*tense
moral—*a*moral	loosened—*un*loosened
responsible—*ir*responsible	flammable—*in*flammable

The terms in the first list are true contradictories; those in the second are not. The prefix *in-*, for example, as it appears in the word "*in*valuable" does not contradict the meaning of the original word; it merely intensifies it.

Care must also be taken in contradicting terms like the following:

religious—irreligious(?)
advantageous—disadvantageous(?)
moral—immoral(?)
legal—illegal(?)

After all, there is a very considerable difference between a book that is *non*religious in content and one that is downright *ir*religious;

between an act that is *a*moral (or nonmoral), as we might say of a brute, and one that is *im*moral; between a *non*legal action and one that is *il*legal. Thus, such terms as those in the second column above are to be regarded as *contraries* rather than as contradictories.

In general, if there is the slightest possibility that one of the conventional prefixes or suffixes may prove misleading, it is advisable to attach the prefix *non-* to the original word as a means of contradicting it. Sometimes, however, the predicate term of a proposition is so complex that it is impracticable to contradict it. In instances of this sort, it is better not to attempt an obversion.

Kinds of Obversion

Before obverting a proposition, *put it into its logical form.* If, then, we apply the rules to each of the four types of single categoricals, we get the following results.

An* A *proposition obverts to an* E *proposition:

OBVERTEND: (*A*) *Every* virtuous person *is* happy.
OBVERSE: (*E*) *No* virtuous person *is* *un*happy.

An* E *proposition obverts to an* A *proposition:

OBVERTEND: (*E*) *No* just act *is* *un*rewarded.
OBVERSE: (*A*) *Every* just act *is* rewarded.

An* I *proposition obverts to an* O *proposition:

OBVERTEND: (*I*) *Some* people *are* *un*talkative.
OBVERSE: (*O*) *Some* people *are not* talkative.

An* O *proposition obverts to an* I *proposition:

OBVERTEND: (*O*) *Some* workers *are not* members of a union.
OBVERSE: (*I*) *Some* workers *are non*-union members.

At this point a student who has a skeptical turn of mind may think that logicians are rather strange people, which, indeed, they would be if they had nothing more to concern themselves with than obversion. In fact, we might conveniently have ignored the subject were it not for the fact that persons frequently are confused when confronted with a statement that contains a double (or even a triple) negation. The following dialogue may help to illustrate our point:

JIM: Yesterday Dad bought Mom a new electric dish-washer, and today she's having a time of it trying to find out how it works. Mom told me confidentially that she'd rather do her dishes the old-fashioned way.

TOM: I suppose she'll have to get used to it, and even after she does, she ought to remember that *there's no modern appliance without its disadvantages.*

JIM: You must be old-fashioned too! Do you mean to say, Tom, that modern appliances don't have their advantages? That's going a little too far, isn't it?

TOM: What I mean, Jim, is that *every modern appliance has its disadvantages.* That doesn't make me old-fashioned, does it? I agree, the modern way is the best. But let's forget about appliances. I hear that your sister's music instructor told her that *she is not without a lack of talent.* Why doesn't she give up her piano lessons, and take up something else?

JIM: Why, that's a compliment, and my sister says so too. So she's going to keep on taking her lessons. . . .

We should note here that the chief practical advantage of knowing how to obvert a proposition consists in the ability to see the *positive implications* of a statement that is purely negative in form. The double negative is a popular device of modern writers and speakers. Thus:

War is not without its ethical implications.

It is not our intention to censure the use of double negation but merely to call attention to the fact of its occasional abuse. In any case, the student of logic should *not* be *un*aware of the means that enable him to see the positive implications of statements that are expressed in a purely negative form.

CONVERSION

Conversion is essentially a process of *interchanging the subject and predicate terms* of a given proposition in such a way that the derived proposition (the converse) is consistent with the meaning of the original (the convertend). Offhand, this may appear to be a rather arbitrary procedure, as, indeed, it would be were we to proceed without a set of rules. For example: "Snakes eat pigs"; therefore, "Pigs eat snakes." Even when we follow the rules and correctly convert the proposition "Some snakes are pig-eaters" to "Some pig-eaters are snakes," the process may still appear, if not arbitrary, at least trivial. Let us turn our attention to a more serious example. We shall then be in a better position to appreciate the utility of conversion as a means, at least, of avoiding incorrect implications.

CONVERTEND: (*A*) All true art has an ennobling effect.

Here we may not imply, as we might be tempted to do, that anything, therefore, which has an ennobling effect—for example, on a civilization—is to be classified as true art. The converse of the above statement is rather:

(*I*) Something that has an ennobling effect is true art.

Here, too, we may say of conversion, as we said of obversion: If the original proposition (the convertend) is true, the derived proposition (the converse) is *necessarily true.*

Rules of Conversion

Before proceeding to the conversion of a proposition, it is necessary to determine whether a proposition is *A, E, I,* or *O* and in so doing *to put the convertend in its logical form.* The rules of conversion proper may be stated as follows:

Rule 1: Keep the quality of the converse the same as that of the convertend.

We have seen that the process of *obversion* of its very nature involves a *change in the quality* of the original proposition. Yet, in *converting* a proposition one must make certain that the converse (the derived proposition) has the *same quality* as the convertend (the original). If the convertend is affirmative, the converse must likewise be affirmative; if the convertend is negative, the converse must also be negative.

Rule 2: In converting a propostion do not overextend a term.

Before converting a proposition it is necessary to determine the quantity of each of the terms in the convertend. In this connection we recall that *the predicate of an affirmative proposition is particular; that of a negative proposition, universal.* Suppose, then, that one of the terms of the convertend is particular (undistributed). To make this same term universal (to distribute it) in the converse would be a violation of Rule 2. The applications of this rule will be set forth in succeeding paragraphs. We should point out, however, that *nothing in the rule forbids a reduction in the quantity of a term.* Thus, if a term that is universal in the convertend becomes particular in the converse, no violation is involved. As a general rule, it should be remembered that, although it is never legitimate (in an implication or an inference) to *overextend* a term, there is nothing that forbids reduction of the term.

Kinds of Conversion

CONVERSION OF AN *A* PROPOSITION. The chief practical importance of conversion lies in the method of converting an *A* proposition, for it is here that Rule 2 of conversion is most frequently violated in practice. In one of our discussions in the note to the student at the beginning of the text, it was noted that some persons think that because all scientific knowledge is organized, therefore (that is, by virtue of this fact), all organized knowledge is of a scientific nature. This may, of course, *seem* logical, as do most fallacies of implication, but let us put it to the test:

CONVERTEND: (*A*) *All* scientific knowledge is organized (knowledge).

CONVERSE: (*I*) *Some* organized knowledge is scientific.

Since the predicate term of our convertend (an *A* proposition) is particular, in transposing it, that is, in making it the subject of the converse, we must *keep it particular.* Since the subject of the converse, then, is a particular term, the converse itself is a particular (*I*) proposition.

Any attempt to convert an *A* proposition to another *A,* instead of to an *I,* is implicitly based on the assumption that the convertend is an *exclusive* proposition (only *S* is *P*).

By way of further example, note the fallacy in the following implication:

Every good Democrat is a good American.

Therefore,

Every good American is a good Democrat.

Such illogic is a common occurrence in everyday life.

Conversion of an *E* Proposition. So long as an *E* proposition is set forth in its logical form, there is little danger here of a rule violation. In converting an *E* proposition it is impossible to overextend a term, since both *S* and *P* are universal.

CONVERTEND: (*E*) No scientist is an ignorant person.
CONVERSE: (*E*) No ignorant person is a scientist.

Care must be taken, however, in the conversion of propositions that involve a negation within one (or both) of the terms. Consider the following proposition:

A person who is not virtuous is not happy.

This proposition does *not* convert to

No happy person is virtuous.

But it *does* convert to

No happy person is nonvirtuous.

Conversion of an *I* Proposition. An *I* proposition converts to another *I.*

CONVERTEND: (*I*) Some ignorant people are prejudiced.
CONVERSE: (*I*) Some prejudiced people are ignorant.

O PROPOSITIONS DO NOT CONVERT. It may *seem* to be perfectly legitimate to imply that because "Some detectives are not policemen," therefore, "Some policemen are not detectives." Granted the independent truth of each of these propositions, the second is not the *converse* of the first. The attempted conversion of the above example is as invalid as the following:

Some Americans are not New Yorkers.
Some New Yorkers are not Americans.

Some engines are not gas-propelled.
Some gas-propelled objects are not engines.

Rule 2 of conversion forbids the conversion of an *O* proposition. Suppose an *O* proposition as convertend and another *O* as the converse. Note below the overextension of the subject term of the original proposition when it appears as predicate of the converse:

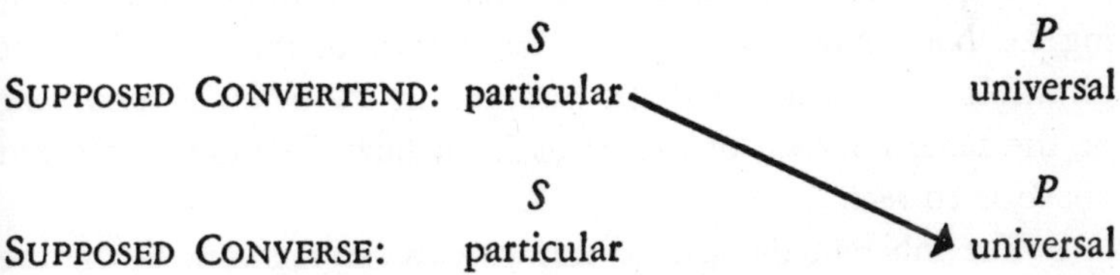

As in the example above, it is as important for the student to know when no implication can be made as it is for him to make a correct implication when it is justified.

METHODS OF MATERIAL IMPLICATION

The *material* implications that follow will help the student to distinguish the *different meanings that terms acquire through usage.* These methods are included mainly because in some way they may help the student become more acutely aware of the flexibility of terms in their meaning.

These methods are not, strictly speaking, eductions. One reason for this is the fact that the derived proposition involves in each case only a change in the matter of the original proposition rather than a change in the *form.* Further, the meaning of the derived proposition adds or detracts something from the meaning of the original statement.

1. *The Method of Added Determinants*

The process known as the method of added determinants may be illustrated by means of the following example:

> A mule is an animal.
> A *stubborn* mule is a *stubborn* animal.

Here it will be noted that each of the terms of the original proposition as restated in the second is *modified,* or *determined,* by the addition of the word "stubborn." Accordingly, we may define this process as a method of *attaching to each of the terms* of a proposition *some modifying word or phrase* which is the same in meaning for both. Note carefully the last phrase of the definition just given: It is necessary that the meaning of the *added determinant* be the same for each of the terms it modifies. The example given above is correct.

The inherent dangers of this process are manifest in the use of a word whose meaning is *relative* to the term that it modifies. Thus:

> A horse and buggy is a means of transportation.
> A *fast* horse and buggy is a *fast*(?) means of transportation.

Clearly, *fast* taken in relation to *horse and buggy* is not *fast* taken in an unqualified sense. Note also:

> A coin is a denomination of money.
> A *large* coin is a *large* denomination of money.

With reference to the last two examples, the student should recall what was said about terms in Chapter 3, namely, that the meaning of a word or a term is not so stable as to justify the naïve assumption that its significance will be the same regardless of its use or context.

2. *The Method of Omitted Determinants*

The method of omitted determinants is simply the reverse of the one just treated. Provided that the removal of a modifying word or phrase does not radically effect a change in the meaning of the original term, the method of omitted determinants is entirely legitimate.

> *Fresh* oranges are *fresh* fruit.
> Oranges are fruit.

Or, let us take an example in which there is but one determinant:

> Plato was a *Grecian* philosopher.
> Plato was a philosopher.

The following examples, however, illustrate how easily this process too may become misleading:

> This pond is *three feet* deep.
> This pond is deep.

> Mary has a new set of *false* teeth.
> Mary has a new set of teeth.

3. *The Method of Complex Conception*

The method of complex conception closely resembles the method of added determinants, for it involves the addition of some new word or phrase. The difference lies in the fact that in complex conception the new word or phrase becomes the *leading part* of each of the terms in the second proposition and the *original* terms are retained only as modifiers. This difference will become clear from an inspection of the examples below:

Added Determinants	*Complex Conception*
A bill is a debt.	A bill is a debt.
An *unpaid* bill is an *unpaid* debt.	The *possessor* of a bill is the *possessor* of a debt.
(Original terms "debt" and "bill" are preserved as the main part of the terms in the second proposition)	(Here the original terms of the first proposition—"bill" and "debt"—are used only as modifiers in the second)

Complex conception is susceptible to the same type of mistake that occurs in the other processes:

Students are citizens.
The majority of students is the majority of citizens.

CONCLUDING REMARKS. With this chapter our study of the second general section of logic is completed, that is, an analysis of propositions from the standpoint of their meaning and implications. In the chapters that follow we shall see how propositions are put to use as part of a process of *reasoning*. To understand how this is done, however, we must have some notion of the nature of reasoning itself. Therefore, reasoning will be the subject of the chapter that follows.

EXERCISES

1. Define *eduction*. Explain your definition.
2. What is *obversion?*
3. (a) State the two rules of obversion. (b) Discuss some of the difficulties involved in the application of these rules.
4. Give your own example of each of the four types of obversion.
5. What is *conversion?*
6. State and explain the two rules of conversion.

7. (a) Why must an *A* proposition be converted to an *I?* (b) Why is it impossible to convert an *O* proposition?

8. Illustrate how an *A* proposition is susceptible to an illogical process of conversion. Give two examples.

9. Give your own examples of the three legitimate types of conversion.

10. Explain what is meant by the *method of added determinants.* Give two examples, one valid and the other invalid.

11. Explain the method of *omitted determinants.* Give two examples, one valid and the other invalid.

12. Explain the difference between the method of *added determinants* and that of *complex conception.*

13. Exemplify the method of *complex conception.*

14. If necessary, put the following propositions in their logical form, and then *obvert* them:

(a) Not every unhealthy person is unhappy.
(b) Almost every chair without a back is uncomfortable.
(c) Many a business venture is unsuccessful.
(d) All wealthy people are not dissatisfied with life.
(e) No professional is unskilled.
(f) Omniscience is a non-human attribute.
(g) Whatever is not good is unpraiseworthy.
(h) Some stories are incredible.

15. If necessary, put the following propositions in their logical form, and then *convert* them *if they are convertible.*

Note: (a) a converted term must bear the same meaning that it had in the convertend; (b) in converting a proposition you do *not* merely change it to the *passive voice*: for example, "Every donkey has long ears" to "Some long ears *are had by* donkeys"; and (c) in converting a proposition it *is permissible* to supply a new word where necessary: for example, "Some professors are learned" to "Some learned *men* are professors."

(a) Some unforgettable events are unforeseen.
(b) Whoever loves God loves his neighbor.
(c) Every stenographer has a boss.
(d) Not every political observer is a disinterested one.

(e) Every eagle has claws.
(f) Most teachers are nonwealthy men.
(g) No university is a high school.
(h) Physical exercise requires energy.
(i) Some people are crabs.
(j) Jane loves Mike.
(k) Some that don't talk *do.*
(l) The United Nations is working toward the cause of peace.
(m) Some immoral actions are not illegal.
(n) A liar is not an honest man.
(o) Not every unexpected guest is unwelcome.
(p) Every Communist is a radical.
(q) Some cars are not convertibles.
(r) All wise men are knowledge seekers.
(s) All businessmen are taxpayers.
(t) Every man is not worthy of honor.

16. Evaluate the following eductions.

(a) If every learned person is a reader of books, it follows that anyone who reads books is learned.

(b) Whatever you dream you imagine, and conversely whatever you imagine you dream.

(c) Some insane people are not morally culpable. It follows from this that some persons who are morally culpable are not insane.

(d) If it is true that all virtuous deeds are not unrewarded, then some virtuous deeds are rewarded.

(e) If every good Christian loves his neighbor, then, clearly, anyone who loves his neighbor is a good Christian.

(f) You say that no good American is a radical. In that case, no radical is a good American.

(g) To state that some people are not unconcerned about their health is to imply that they are concerned.

17. The purpose of this exercise is to make combined use of obversion and conversion. In each part decide whether the example given is valid or not by following out the suggested procedures.

(a) *If all your answers are correct, then none of the incorrect answers (on this sheet) are yours.*

ORIGINAL PROPOSITION: All your answers are correct.

Obvert this proposition, and convert the obverse.

Note: If you have worked out this example correctly, your last proposition is the *partial contrapositive* of the original.

(b) *If every virtuous person is happy, then every unhappy person is nonvirtuous.*

ORIGINAL PROPOSITION: Every virtuous person is happy.

Obvert this proposition; convert the obverse; obvert again.

Note: Your last proposition is the *full contrapositive* of the first. If your answer is correct, the *S* term of your last proposition should be the contradictory of the *P* term of the original; the *P* term of your last proposition should be the contradictory of the *S* term of the original.

(c) *If all wealthy men are financially secure, then some nonwealthy men are financially insecure.*

ORIGINAL PROPOSITION: All wealthy men are financially secure.

Obvert this proposition; convert the obverse; obvert again; convert again.

Note: Your last proposition is the *inverse* of the original. If your last proposition is correct, it is an *I* proposition whose *S* and *P* terms are the contradictory of the *S* and *P* terms of the original proposition.

18. Can you figure out a way to justify the following eduction: *If some gamblers are not unlucky people, then some lucky people are gamblers?*

19. Determine whether the method of implication used in each of the following statements is by added determinants, omitted determinants, or complex conception. Determine also whether the example in question is legitimate or illegitimate. In some of the examples there may be room for a difference of opinion. If so, give reasons for working out the example as you did.

(a) The mouth is part of an organism.
The mouth of a horse is part of a horse's organism.

(b) Some people have a lack of hair.
Some people have hair.

(c) A hobby is a source of enjoyment.
A money-making hobby is a money-making source of enjoyment.

(d) Some people are in love with money.
Some people are in love.

(e) A novel is a book.
The end of a novel is the end of a book.

(f) Inflation means high prices.
The evil of inflation is the evil of high prices.

(g) A needle is an instrument.
A large needle is a large instrument.

(h) He who tells jokes has a sense of humor.
He who tells poor jokes has a poor sense of humor.

(i) A dangerous sport is a dangerous game.
A sport is a game.

(j) Ice cream is made with flavoring.
Chocolate ice cream is made with chocolate flavoring.

(k) Money is power.
Unlimited money is unlimited power.

(l) Food is nourishment.
Rich food is rich nourishment.

9

The Nature of Deductive Reasoning

Judgment and Reasoning
Reasoning and First Principles
Reasoning and New Knowledge
The Unity of the Reasoning Act
Validity and Truth

INTRODUCTORY REMARKS. The purpose of the present chapter is to help the student gain some insight into the nature of the act of reasoning. Logic, it is true, is not exclusively a matter of reasoning, but the study of inference and the laws that govern it comprise the most important section of logic. Thus, a good part of what the student has thus far studied has been a preparation for the matter to be explained in this and succeeding chapters.

JUDGMENT AND REASONING

Reasoning is the most *complex* of the three acts of the mind. Is it also the most *important?* Considered *in and by itself* the most important act of the mind is the one by which the intellect formally knows something to be true. Since, as we have seen, it is only in the act of judgment that we attain to truth in its strict and proper sense, judgment, in and by itself, and not reasoning, is the most important of the three acts of the mind.[1]

The intrinsic importance of the act of judgment becomes even more evident if one considers that reasoning, as opposed to judgment, is a process *that is never performed for its own sake.* Reasoning, in other words, is never an end in itself but is merely a means toward an end, the end always being some new truth that is attained in an act of *judgment.* It is precisely, then, in its role as a means to an end that the importance of reasoning lies.

We should also note here that the content, or *matter,* that is involved in an act of reasoning is the very content of the judgments themselves that we employ in the reasoning process. Thus, although the judgments that we employ in reasoning are true or false, the reasoning process itself is spoken of as either *valid* or *invalid.* If we do speak of reasoning as "true" or "false," we do so only by way of analogy.

REASONING AND FIRST PRINCIPLES

The *need* for reasoning argues an imperfection in the human intelligence. Indeed, *there would be no need for reasoning if man could know all truth by intuition.* What we know by intuition we know directly and immediately, there being no need for invoking some other truth or truths as a medium of further understanding. A truth, then, that is known by intuition is known in a better way than one that is known by reasoning because it is one that is *immediately intelligible* to the mind which grasps it.

In actual fact, there are some truths that man knows by intuition and others that he knows only by a process of reasoning. Apart from what he knows about the objects of his immediate sense experience, the truths that man knows by intuition are relatively

[1] There are, it is true, certain judgments (*practical* judgments) that function only as a means to an end, the end being the performance of a certain action. Speculative judgments, however, in which the mind rests content in its contemplation of the truth, are not related to anything, except accidentally, as a means to an end. It is this type of judgment that we have in mind.

few, *although they are fundamental.* The intuitions to which we are referring are not the "hunches" that many persons (especially women?) have or claim to have; they are something far more *objective* and *universal.* In a word, we are referring to the *self-evident truths of first principles,* truths that are common to *all* men.

Almost no one, of course, except a philosopher will go to the trouble of explicitly formulating these truths. In fact, the "man in the street" or even the student in the classroom might be rather mystified to hear a philosopher say that "a thing cannot be and not be at the same time and in the same respect." The principle just stated, that is, *the principle of noncontradiction,* is so fundamental that neither the man in the street nor the philosopher could form a single judgment without it. Indeed, the logical significance of this principle becomes forcefully apparent when we consider that it forbids one to assign contradictory predicates to one and the same subject as regarded from the same point of view. Of course, one can say of a man *from different points of view* that he is both a father and not a father. Thus, he is a father with respect to his son and not a father with respect to his own father. Yet, it is impossible to think of a man both as *a father and not a father* with respect to his own son. A man is *either a father or not a father* with respect to any individual, including himself.

The importance of first principles is evidenced by the fact that they are the starting points of all human knowledge and, as a result, the starting point of *every act of reasoning* that proceeds from them. Without these truths we could not reason at all. Further, all our reasoning must proceed in accordance with the demands or exigencies of these truths, that is, in such a way that it does not contradict them.[2] It would be a hopeless confusion of human thought if one were to "reason" thus:

Every man has the ability to laugh.
Jonathan *is* a man.
Jonathan does *not* have the ability to laugh.

[2] It is part of the science of epistemology to expose the inherent contradictions involved in any (skeptical) attempt to refuse the *evidence* of first principles. Here, too, we should point out that, because of their self-evidence, it is incorrect to speak of first principles as "suppositions" or "assumptions."

REASONING AND NEW KNOWLEDGE

The *significance* of reasoning lies in the fact that it is a means—for man a *necessary* means—of advancing man's knowledge beyond the frontiers of the limited truths that he knows by intuition. What we come to know by a reasoning process is not, of course, self-evident, as is our knowledge of first principles. Yet, reasoning is a process by which we *do* come to know something that was heretofore unknown. But how?

The necessary condition for our coming to know anything new is that the new element in our knowledge be somehow *related* to what was known *previously*. In a sense, we never come to know something that is *completely* new. Indeed, it is of the very essence of the reasoning process that *by virtue of certain known truths* we advance to a knowledge of some new truth that is intimately connected with and virtually contained in the others. What becomes *actually* known in a conclusion was *potentially* known in the premises that produced it.

Clearly, one cannot by the mere juxtaposition of two disparate truths somehow use these truths as a medium for arriving at a new judgment. There is no logical connection, for example, between the two following propositions:

> Brazil is one of the world's greatest coffee centers.
> The baby is crying for its bottle.

Since there is no relationship between these propositions, no conclusion is derivable from them. Only if two propositions are related to each other in certain definite ways, as set forth by the rules of logic, is it possible to draw a conclusion. Note the two following propositions:

> Reading material which deals only with matters of current interest will be of little use to future generations.
> Most magazines are exclusively concerned with matters of current interest.

The logical connection between these two propositions is such as to lead naturally to the conclusion that

Most (of today's) magazines will be of little use to future generations.

THE UNITY OF THE REASONING ACT

In Chapter 4, on judgment, we noted that judgment, taken in its most basic sense, is an act, or operation, of the mind that unites or disunites two distinct objects of thought. By way of comparison and contrast, reasoning in *its* most basic sense is an act by which the intellect unites *two distinct judgments,* and in this very act it knows some new truth as causally related to the others.[3]

We have said that reasoning is the most *complex* of our mental acts. The reason for this is that the elements involved are more complex. But the act of reasoning itself, in spite of the complexity of its *matter,* has a *formal* unity of its own. Accordingly, the student should be careful to avoid the mistaken impression that reasoning is *merely* a successive consideration of two distinct judgments. *Formally* and *essentially* an act of reasoning in its most strict and proper sense takes place when, *in perceiving the logical relationship that exists between two judgments, we see in that relationship some new truth which follows of necessity from the others.*

VALIDITY AND TRUTH

Under what conditions does reasoning in its most strict and proper sense lead to new knowledge? The answer to this question is seen in *the connection that exists between validity and truth,* and it is precisely this: given two propositions that are *known to be true* and that are *logically connected,* we come to the knowledge of a

[3] This definition obviously does not make provision for so-called inductive "reasoning." If reasoning, of course, were to be defined as *any* act or series of acts by which we come to know something that is not self-evident, then such a definition would include induction. Such a definition, however, would make it difficult to determine where the *formal unity* of the reasoning act lies. Moreover, to state that induction is reasoning is, to say the least, a somewhat ambiguous proposition. As we shall point out in the last chapter, induction clearly *involves* reasoning—*deductive* reasoning, but whether the procedures of induction are inherently resolvable to any specific form of reasoning is another question.

third. This third proposition (the conclusion) *must be true* if the propositions from which it derives are *true* and if the reasoning process itself is *valid*. Given the fulfillment of these two conditions, *the conclusion cannot be other than true.*

On the other hand, if either of these two conditions is lacking, there can be *no guarantee* of the truth of the conclusion. Accordingly, even if a person reasons from *true* premises and his reasoning is *invalid,* his "conclusion" will be doubtful; even if a person reasons *validly* from premises, one or both of which are *false,* his "conclusion" will again be doubtful. With respect to the latter statement it should be noted that if logical validity is to have any real significance, it *presupposes* the truth of the premises. Thus, if a person reasons from premises that are false, his reasoning, however faultless it may be, is to no avail.

The points we have just set forth concerning validity and truth are summarized in the following table:

	Premises	*Conclusion*
1	both true	doubtful (true or false)
	reasoning invalid	invalid
2	one or both false	doubtful (true or false)
	reasoning valid	valid (but insignificant)
3	*both true*	*necessarily true*
	reasoning valid	*valid*

From the above considerations it should be clear that, although the truth of the premises and the validity of a reasoning act as such are distinct, *they should never be separated in practice.*

CONCLUDING REMARKS. If it seems at times that the logician is more interested in validity than in truth, the reason is that validity is his area of concentration. Indeed, a logician cannot afford to assume an attitude of indifference to truth, for the whole meaningfulness of logic is that it serve as an instrument for truth. If we isolate the form for the sake of learning it, or for some other purpose, we must also, if logic is to be worth while, restore it again, to the *matter* for which it is intended.

EXERCISES

1. Why is judgment the most important of the three acts of the mind?

2. Comment on the statement: "Reasoning is never performed for its own sake."

3. Comment on the statement: "The need for reasoning argues an imperfection in the human intelligence."

4. Would reasoning be possible without a knowledge of first principles?

5. *How,* in the process of reasoning, does the intellect proceed from truths previously known to *new* truths?

6. Carefully explain the connection that exists between validity and truth.

7. Comment on the following statement: "Validity and truth should never be separated in practice."

8. Due to psychological associations people frequently try to "make something" of two propositions which are not logically related to each other as premises. The purpose of the following *informal* exercise is to call attention to this fact. In your own opinion, which of the following sets of propositions are *logically* related to each other (*i.e.,* as premises in an argument), and which are not? Give reasons for your answers.

(a) Everything that is good is praiseworthy.
Pride is the worst of all vices.

(b) Hamburgers are popular in America.
Some comedians too are popular.

(c) Cleanliness is next to godliness.

There are some saints who never change their hair-shirts.

(d) Many artists, especially opera stars, are temperamental.
Baseball players, it is said, are superstitious.

(e) Men have intelligence.
Brutes, on the other hand, do not.

(f) The Marxists say that religion is the opiate of the people.
Some people are "leftists."

(g) Brevity is the soul of wit.
Some people I know are "long-winded."

(h) Horseradish and beer sometimes make people cry.
All mourners do not weep.

(i) Some antique collectors are wealthy men.
Many wealthy men are in love with the past.

(j) Some clocks do not chime.
A sundial is an instrument for telling time.

10

11/26/58

The Categorical Syllogism

NATURE • STRUCTURE • PRINCIPLES

Difference between an Apparent and a Real Syllogism

Categorical Syllogism Defined

Matter and Form of Categorical Syllogism

Fundamental Principle of Syllogistic Reasoning

Syllogistic Axioms

INTRODUCTORY REMARKS. Whether the student realizes it or not, he makes constant use of the categorical syllogism in one or another of its forms in his everyday reasoning. How this is done will be explained in Chapter 12. The purpose of this chapter and of the one that follows is to analyze the fundamental *theory* of the syllogism and to provide the means of ensuring its correct application. The present chapter is limited to an explanation of the nature, structure, and principles upon which syllogistic reasoning is based.

DIFFERENCE BETWEEN AN APPARENT AND A REAL SYLLOGISM

The history of logic has been marked with many misunderstandings concerning the real value of syllogistic reasoning as a means of bringing forth new knowledge, and most of these are in existence even today. Especially since the time of Francis Bacon (1561-1626), there has been a tendency in some circles either to minimize the importance of syllogistic reasoning or to deny its value altogether on the grounds that all such reasoning is circular. The purpose of the remarks that follow is to prevent any such misunderstanding on the part of the student, and to do this it is necessary to distinguish between a merely *apparent* syllogism and a *genuine* one, that is, genuine in the sense of leading the reasoner on to new knowledge.

It is of fundamental importance to point out here the fact that the known truths or principles upon which a categorical syllogism is based are truly principles[1] and are not merely the result of a collection of singulars. Although the three following propositions have the appearance of a syllogism, they do not constitute a true syllogism:

1. All the books in my library bear my signature.
2. Tolstoy's *War and Peace* is one of the books in my library.

Therefore(?),

3. This book (Tolstoy's *War and Peace*) bears my signature.

In this example there is no movement or progression of thought. The knowledge that I have of proposition 1 can be had only by a process of complete induction whereby, after examining each book in my library (including Tolstoy's *War and Peace*), I know that it bears my signature. My knowledge of proposition 1, then, is partly the *result*—and *in no way the cause*—of my knowing that Tolstoy's *War and Peace* is one of these books.

[1] True principles are genuine "starting points" from which further knowledge may proceed.

Let us take another example:

1. All the New England states voted Republican in the presidential election of 1952.
2. Vermont is a New England state.

Therefore(?),

3. Vermont voted Republican in the presidential election of 1952.

Here, again, the knowledge of proposition 3 is *not dependent* upon proposition 1. On the contrary, the truth assented to in proposition 1 is partly the result of the *previous* knowledge that Vermont voted Republican.

If syllogistic reasoning were based (as in the examples above) upon truths which by their very nature presuppose a knowledge of the conclusion that they are intended to prove, then all syllogistic reasoning would be *circular*. The syllogism could not, in this case, be productive of any *new knowledge,* scientific or otherwise. Compare the examples above with the following one:

1. No action that is merely a means to an end is performed for its own sake.
2. Walking is an action that is merely a means to an end.

Therefore,

3. Walking (is an action that) is not performed for its own sake.

In this example proposition 1 is not contingent upon a mere enumeration of singulars. Rather, it represents a judgment to which assent is given *independently* of the knowledge that walking, eating, sleeping, and so on, are not actions performed for their own sake. Knowing as a *universal truth* that

1. No action that is merely a means to an end is performed for its own sake

and knowing that

2. Walking is merely a means to an end

a person *comes to know as a result* of the connection that exists between these two propositions that

3. Walking (is an action which) is not performed for its own sake.

Proposition 3 represents a genuine movement of thought, a real advance in knowledge, and is not a mere reaffirmation of what had been known "all along." It is true, of course, that a person in knowing proposition 1 *potentially* knew the third; yet, *actually* he comes to know the third only as the result of seeing it as a *new* truth dependent upon the other two.

CATEGORICAL SYLLOGISM DEFINED

The student is already in a fair position to know what is meant by a "syllogism." The following definition is that set forth by Aristotle. For Aristotle a syllogism is a discourse in which, certain things being stated [that is, the premises], something other than what is stated [that is, the conclusion] follows of necessity from their being so. (*Prior Analytics,* Bk. I, Ch. I, 24b, 18)

This definition is a very general one and applies accordingly to every kind of syllogism, categorical and noncategorical alike. Our present concern is with the categorical syllogism, so called because each of the propositions involved—premises and conclusion alike—is categorical. We may define a *categorical syllogism as an argumentation in which two terms, by virtue of their identity or nonidentity with a common third, are declared to be identical or nonidentical with each other.*

THE MATTER AND FORM OF THE CATEGORICAL SYLLOGISM

As to its *matter,* or composition, the categorical syllogism consists of three propositions and of three terms within those propositions. In the example that follows the first two propositions are the *premises* (sometimes called the "antecedent"); the third is the *conclusion* (the "consequent") that is usually signified by the word "therefore":

All human agreements are subject to violation.
All peace treaties are human agreements.

Therefore,

All peace treaties are subject to violation.

With respect to the *terms* that appear within these three propositions, note that, although there are only *three distinct terms, each of them appears twice* within the syllogism.

All *human agreements* (1) are *subject to violation* (3).
All *peace treaties* (2) are *human agreements* (1).
All *peace treaties* (2) are *subject to violation* (3).

These three terms are designated thus:

1. *The Middle Term (M)*

This term appears in each of the premises but *never* in the conclusion. The middle term is the heart of the syllogism, since it is the means by which it is possible to connect the other two terms in the conclusion. It is the *common standard of reference* and serves to unite in the conclusion the other two "extremes." In the example above the middle term is "human agreements."

2. *The Subject Term (S)*

This term, also called the *minor* term of the syllogism, appears once in the premises and once in the conclusion. It is called the *subject* term because it is always the *subject of the conclusion.* "Peace treaties" is the subject term of the syllogism above.

3. *The Predicate Term (P)*

The predicate, or *major* term, of the syllogism likewise appears once in the premises and once in the conclusion. It is always the *predicate of the conclusion.* The predicate term of our example is "subject to violation."

It is important that the student realize that prior to his study of the syllogism he had been considering terms *only as parts of a proposition.* He must now accustom himself to a consideration of terms as *parts of a syllogism.* Henceforth, the letters *S* and *P* will be used to signify, not the subject or predicate of an isolated proposition, but the *subject* or *predicate terms* of the syllogism as such.

Up to this point we have referred indifferently to the "premises" of a syllogism, not having as yet distinguished between the *major* and the *minor* premise. The means of determining the respective premises of a syllogism is simple. The *major premise* is the one in which the predicate, or *major term,* appears (the *P* term of the conclusion). The *minor premise* is the one in which the subject, or *minor term,* appears (the *S* term of the conclusion). Thus:

MAJOR PREMISE:

M *P*

All human agreements are *subject to violation.*

MINOR PREMISE:

S *M*

All *peace treaties* are human agreements.

CONCLUSION:

S *P*

All *peace treaties* are *subject to violation.*

The student may be interested in learning why the *P* term, since it determines the major premise, is called the *major term.* The reason is simple. Generally speaking, the predicate of a proposition has a wider extension than does the subject. Since the predicate term of the syllogism is the predicate of the conclusion, it has a wider extension than the subject and is, therefore, called the *major* term. Since the subject term of the conclusion is of lesser extension, it is accordingly designated as the *minor* term.

Note that in the example given above the major premise is given first, and the minor, second. This is the *proper* and *ordinary* method of presentation, although, as we shall see in a subsequent chapter, it is not always followed in practice.

In concluding our treatment of the *matter* of the syllogism, we might add that the three terms are sometimes referred to as the *remote* matter and that the three propositions are referred to as the *proximate* matter of the syllogism.

With respect to *form,* we distinguish in every categorical syllogism both its *mood* and its *figure.* The mood of a syllogism is *the respective designation of the premises and conclusion as A, E, I, or O propositions.* In the example given above, both the premises and the conclusion are *A* propositions; therefore, we signify its mood thus: *AAA* (major *A,* minor *A,* conclusion *A*). The *figure* of a syllogism is *the position of the middle term, as taken in both of the premises.* In the example above the figure of the syllogism may be thus represented:

Major	*M–P*
Minor	*S–M*
Conclusion	*S–P*

Here the middle term is the *subject of the major premise* and the *predicate of the minor.*

More will be said later as to the various combinations of moods and figures and what is required for the validity of a syllogism. For the present it is enough for the student to know what these terms signify and to know that the mood and the figure constitute the *form of the syllogism.*

FUNDAMENTAL PRINCIPLE OF SYLLOGISTIC REASONING

Important as it is for the student to be conversant with the mechanics of syllogistic reasoning, he should also have a grasp of the principles upon which it is based. There is one such *universal* principle which may be stated in two parts as follows: *Two things that are identical with a common third are identical with each other;* and *two things, of which one is identical with a third and the other nonidentical, differ from each other.*

In a moment, we shall illustrate both parts of this principle. However, we should first explain the reason for our choice of words "identical" and "nonidentical" rather than the words "equal" and "unequal." These words were chosen so as to prevent the possible confusion of logical identity or nonidentity with mathematical equality or inequality. Granted that logic and mathematics are from an *extensional* point of view analogously related to each other, the fundamental fact remains that the relationships with which logic deals are essentially of a qualitative denomination. When, therefore, the logician states that two things identical with a common third are identical with each other, the identity of which he speaks is primarily a logical identity of a comprehensional nature, that is, an identity in *meaning,* and not a mere mathematical equivalence.[2]

Note, then, how the principle stated above (taken in its affirmative part) is applied to the theory of the syllogism:

MAJOR: 1. Every organism is endowed with life.
MINOR: 2. A cat is an organism.
CONCLUSION: 3. A cat is endowed with life.

By reason of the identity that is separately established in the premises between the terms "endowed with life" and "cat" with the middle term "organism," we are justified in identifying these same two terms ("cat" and "endowed with life") in the conclusion. The three steps involved in this syllogism may be diagrammatically presented thus:

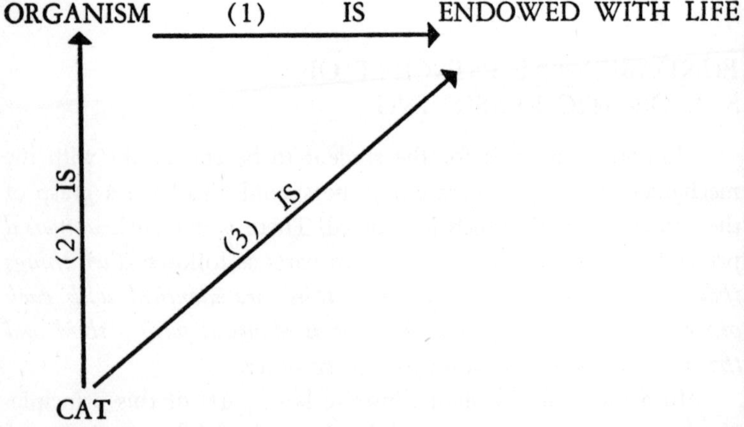

[2] The student should be aware, however, that in logic both the *comprehensional* and *extensional* manner of regarding terms are legitimate. As a matter of fact, both points of view must be taken into account. Any attempt, therefore, to reduce the meaning (comprehension) of terms to their extension is erroneous. The error in question is that of *nominalism.*

We may illustrate the second part of this principle by means of the following syllogism:

MAJOR: 1. No purely material substance is an organism.
MINOR: 2. A rock is a purely material substance.
CONCLUSION: 3. No rock is an organism.

Here we designate (in the major) the *non*identity of the *P* term "organism" with the *M* term "purely material substance." In the minor we declare the *S* term "rock" to be identical with the *M* term "material substance." Accordingly, in the conclusion we declare the two extremes (*S* and *P*) "rock" and "organism" to be nonidentical with each other. Each step is traced in the following diagram:

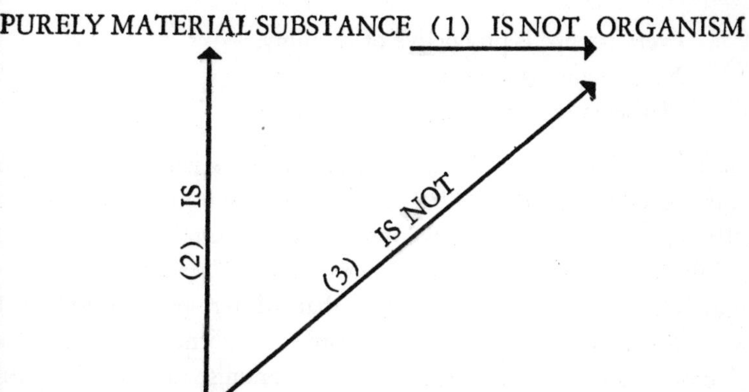

SYLLOGISTIC AXIOMS

In a preceding paragraph we explained that by the term "figure" of a syllogism, we meant the position of the middle term in the premises. There are four combinations of figures which will be treated in the next chapter (pages 194-195). It is necessary, however, to introduce here Figure 1, the most common and typical of the four. Figure 1 is the form in which *M* is placed as *subject of the major premise* and as *predicate of the minor* (*M–P, S–M*) and always takes the form "All (or no) *M* is *P; S* is *M;* therefore, *S* is (or is not) *P.*" We speak of this figure here because the axioms we are about to present (unlike the twofold principle just set forth) are applicable in a direct sense only to this figure of the syllogism. The importance of these axioms is rooted in the fact that Figure 1 is more basic than any of the other figures.

> ***Axiom 1: Whatever can be affirmed of a logical whole can be affirmed of its logical parts.***
>
> ***Axiom 2: Whatever can be denied of a logical whole can be denied of its logical parts.***

The following example may be taken as an illustration of Axiom 1.

> Every science is productive of certainty.
> Mathematics is a science.
> Mathematics is productive of certainty.

The *logical whole* of the above example is "science"; the *logical part* is "Mathematics." What is affirmed of the logical whole (in the major premise), namely, "productive of certainty," is affirmed of the logical part in the conclusion, namely, "Mathematics is productive of certainty." Note, then, that with respect to Axiom 1 it is the function of the major premise to affirm something of a logical whole, the function of the minor premise to relate a logical part to this same logical whole, and the function of the conclusion to affirm of the part what had been previously affirmed (in the major) of the whole.

To illustrate Axiom 2 let us take the following example:

> No person is a mere piece of property.
> A slave is a person.
> No slave is a mere piece of property.

The *logical whole* of this example is "person"; the *logical part* is "slave." What is denied of the logical whole in the major, namely, "mere piece of property," is denied of the logical part in the conclusion, namely, "No slave is a mere piece of property." In the example given it is the function of the major to deny something of a logical whole, the function of the minor to relate (affirmatively) the logical part to the logical whole, and the function of the conclusion to deny of the logical part what had been previously denied (in the major) of the logical whole, "mere piece of property."

CONCLUDING REMARKS. The fundamental theory of the syllogism, as we have just explained it, is relatively easy to grasp. Yet, to ensure its correct application it is necessary also to examine the rules. Such is the burden of the next chapter.

EXERCISES

1. Explain why the following "syllogism" does not contain a true act of inference:

   Every automobile in this parking lot is American-made.
   Smith's automobile is in this parking lot.
   Smith's automobile is American-made.

2. Indicate which of the following examples are genuine syllogisms and which are not. Explain your answers.

   (a) Every president has the power to execute the nation's laws.
   Abraham Lincoln was a president.
   Abraham Lincoln had the power to execute the nation's laws.

   (b) All of the freshmen in our school are graduates of the local high school.
   Jacobs is one of the freshmen in our school.
   Jacobs is a graduate of one of the local high schools.

(c) No good businessman is in the habit of making poor investments.
Jones is a good businessman.
Jones is not in the habit of making poor investments.

(d) Damp climates are not conducive to sound health.
Some sections of the United States are characterized by the dampness of their climate.
Some sections of the United States are not conducive to sound health.

(e) All of the trucks in our fleet have Diesel engines.
This semitrailer is one of the trucks in our fleet.
This semitrailer has a Diesel engine.

(f) No one living in our block is a member of the Chamber of Commerce.
Smith lives in our block.
Smith is not a member of the Chamber of Commerce.

3. Define *categorical syllogism.*

4. Explain the function of the middle term (*M*) of a syllogism.

5. What is meant by the *subject* and *predicate* terms of a syllogism?

6. How does one determine which of the premises is the major and which is the minor?

7. What is meant by the *mood* of a syllogism? the *figure?*

8. (a) Give the *S, P,* and *M* terms of the following syllogism. (b) Give its mood and figure.

No capitalist is a pauper.
Some executives are capitalists.
Therefore, some executives are not paupers.

9. State the two parts of the *fundamental principle* which underlies every categorical syllogism.

10. (a) Exemplify the two parts of this principle through your own examples, using as parallels those given in the text. (b) Explain how the principle is verified in your own examples.

11. State the two axioms of the first figure.

12. (a) Draw up two of your own examples, paralleling those in the text, to illustrate each of these axioms. (b) What is the logical whole in each of your examples? What is the logical part?

11

The Categorical Syllogism

RULES • MOODS • FIGURES

Rules of the Syllogism
Explanation of the Rules
Corollaries
Valid Moods of the Syllogism
Figures of the Syllogism
Suggestions for Determining Validity
How to Construct a Simple Syllogism

INTRODUCTORY REMARKS. The scientific requirements of syllogistic reasoning, although comparatively few and simple, are extremely important. If logic is to have any significant effect on a student's thinking, observance of the rules that we are about to set forth must become second nature to him. It is not enough simply to learn these rules by rote. Above all else, the student must know how to put the rules to use.

RULES OF THE SYLLOGISM

Most logicians present seven rules of the syllogism—or more. It is a simpler procedure, we believe, to give only five rules, and to treat two of the statements usually listed as rules as corollaries. These five rules of the syllogism are:

1. *The syllogism should consist of no more than three terms.*
2. *The middle term must be universal in at least one premise.*
3. *No term which is particular in a premise may be made universal in the conclusion.*
4. *No conclusion can be drawn from two negative premises.*
5. *A negative premise requires a negative conclusion.*

The rules are either a direct or an indirect application of the principles and axioms studied in the preceding chapter. Their purpose is to ensure the practical application of the underlying theory of the syllogism. It will be of considerable help in learning these rules to note that *Rule 1* pertains to the very structure of the syllogism; *Rules 2 and 3* pertain to the quantity of the terms; and *Rules 4 and 5* pertain to the quality of its propositions.

Some authors include as rules of the syllogism the two following statements:

1. The syllogism must consist of only three propositions.
2. The middle term should never appear in the conclusion.

The student will do well to note that these two statements merely emphasize what we have already said in the preceding chapter concerning the structure of the syllogism. Once this point is understood, there is little danger of any violation. Hence, there is no real need to include them in the list of rules.

EXPLANATION OF THE RULES

Rule 1: The syllogism should consist of no more than three terms.

Since, as we have already said, this first rule is a requirement of the very structure of the syllogism, we need look no further to justify it. Let us examine, for instance, the two following propositions for the number of terms they embody:

To err is *human.*
To forgive is *divine.*

These two propositions simply do not comprise a syllogism, nor is anyone likely to attempt to draw a conclusion from these two propositions. The importance of Rule 1 becomes evident, however, when we recall that frequently we have an arrangement in which there are *apparently* only three, but *actually* four, terms.

MAJOR: Every *square* is *four-sided.*
MINOR: Your *jaw* is *square.*
CONCLUSION: Your *jaw* is *four-sided.*

From a *purely formal* point of view, the above argument would have to be regarded as *valid,* inasmuch as it presents the *appearance* of a three-term construction: "four-sided" (*P*), "square" (*M*), and "jaw" (*S*). However, the syllogism as it stands above is *invalid* on material grounds,[1] that is, it is invalid inasmuch as the *meaning* of the intended middle term "square" is different in each of the premises. Thus, although the same *word* is employed as middle term, the *term* itself is different in each case because it "stands for" two different things. Accordingly, the argument is really a four-term construction.

The name of the fallacy that violates Rule 1 is the *fallacy of*

[1] Although the term "validity" usually has reference to the *form* of an argument, it is not incorrect to speak of an argument as invalid on *material* grounds. Validity has reference *essentially* to the internal consistency of our reasoning acts. If, then, a reasoning act is inconsistent with regard to the *meanings* it employs, it is inconsistent on material grounds, and for this reason too it is *invalid.*

four terms. The most typical instance of this fallacy is that in which the *middle term* has two different meanings, as in the example above. This violation, which is a particular instance of the fallacy of four terms, is specifically referred to as the *fallacy of the ambiguous middle.*

Before we pass on to a study of the second rule of the syllogism, we shall give more examples of the *fallacy of four terms,* that is, examples in which the *S* or the *P* term has a different meaning in the conclusion than it has in the premises. At this point, however, there is more to be said of the *fallacy of the ambiguous middle term.*

In order that a syllogism may be valid, the middle term of the syllogism must have the same meaning in one premise as it has in the other. If its meaning in either premise, as compared with its meaning in the other, is *analogous* or *equivocal,* no legitimate conclusion can be drawn. In the example already given the meaning of the term "square" with reference to "jaw" is only *analogous.*

The employment of the ambiguous middle is an inexhaustible source of jokes, and we need not look very hard to find them. Not all instances of this fallacy, however, are as obvious as those used in jest. Hence, there is need for caution if there is only the slightest suspicion that the meaning of the middle term is shifting within the course of a syllogistic argument. Note the following example in which the fallacy of the ambiguous middle (though not too difficult to detect) is somewhat more plausible—and therefore more deceptive—than the one already set forth:

MAJOR:

A division in the government of a nation is unfavorable to that nation's welfare.

MINOR:

The legislative, judicial, and executive branches of the U.S. government are a division in the government of a nation.

CONCLUSION:

The legislative, judicial, and executive branches of the U.S. are (a division) unfavorable to that nation's welfare.

Or take an even more plausible example:

MAJOR:

Anyone who "quarrels with a fact" is being unreasonable.

MINOR:

Some lawyers (in courtroom cases) "quarrel with the facts."

CONCLUSION:

Therefore, some lawyers (in courtroom cases) are being unreasonable.

This argument seems entirely acceptable, which, indeed, it would be if the middle term meant the same thing in both premises. But what does it mean to "quarrel with a fact"? In the major premise the expression apparently has reference to something that is *really* a fact, that is, a *proved* and *established* fact. If "fact" is taken thus, then, clearly it is unreasonable to "quarrel with a fact." But in the middle term as it appears in the minor premise, there is some doubt that this is what is really meant. It may very well be that a lawyer (in a courtroom case) is merely "quarreling" with something that is *alleged* to be a fact. If this is the sense of the minor, then obviously the conclusion does not follow that some lawyers (in doing this) are "unreasonable." The fallacy would thus be one of an *ambiguous middle term.*

At this point it is important for the student to realize that the more *abstract* the terms of an argument, the more difficult it becomes to detect the presence of this fallacy. Accordingly, one should (whenever necessary) *define* the meaning of his terms. An incredible amount of fruitless argumentation results from failure in an argument to define the meaning of such terms as appear in the following—and very incomplete—list:

progress	free enterprise
democracy	music
religion	art
education	beauty
peace	philosophy
capitalism	nationalism

As a further instance of the fallacy of the ambiguous middle, note the following example:

> The citizens of our community contributed a million dollars to the local charity drive.
>
> John Smith did not contribute a million dollars to the local charity drive.
>
> John Smith is not a citizen of our community.

The function of the middle term in this example is destroyed because in the major premise it is collectively applied to its subject but in the minor it is divisively applied. In general, any argument in which the *supposition* of a term varies from one premise to another is invalid.

Curiously enough, there are many syllogisms which, although *formally* composed of four terms, *materially* (that is, from the standpoint of meaning) are *resolvable* into three. Note the example:

> Anyone who *knows the science of reasoning* is a competent judge of a sound argument.
>
> Some students in our class *know logic.*
>
> Some students in our class are competent judges of a sound argument.

In spite of the fact that the middle term of this syllogism is *differently worded,* its meaning *for the purposes of the argument given* is the same. Materially, then, we should have to consider the argument valid.[2] In their actual use many syllogisms are of an

[2] *Formally,* of course, this example may be considered as an abbreviated statement of two distinct syllogisms which, if fully set forth, would appear thus:

1. Anyone who knows the science of reasoning knows logic.
   Some students . . . know the science of reasoning.
   Some students . . . know logic.
2. Anyone who knows logic is a competent judge of a sound argument.
   Some students . . . know logic.
   Some students . . . are competent judges of a sound argument.

In actual practice such a resolution would be not only tedious but quite unnecessary. Therefore, *as long as one is certain* that the meaning of a term is the same (even though the wording is in some respects different), an argument of this sort may be handled as a *single* syllogism.

apparent four-term construction. Whether such arguments are to be considered valid or not depends in part upon the equatability of the meaning of the terms as stated within the *context* of the argument.

It is precisely on this last point that people most often *assume* (within the course of an argument) that two terms that are differently worded are the *same* as to their meaning. Needless to say, this assumption is frequently unwarranted and for that reason is the source of many mistakes in reasoning. Consider the following example:

MAJOR:	Every man	is *rational.*
MINOR:	John	is a man.
CONCLUSION:	John	is *intelligent.*

Here is another example of a four-term construction, although without an ambiguous middle. In this example the *P* term of the conclusion is different from the *P* term as it appears in the major premise. Now, if the words "rational" and "intelligent" were equatable in their meaning, if only for the purposes of the argument, there would be very little objection on this score. Since "rational," however, means *having the capacity to be intelligent,* it does not follow that John as a man is *actually* intelligent. Hence, the terms "rational" and "intelligent" are *two different terms,* and the syllogism as it stands is invalid.

With regard to the example above, note also that insertion of the term "intelligent" in place of "rational" is an obtrusion that very few people would accept if the syllogism were presented *exactly as it appears here.* In actual argumentation, however, an error of this sort is far less easily detected. The reason for this is that few arguments appear in a strictly logical form. *In actual discourse,* there is frequently a great deal else that appears between one premise and another and between the premises and the conclusion itself.

To conclude our treatment of Rule 1, note another example of a four-term construction:

MAJOR:

Anyone who weakens his physical constitution is endangering his health.

MINOR:

Drunkards weaken their physical constitution.

CONCLUSION:

People who take intoxicating drinks are endangering their health.

Again, if the subject term as it appears in the conclusion were simply equatable with the subject term of the minor premise, this argument, even as it stands, could be considered valid. Now it is true, of course, that *all drunkards are people who take intoxicating drinks,* but it is not true *conversely* (that is, by an illicit process of conversion) that *anyone who takes intoxicating drinks is a drunkard.* Thus, the subject term as it appears in the conclusion is really another term, and the argument as it stands is invalid.

Rule 2: The middle term must be universal in at least one premise.

The student already knows that it is the function of the middle term to serve as a common point of reference for uniting or disuniting *S* and *P* in the conclusion. Yet, if the middle term is taken *particularly* (that is, as an *undistributed* term) in *both* premises, there is no guarantee that *S* and *P* are being referred to the *same part* of *M*. Thus, it may be said that everyone who has pneumonia is *sick;* it may be said further that everyone who has the measles is *sick;* yet this does not prove that whoever has the measles has pneumonia. People who have pneumonia and people who have the measles belong to *two different parts of the extension* of those who are *sick.* In order, then, to unite or disunite the two terms of the conclusion (*S* and *P*), the middle term must be taken *universally* (that is, it must be distributed) in at least one of the premises. In the absence of this condition no valid conclusion can be drawn.

In order to ensure the practical application of this rule, the student should recall the chart (given in Chapter 5) as to the extension of both of the terms in each of the four types of propositions (*A, E, I, O*). He will again note that the predicates of *A* and *I* propositions are *particular* and that those of *E* and *O* propositions are *universal.* With this in mind he should note the quantity of the *M* term (signified by the small letter *p*) in both premises of the following example:

MAJOR:

	Pu	*Mp*
(*A*)	Everything *worth while*	is *difficult of attainment.*

MINOR:

	Su	*Mp*
	All *virtue*	is *difficult of attainment.*

CONCLUSION:

	Su	*Pp*
(*A*)	All *virtue*	is *worth while.*

The reason why *M* is marked "*p*" in both of the premises above is simply that it happens to appear in both premises *as predicate of an affirmative proposition* (an *A*). Keep in mind, then, that the predicate of an affirmative statement (*A* or *I*) is *particular.* The fallacy, therefore, in the above example is that of an *undistributed middle* (*MpMp*).

The intended conclusion of the example just presented seems *plausible* enough because it *happens* to be true. But the logician does not judge the validity or invalidity of a syllogism by the possible truth of the conclusion. This conclusion is *invalid* because of the *fallacy of the undistributed middle* (not to be confused with the *ambiguous middle*). In the above example *S* and *P* (*virtue* and *worth while*) *happen* to fall within the same part of the extension of *M* (*difficult of attainment*). Yet this *material* coincidence of *virtue* (*S*) and *worth while* (*P*) with *difficult of attainment* (*M*) takes place in spite of the invalidity of the form (*MpMp*). Note the presence of the same fallacy in an example where there is no such coincidence of matter:

Pu	*Mp*
Everything *worth while*	is *difficult of attainment.*
Su	*Mp*
Carrying coals to Newcastle	is *difficult of attainment.*
Su	*Pp*
Carrying coals to Newcastle	is *worth while.*

Even a nonlogician, if confronted with this line of "reasoning," would suspect that there is something wrong—but in this case only because the conclusion is taken as false or ridiculous. Yet, as we must repeatedly insist, *the validity or invalidity of a conclusion is in no way to be adjudged by its material truth or falsity.* The fact that most people accept or reject an argument according as they consider the conclusion to be *true* or *false* is itself the most cogent indication of the need (spoken of in the introductory remarks to the student in this text) for a scientific knowledge of logic. Indeed, the plausibility or nonplausibility of the conclusion is no basis for judging the validity of an argument .

In order, then, that a syllogism may be valid, the middle term must be *universal,* or *distributed,* in one of the premises—either the major or the minor. Further, although the middle term is often found to be universal in *both* premises, it is *not necessary* for it to be. The fact that *M* is taken universally in at least one of the premises precludes the possibility of our identifying *S* and *P* with two distinct parts of *M.*

Rule 3: No term that is particular in a premise may be made universal in the conclusion.

This rule is the counterpart of the syllogism of rules already studied under the square of opposition and conversion. The fallacy that violates this rule may be designated generically as the *fallacy of overextension.* In order to appreciate the need for this rule the student should note that *the terms S and P are related to each other in the conclusion only to the extent to which they are related to M in the premises.* Thus, if either of these terms (*S* or *P*) is particular in a premise, it must remain particular in the conclusion. To make such a term universal in the conclusion would be to overextend it. Indeed, to overextend a term in the conclusion would be the equivalent of inserting more in the conclusion than the premises themselves warrant. Remember that the conclusion is the effect of the premises, and no effect can be greater than its cause. This violation takes the form of the overextension of *S* or of *P* in the conclusion. These forms are respectively designated as the *fallacy of the illicit minor* and the *fallacy of the illicit major.*

In order to detect the presence of either of these fallacies, the student must again be reminded of the need for marking off the quantity of each of the terms in the syllogism. This can be done only by considering each of the propositions (major, minor, and conclusion) as *A, E, I,* or *O* and by remembering the rules governing the quantity of predicate terms.

Fallacy of the Illicit Minor

The *S* term of the syllogism is always the subject of the conclusion. Since the *fallacy of the illicit minor* is an overextension of the *S* term in the conclusion, this violation can occur only when the conclusion is a universal proposition (*A* or *E*). Thus:

Mu	*Pp*
Every *good singer*	is a *diaphragmatic breather.*
Mu	*Sp*
Every *good singer*	is a *person with a pleasant voice.*
Su	*Pp*
Every *person with a pleasant voice*	is a *diaphragmatic breather.*

Here the *S* term (of the syllogism) *as predicate of an affirmative premise* (the minor) is particular (*Sp*). Accordingly, it must remain particular as subject of the conclusion. The above syllogism would be *valid* if the conclusion were to read

Sp
Some *person with a pleasant voice* is a diaphragmatic breather.

Fallacy of the Illicit Major

This fallacy occurs when a *P* term that is particular in the major premise is made universal in the conclusion. Since negative propositions alone have universal predicates, this fallacy can occur only when the conclusion is a *negative proposition* (*E* or *O*).

Mp	*Pp*
Some *commercial vehicles*	are an *obstruction to passenger traffic.*
Su	*Mu*
None *of the equipment of our corporation*	is a *commercial vehicle.*
Su	*Pu*
None *of the equipment of our corporation*	is an *obstruction to passenger traffic.*

Rule 4: No conclusion can be drawn from two negative premises.

The reason for this rule is plain and simple. If both premises are negative, *S* and *P* are both *excluded* from the extension of the *intended* middle term. In this case there really is no middle term and hence no syllogism:

Some river fish are not tasty.
The sailfish is not a river fish.
Conclusion?

There is little probability that anyone will attempt to draw a conclusion. The following example, however, does seem quite plausible:

No nongraduate student is eligible for an M.A.
No freshman is a graduate student.
No freshman is eligible for an M.A.

Because both of its premises are negative, this example as it stands is *formally invalid.* Yet, by *obverting* the *E* proposition of the minor to *A* ("Every freshman is a nongraduate student") we can get a valid syllogism:

No nongraduate student is eligible for an M.A.
Every freshman is a nongraduate student.
No freshman is eligible for an M.A.

Opportunities for validating this type of premise arrangement are somewhat rare, since the change is (as in our example) conditioned by the negation that exists within the middle term of the major premise (namely, "nongraduate").

Rule 5: A negative premise requires a negative conclusion.

If one of the terms agrees with *M* and the other disagrees, we can only conclude that the two extremes (*S* and *P*) must *disagree* with each other. Given the two following premises:

No dude rancher is an expert at roping steers.
Some Indians *are* experts at roping steers.

One has no choice but to conclude that

Some Indians are *not* dude ranchers.

COROLLARIES

In addition to studying the rules just explained, it will be to the student's advantage to give some attention to the two following corollaries:

1. *No conclusion can be drawn from two particular premises.*
2. *If one premise is particular, the conclusion must be particular.*[3]

[3] As a help for remembering Rule 5 and Corollary 2 the student should take note of the following maxim: *The conclusion always follows the weaker part.*

Here we should make it perfectly clear that the above corollaries are merely *specific applications* of requirements already set forth by Rules 2 and 3 of the syllogism. *They do not really add anything to the rules themselves,* and it is for this reason that we do not include them in our list of rules. Yet they do serve a practical purpose. The violation of one of these corollaries is an immediate indication of the presence of one of the three following fallacies: *the fallacy of the undistributed middle, the fallacy of the illicit minor, and the fallacy of the illicit major.* How this comes about is made clear by the following *inductive* proofs.

Corollary 1: No conclusion can be drawn from two particular premises.

Any combination of two particular premises automatically involves a violation of either Rule 2 or Rule 3. To see why this is so, let us explore the two possibilities.

1. A Combination of Two I *Propositions*

Suppose we were to employ two *I* propositions as our major and minor premises. Since the subject and predicate terms of these propositions are both particular, we would have a premise arrangement in which all of the terms are particular (undistributed). Regardless, then, of where the *M* term appears in either of these premises, it would be *particular* in both of them. Hence, we have the fallacy of the *undistributed middle.* This means a violation of Rule 2.

2. A Combination of an I *and an* O *Proposition*

With this combination of premises we would have only *one* universal term, namely, the predicate of the *O* proposition. In order to avoid an *undistributed middle,* it is necessary to reserve the predicate of the *O* proposition for the placement of the *M* term. Next, consider that the conclusion of our syllogism must be negative, since one of our premises (the *O* proposition) is negative. The predicate of the conclusion, then, would be *universal* (*Pu*). Yet the only universal term we had in our premises has already been used for the placement of *M*. This means that the *P* term, whether it appears as subject or predicate of the major premise, will be *particular;* hence, the fallacy of the *illicit major.* Any attempt, then, to conclude from an *I* and an *O* combination would result in the fallacy of either the *undistributed middle* or the *illicit major.*

Corollary 2: If one of the premises is particular, the conclusion must be particular.

1. A Combination of Two Affirmative Premises

With this combination, if one premise is universal (an *A* proposition) and the other particular (an *I* proposition), we have only *one* universal term, namely, the subject of the universal premise (the *A* proposition). To avoid the *undistributed middle* we must use the subject of our *A* proposition for the placement of *M.* Since, then, the remaining terms are particular, the *S* term too is particular (in the minor premise). In order to avoid an *illicit minor,* we must keep it particular as subject of the conclusion (*Sp*). The conclusion itself, therefore, will be a particular proposition (*I*).

2. A Combination in Which One Premise Is Affirmative and the Other Negative

If one premise of this combination is universal and the other is particular (both cannot be particular), these possibilities arise: an *E and an I* proposition and *an A and an O.* In either of these combinations we have *two* universal terms: the subject of the universal premise and the predicate of the one that is negative. One of these terms must be used for the placement of *M* to avoid an *undistributed middle.* Moreover, since one of the premises is negative, the conclusion will be negative, and the predicate of the conclusion *universal.* To avoid an *illicit major* the remaining universal term must distribute the *P* term in the major premise. The *S* term, then, as one of the remaining *particular* terms, must be *kept* particular in the conclusion; otherwise, we would have an *illicit minor.* To avoid an illicit minor the *conclusion itself must be particular* (an *O* proposition).

A careful analysis of the proof just given reveals that a violation of Corollary 2 involves a violation of either Rule 2 or Rule 3 of the syllogism and, accordingly, also the fallacy of an undistributed middle, an illicit major, or an illicit minor.

VALID MOODS OF THE SYLLOGISM

In the preceding chapter, a syllogistic *mood* was defined as the respective designation of the premises and conclusion as *A, E, I,* and *O* propositions. Thus, if we use the letters *AII* (in that order) the purpose is to indicate the following type of syllogism:

MAJOR:	*A* proposition
MINOR:	*I* proposition
CONCLUSION:	*I* proposition

If we simply use the letters *AI,* we intend merely to indicate the major and minor premises without considering the conclusion.

Now that we have studied the rules of the syllogism, together with their corollaries, we are prepared to ask the question: *How many different kinds of moods are there?* Theoretically, with respect to only the major and minor premises, there are sixteen possible moods:

AA	*EA*	*IA*	*OA*
AE	*EE**	*IE*	*OE**
AI	*EI*	*II**	*OI**
AO	*EO**	*IO**	*OO**

The question that immediately arises, therefore, is this: How many of these moods are valid? The answer is not too far to seek. The moods that are marked by an asterisk(*) are invalid because they stand for either *two negative premises* (see Rule 4) or *two par-*

ticular premises (see Corollary 1). The mood *OO* is invalid on both counts. The invalidity of the *IE* mood (not marked by an asterisk) is not quite so apparent. Note first that the *major* premise is an *I* proposition. This means that the *P* term, whether it appears as subject or predicate of the major premise, is *particular* (*Pp*). However, since the minor premise (*E*) is negative, the conclusion must be negative. Since this is so, the *P* term in the conclusion would be universal (*Pu*). Any attempt, therefore, to use an *IE* mood would result in a fallacy of *illicit major* (Rule 3).

By the process of elimination the following *eight* valid moods are all that remain:

AA	*EA*	*IA*	*OA*
AE			
AI	*EI*		
AO			

It cannot be assumed, however, that all of these eight remaining moods are *always* valid, for the figures in which they appear must be taken into account. In other words, we should not conclude that when a syllogism is in one of the above eight moods, it is automatically valid. The point of our present inquiry is simply to indicate that if a syllogism is to have any chance at all of being valid, it must fall within one of these moods.

FIGURES OF THE SYLLOGISM

We have already explained that the *figure* of a syllogism is the disposition of the middle term in the premises. There are four possible combinations of figures:

	Figure 1	Figure 2	Figure 3	Figure 4
MAJOR:	*M—P*	*P—M*	*M—P*	*P—M*
MINOR:	*S—M*	*S—M*	*M—S*	*M—S*
CONCLUSION:	*S—P*	*S—P*	*S—P*	*S—P*

Figure 1 is the most common figure of the syllogism—most common because it is the most *natural*. The student may already have observed that most of the syllogisms given thus far in the text have been cast in the form of Figure 1 (the "perfect" figure). Note, then, that in this figure the *M* term is subject of the major premise and predicate of the minor. Figures 2 and 3, although of less common occurrence, are important. By way of contradistinction, note that in Figure 2 the *M* term is the *predicate* and that in Figure 3 it is the *subject* of both of the premises. Figure 4 (the Galenic figure[4]) is the reverse of Figure 1 and therefore the most uncommon.

PRACTICAL SUGGESTIONS FOR DETERMINING THE VALIDITY OF A CATEGORICAL SYLLOGISM

Theoretically, the student is now in a position to judge whether any given categorical syllogism is valid or invalid. In this chapter and in the one preceding the syllogism has been presented from the following points of view:

1. Fundamental theory and principles.
2. The *matter* of the syllogism, namely, its terms (*S, M, P*) and propositions (major, minor, and conclusion).
3. The five rules and their corresponding fallacies.
4. The two corollaries.
5. The eight valid moods.
6. The four figures.

Yet, a mere theoretical acquaintance with the various phases of syllogistic reasoning is not of itself an adequate guarantee of a genuine *working knowledge* of the syllogism. With this thought in mind we shall devote ourselves in the remainder of this chapter to a variety of practical considerations with respect to what we might call the *method of fallacy detection* and the *method of syllogistic construction.* Indeed, in order that the student may realize the full value of logic, he must be provided with the means for criticizing an unsound argument when he hears it (method of fallacy detec-

[4] The Galenic figure is named for the physician Galen (131-200).

tion) and the means for drawing up an argument of his own (method of construction).

In connection with the method of fallacy detection we shall set forth here a number of practical suggestions for determining the validity or invalidity of *ready-made* categorical syllogisms. For the present we shall deal only with relatively simple syllogisms in which the major, minor, and conclusion are each expressed—and expressed in their proper order.

Let us examine the following syllogism:

Not every public official is elected.
A mayor is a public official.
A mayor is not elected.

First ask the question: *Is there a fallacy of four terms?* What this usually amounts to in practice is the question of whether or not there is a *fallacy of the ambiguous middle.* In the example just given, it should be clear that the *M* term "public official" has the same signification in both of the premises. So, we shall have to look further.

The next step is to put the syllogism in its logical form, marking off each proposition as *A, E, I,* or *O* in order to determine the mood. Thus:

O Some public officials are not elected.
A Every mayor is a public official.
E No mayor is elected.

A glance at the *mood* of the syllogism (*OAE*) should immediately show us that there is something wrong, for we have here a direct violation of Corollary 2. Let us proceed, then, to specify (in addition to the mood) the figure and the quantity of each of the terms thus:

O	*Mp*	*Pu*
A	*Su*	*Mp*
E	*Su*	*Pu*

Now that we have our syllogism in skeleton form, any defects that it contains must become immediately apparent. We should now examine our syllogism for one or more of the following fallacies in the order given:

Undistributed middle
Illicit minor
Illicit major

A glance at the *M* term shows us that it is *particular* in both premises (*MpMp*); hence, it is an *undistributed middle* and an *invalid* syllogism.

Let us take another example:

A slave is not allowed the free exercise of his natural rights.
Most Americans are not slaves.
Most Americans are not allowed the free exercise of their natural rights.

Is there a possible violation of Rule 1? Clearly, the middle-term "slave" has an identical signification in both premises. What is the mood? The major is an *E* proposition, the minor an *O*, and the conclusion an *O*. Thus: *EOO*. Immediately we adjudge the example to be invalid on account of the mood: No conclusion from *two negative premises* (Rule 4).

Again:

All true art is beautiful.
Some contemporary sculpture is not true art.
Some contemporary sculpture is not beautiful.

Ambiguous middle? No, the term "true art" has the same signification. Is the mood, generally speaking, valid? Yes, *AOO* is *generally* (that is, without regard to the figure in which it appears) valid. Accordingly, we must skeletonize our syllogism thus:

A	*Mu*	*Pp*
O	*Sp*	*Mu*
O	*Sp*	*Pu*

We can now detect immediately the presence of an illicit major

(*PpPu*). Hence, the syllogism is invalid, because of the over-extension in the conclusion of the *P* term "beautiful."

Once the student has formed the *habit* suggested by the method applied to the above examples, he should have little difficulty in determining whether or not a syllogism is valid and if invalid what fallacy occurs. In general, then, in examining a syllogism for its validity, it is necessary to do two things:

1. *To give attention to the middle term.*

This term is easy to locate, since it is the only term that appears in *both premises* and *never* in the conclusion. Once the middle term is located, the next step is to look for a possible violation of Rule 1. If the middle term is ambiguous, one need look no further to know that the syllogism is invalid.

2. Next to set forth the *mood,* the *figure,* and the *quantity of each of the terms.*

In short, we must determine the *form* of the syllogism. Any deficiency in the form will point to the presence of one of the remaining fallacies.

HOW TO CONSTRUCT A SIMPLE SYLLOGISM

Before we conclude this chapter, a word as to the means of constructing a simple, categorical syllogism is in order. First, let us recall the two following fundamental facts:

1. The *conclusion* is what we are attempting to prove.
2. The *premises* are the means whereby it is proved.

In constructing a syllogism, then, we must know first *what* we want to prove. For the purpose of illustration, suppose we want to prove the following proposition:

Some nations are unsuited for self-rule.

Since this proposition will be our conclusion, we already have the *S* and *P* terms of the syllogism. In the order of terms, all that we need look for is *M*. The search for a middle term is facilitated simply by asking the question: *Why?* Indeed, there are as many possible middle terms as there are *reasons* for the proposition that we maintain. Suppose, then, that we consider *incapacity for producing responsible leadership* as the reason why some nations are unsuited for self-rule. This will be our *middle term.* Identifying the *S* term "some nations" with the middle term, we may concretely express our *minor premise* in the form of the following proposition:

> Some nations are incapable of producing responsible leadership.

In setting forth our major premise we shall have to identify the same middle term of the minor with the predicate of the conclusion. The problem, then, is to express *concretely* in the form of a proposition the identification of the two terms "incapacity for responsible leadership" and "unsuitability for self-rule." This may be done (with the required changes in the wording of our terms) by means of the following statement:

> Any nation incapable of producing responsible leadership is unsuited for self-rule.

Our entire syllogism, then, should read:

> Any nation incapable of producing responsible leadership is unsuited for self-rule.
> Some nations are incapable of producing responsible leadership.
> Some nations are unsuited for self-rule.

Note that the syllogism is cast in the first figure, and it is valid.

A word is in order as to the means of supplying premises for a *negative* conclusion. Let us take the following as our conclusion:

> Some marriages are not happy.

Here, again, we have in our conclusion both the *S* and the *P* terms of the syllogism we wish to construct. In looking for a middle term we must seek out a reason for the proposition just stated. Why are some marriages not happy? Because of too much quarreling.

Roughly, "excessive quarreling" will be our middle term. Identifying *S* with *M*, we may state our minor thus:

> Some marriages are characterized by excessive quarreling.

The remaining assumption is that

> No marriage that is characterized by excessive quarreling is a happy one.

This will be our major premise. Note that in this premise we have denied a relationship between the middle term (already used in the minor) with the predicate of the conclusion. In point of form, then, our syllogism would read thus:

E No *M* is *P*.
I Some *S* is *M*.
O Some *S* is not *P*.

CONCLUDING REMARKS. There is, of course, no infallible method of directing the student to the correct formulation of a syllogism by a purely *mechanical* process. No mere mechanical process can in any way substitute for an understanding of the nature of syllogistic reasoning as discussed in our previous chapter. To the extent, however, that the student combines his understanding of the underlying theory of the syllogism with the suggestions just presented, he may find these suggestions of considerable help in drawing up a valid argument of his own.

EXERCISES

Part I

1. Explain the practical importance of Rule 1 of the syllogism. Exemplify.
2. Give an informal proof of Rule 2 of the syllogism.
3. Give your own example of a syllogism with an *undistributed middle* in which the conclusion seems *plausible.* Pattern your example according to the form of the one given in the text.

By changing the *S* term of your example draw a conclusion that is not plausible.

4. How, in your opinion, do most people gauge the validity or nonvalidity of an argument?

5. What is meant by the fallacy of *overextension?* the *illicit minor?* the *illicit major?*

6. Give an informal proof of Rule 3.

7. Comment on the following statement: An illicit minor can occur only in a syllogism in which the conclusion is an *A* or an *E* proposition.

8. Comment on the following statement: An illicit major can occur only in a syllogism in which the conclusion is an *E* or an *O* proposition.

9. Briefly explain the reason for Rule 4 of the syllogism.

10. Briefly explain the reason for Rule 5 of the syllogism.

11. Citing the appropriate rule (or corollary), determine which of the following moods are always invalid:

AA	*EA*	*IA*	*OA*
AE	*EE*	*IE*	*OE*
AI	*EI*	*II*	*OI*
AO	*EO*	*IO*	*OO*

12. Are the remaining moods valid for *any* syllogism?

13. Explain the position of the middle term with respect to the four figures of the syllogism. Which of these figures is most commonly used?

14. What procedure is to be used in examining a syllogism for its validity?

15. Review some of the hints that were given in the text for constructing a categorical syllogism.

Part II

In accordance with the suggestions given in the text, examine each of the following examples for their *validity*. Decide in each case of an invalid syllogism which rule is violated, and name the fallacy. The propositions in each example are to be taken as major, minor, and conclusion, respectively.

Note:

a. If there is the need for so doing, place each proposition into its logical form.

b. In working out this exercise do not confuse "words" with "terms." Frequently two different *terms* in an argument contain one or more of the same *words,* but this of itself does not make the *terms* identical. Terms are identical only if they are identical in meaning.

c. By the same token, if a term, let us say, as it appears in the conclusion contains some new word that it did not contain in the premise, this of itself is not enough to invalidate the argument. Often it is necessary in order to make a syllogism read intelligibly to fill in a word or two. So, again, the question is whether the *meaning* is the same.

1. No irresponsible person is worthy of high position.
   Criminals are irresponsible persons.
   Criminals are not worthy of high position.
2. All art is not religious.
   Raphael's "Madonna and the Child" is a work of art.
   It is not a religious work of art.
3. Not every science is practical.
   Logic is practical.
   Logic is not a science.
4. Every physician is a doctor.
   Some doctors are dentists.
   Some dentists are physicians.
5. Every true patriot respects his country's flag.
   Some politicians are true patriots.
   They respect their country's flag.
6. No invalid syllogism is a sound argument.

No true act of reasoning is an invalid syllogism.
No true act of reasoning is a sound argument.

7. Not every valid syllogism is based upon true premises.
Most arguments are based upon true premises.
Most arguments are valid syllogisms.

8. The middle term of a syllogism is found in each of the premises.
No middle term appears in the conclusion.
No term appearing in the conclusion is found in each of the premises.

9. Every syllogism is not valid.
This is a syllogism.
It is not valid.

10. All inflammable liquids are potentially dangerous.
Some cleaning fluids are inflammable.
Some cleaning fluids are potentially dangerous.

11. Most grammarians disapprove of the use of slang.
My sister disapproves of the use of slang.
My sister is a grammarian.

12. All practical jokers have a perverted sense of humor.
All practical jokers are nuisances.
Every person who is a nuisance has a perverted sense of humor.

13. No fast talker is easy to understand.
Some "fast" talkers are hard to believe.
Some people who are hard to believe are not easy to understand.

14. Lying is not morally permissible.
A so-called "white lie" is really a lie.
A so-called "white lie" is not morally permissible.

15. All exceptional people are not brilliant.
 Most geniuses are exceptional people.
 Most geniuses are not brilliant.

16. Every literary masterpiece is worth reading well.
 Most textbooks are not literary masterpieces.
 Most textbooks are not worth reading well.

17. Whoever is uneducated is unlearned.
 Some people who are not learned are readers of books.
 Some people who read books are uneducated.

18. A bad habit is easy to acquire.
 A bad habit is difficult to lose.
 Whatever is difficult to lose is easy to acquire.

19. Every virtue is a good habit.
 Some good habits are acquired by repeated effort.
 Some qualities acquired by repeated effort are virtues.

20. Not every animal that is responsible to its master's will is a dog.
 A fox terrier is a dog.
 A fox terrier is not responsive to its master's will.

21. Every operation performed without the use of an anesthetic is painful.
 No appendectomy is performed without the use of an anesthetic.
 No appendectomy is painful.

22. No unjust act is commendable.
 Some unjust acts are crimes.
 No crime is commendable.

23. Anyone who works deserves to eat.
 But some people who work do not like to eat.
 Therefore, some people who don't like to eat don't deserve to eat.

24. Anyone who enjoys good music enjoys opera.
Some people who enjoy good music do not like jazz.
Some people who do like jazz do not enjoy opera.

25. All self-evident truths are indemonstrable.
First principles are self-evident truths.
First principles are indemonstrable.

26. Anything well written is legible.
Some novels are not well written.
Some novels are not legible.

27. Not everyone who knows how to read knows how to write.
Most children know how to read.
Most children do not know how to write.

28. Every individual is worthy of respect.
A criminal is an individual.
A criminal is worthy of respect.

29. All diseases are not incurable.
Tuberculosis is not incurable.
Tuberculosis is not a disease.

30. Whatever is worth doing is worth doing well.
Some assignments are not worth doing.
Some assignments are not worth doing well.

Part III

It was explained in the text that, *generally* speaking, there are eight valid moods of the syllogism. The purpose of this exercise is to determine which of these eight moods are valid for Figure 1, for Figure 2, and for Figure 3. For each mood that you find valid, supply the correct conclusion (*A, E, I,* or *O*). It is advisable to make a written summary of your results.

1. FIGURE 1:

(a) *A Mu—Pp*	(b) *A Mu—Pp*	(c) *A Mu—Pp*	(d) *A Mu—Pp*
A Su—Mp	*E Su—Mu*	*I Sp—Mp*	*O Sp—Mu*
(e) *E Mu—Pu*	(f) *E Mu—Pu*	(g) *I Mp—Pp*	(h) *O Mp—Pu*
A Su—Mp	*I Sp—Mp*	*A Su—Mp*	*A Su—Mp*

2. FIGURE 2:

(a) *A Pu—Mp*	(b) *A Pu—Mp*	(c) *A Pu—Mp*	(d) *A Pu—Mp*
A Su—Mp	*E Su—Mu*	*I Sp—Mp*	*O Sp—Mu*
(e) *E Pu—Mu*	(f) *E Pu—Mu*	(g) *I Pp—Mp*	(h) *O Pp—Mu*
A Su—Mp	*I Sp—Mp*	*A Su—Mp*	*A Su—Mp*

3. FIGURE 3:

(a) *A Mu—Pp*	(b) *A Mu—Pp*	(c) *A Mu—Pp*	(d) *A Mu—Pp*
A Mu—Sp	*E Mu—Su*	*I Mp—Sp*	*O Mp—Su*
(e) *E Mu—Pu*	(f) *E Mu—Pu*	(g) *I Mp—Pp*	(h) *O Mp—Pu*
A Mu—Sp	*I Mp—Sp*	*A Mu—Sp*	*A Mu—Sp*

Part IV

a. Supply an appropriate middle term for each of the following (incomplete) syllogisms.

b. Set forth the form (mood, figure, and quantity of terms) of each syllogism after you have worked it out.

c. Compare the results of (b) with the results of Part III.

1. Every ——— is trustworthy.
   Every honest person is ———.
   Every honest person is trustworthy.

2. Every ——— is clever.
   Some students are ———.
   Some students are clever.

3. No one ——— is a traitor to his country.
   Every good citizen is ———.
   No good citizen is a traitor to his country.

4. No ——— is just.

Some wars are ———.
Some wars are not just.

5. Every conservative person is ———.
No gambler is ———.
No gambler is conservative.

6. Whatever is educational is ———.
Some entertainment is not ———.
Some entertainment is not educational.

7. No pleasant conversationalist is ———.
Every bore is ———.
No bore is a pleasant conversationalist.

8. No well-patronized establishment is ———.
Some stores are ———.
Some stores are not well patronized.

9. Every ——— is a permanent source of enjoyment.
Every ——— is a literary masterpiece.
Some literary masterpiece is a permanent source of enjoyment.

10. Every ——— is useful.
Some ——— is science.
Some science is useful.

11. No ——— is a man-eater.
Every ——— is an animal.
Some animals are not man-eaters.

12. No ——— is man-made.
Some ——— are beautiful.
Some beautiful things are not man-made.

13. Some ——— are wealthy.
All ——— are generous.
Some generous people are wealthy.

14. Some ——— are not misers.

All ——— are thrifty.
Some thrifty people are not misers.

Part V

Applying the suggestions made in the text, construct a valid syllogism for each of the following conclusions.

1. Some business enterprises are not a success.
2. Some of the students in our class deserve good marks.
3. Big-game hunting is a dangerous sport for amateurs.
4. Most libraries are suitable places for study.
5. Some drivers are careless.
6. Cancer is an insidious disease.
7. No good deed is unrewarded.
8. Most children are interested in cowboy movies.
9. Some syllogisms are not valid.
10. Some food is not easily digested.

12

Argumentative Discourse

Demonstrative and Probable Reasoning

The Enthymeme

Practical Suggestions

Further Considerations

INTRODUCTORY REMARKS. Frequently there is a question in the mind of the student as to the *practical* value of the theory of the syllogism as he has studied it in the preceding chapters. Moreover, even if a student is convinced of the relevancy of syllogistic reasoning for everyday use, there is the question of *how* to apply it. In the chapter just completed we did, of course, indicate some of the means of detecting fallacies and drawing up a syllogism of one's own. These considerations, however, were in the main limited to syllogisms as taken in their *logical form.* So the question of how to relate syllogistic theory to *everyday argumentative discourse* still remains. It is the purpose of this chapter to provide the basic means for accomplishing the objective just stated.

Suppose, however, that a student does become proficient in the application of his logic to the problems of everyday discourse. He would be deluding himself very seriously were he to think for a moment that *the same kind of certainty* can be had in matters of politics, for instance, as in mathematics. *Even with the best application of reasoning,* there are certain fields of human inquiry which do not *of themselves* admit of the same kind and degree of certainty as that found in the stricter types of sciences. Indeed, it is unreasonable to demand a higher degree of certainty in *any* field of inquiry, scientific or otherwise, than the nature of the subject itself allows. Failure to take this element into account has on occasion led to the most tragic of historical consequences, as, for example, when Descartes attempted to introduce into all of the sciences the same kind of certainty as obtains in mathematics. For our own purposes, then, it will be necessary, before taking up our practical suggestions, to draw the general distinction between *demonstrative* and *probable* reasoning.

DEMONSTRATIVE AND PROBABLE REASONING

We are in a fair position at this point to realize that logic is in the main concerned with the *validity* of our reasoning processes. Viewed in this light, logic is largely concerned with the correctness of the form of an argument in contradistinction to the truth of its matter. Yet, in view of the fact that the relationship of formal validity to truth is that of a means to an end, it would be a mistake to neglect altogether the study of argumentation considered also *from the standpoint of its matter or content.*

It is true, of course, that whether reasoning concerns itself with the affairs of everyday life or with matters of scientific import, the process in its purely *formal* aspects is *essentially the same.* Thus, whether we reason concretely about the affairs of our everyday practical existence or whether we reason in the realm of scientific abstraction, a syllogism will be equally valid or invalid, depending mainly upon the correctness of its form. So, too, if a conclusion *follows* from its premises, it *necessarily follows,* that is, in a manner that is due to the necessity of the *form.*

As we have already seen in our proof of the third rule of the syllogism, the premises are the cause of the conclusion, and the conclusion itself is purely and simply the effect of the premises from which it derives. Since no effect can exceed its cause, the *kind* of truth that the premises produce in the conclusion will depend upon the *kind* of truth that the premises themselves express. Accordingly, if we reason validly from premises that are only *probably* true, we can at best arrive at a *probable* conclusion. On the other hand, if we reason from premises that are rooted in scientific *certainty,* the conclusion too will be endowed with the same kind of *certainty.* In short, the truth of the conclusion is proportional in its nature to the truth of the premises upon which it is based.

Note, then, the difference between the two following syllogisms with respect to the matter, or content:

No conscientious citizen will fail to cast his vote in an important election.
Smith is a conscientious citizen.
Therefore, Smith will not fail to cast his vote in an important election.

No nonliving substance is capable of organic growth.
Mercury is a nonliving substance.
Therefore, mercury is not capable of organic growth.

From the standpoint of *form* these syllogisms are identical, and both are *equally valid.* A comparison, however, of the nature of the truth expressed in the major premise of the first syllogism with that given in the second syllogism will reveal an important difference in their *matter.*

The major premise of the first syllogism is suitable for general acceptance. Yet, the universality of the truth that it expresses is inferior to that expressed in the major premise of the second syllogism. Thus, although a proposition of this sort is true as the basis of an argument that is solidly probable, it cannot serve as a principle of *scientific* reasoning. Any number of contingencies which might lead to an exception in the truth we are stating are possible.

What we state is, of course, true, but it is not true in such a way that it *could not be otherwise.*

Needless to say, most argumentation is of a nonscientific nature, lacking as it does the required degree of necessity in the truth of its matter, or content. Such argumentation, however, is far from being worthless. Thus, *even though we may reason from premises that are only probably true* (and do admit of possible contradiction), *the conclusions that we arrive at are frequently of the utmost practical value.* The reasoning, for instance, that enters into the making of a foreign-policy decision is on a nonscientific level. Yet, in the consequences that such a decision involves, the reasoning employed is of paramount practical value.

THE ENTHYMEME

In its original Aristotelian usage an *enthymeme* is a syllogism which, in its suppressed major premise, is based upon truths that are only probable and nonscientific. Thus, if we infer that Smith hates Jones because he is envious of Jones, our reasoning rests on the assumption, which is *probably* true and generally accepted, that

Men hate those of whom they are envious.

This major premise is *suppressed* because it lacks the degree of certainty that is required for a strictly scientific truth.

Here we should further state that for Aristotle the term "enthymeme" is to be applied also to an *argument that is taken from a sign* (*Prior Analytics,* Bk. II, Ch. 27, 70a). Thus, it is "argued" from the redness of a person's cheeks that he is shy or embarrassed; from the cloudiness of the sky that it will rain; from the uncouthness of a person's appearance that he is uncultured; from the discolor of a piece of meat that it is old; from the hardness of a loaf of bread that it is stale. Examples of this kind could be multiplied indefinitely. From the few that we have given it should be clear that much of our everyday "reasonings" are of precisely this kind. Under ordinary circumstances the "argument" from a sign leads to no necessary conclusion, and the *failure to take this into account is the source of an incredible number of mistakes which people commit in their everyday life.*[1] At their best most "sign arguments" only provide one with a *clue* to a problem which must be solved by the use of induction, and induction is not *per se* a simple matter of inference (see Chapter 15).

As it is employed in modern usage, an enthymeme is understood to be *any* kind of syllogism (that is, regardless of its matter) in which one of the propositions (major, minor, or conclusion) is suppressed. Taken in this sense an enthymeme may be defined as *an abbreviated syllogism that implies either one of its premises or its conclusion.*

In the study of the enthymeme as thus defined, we encounter the syllogism as it occurs in common, everyday speaking and writing. Indeed, it very seldom happens that in the reading of an argumentative piece of discourse we find a neat, full-fledged syllogism with a conveniently arranged major, minor, and conclusion. A reader would be somewhat taken aback if he read something like the following in the editorial of his evening newspaper:

No incompetent is deserving of re-election.
Mr. X is an incompetent official.
Therefore, Mr. X is not deserving of re-election.

It is more than likely that the same bit of argumentation (with a considerable amount of rhetorical fill-in) would be expressed in some such way as the following:

1. Being an incompetent official, Mr. X does not deserve to be re-elected.

[1] This is especially true if the sign argument in question is based merely on a *conventional* sign. Thus, it is fallacious to think that because the term "invaluable" contains the prefix "in" the term in question means *"not valuable"* (see *fallacy of parallel word construction,* Chap. 14). If, on the other hand, a sign argument is based on a *natural sign,* there is perhaps less likelihood of going astray, although here, too, the sign should be taken only as a clue for a problem that is to be solved on its own merits by means of induction, that is, by further observation, hypothesis, and the experimental testing of hypothesis. Thus, gray hair is *under certain conditions* a sign of advancing age; a cloudy sky is *under certain conditions* a sign of rain; a persistent cough is *under certain conditions* a sign of tuberculosis.

2. Incompetent officials are hardly deserving of re-election. Mr. X should be rejected at the polls.
3. Incompetency in office is hardly a brief for re-election. Is there anyone in this community who has a reasonable doubt as to the incompetency of Mr. X?

Offhand, the three statements above seem a far cry from the syllogism as studied in the last few chapters. Yet, in spite of their verbal dissimilarity, each of these statements is *logically identical* with the syllogism presented above.

It is of the utmost practical importance that the student begin at this point to penetrate beyond the rhetorical word combinations of common parlance to reach an understanding of the basic skeleton of the argument. Note, then, that the logical structure of the above enthymemes is as follows:

1. SUPPRESSED MAJOR
   Mr. X is an incompetent official.
   Mr. X is not deserving of re-election.

2. No incompetent official is deserving of re-election.
   SUPPRESSED MINOR
   Mr. X is not deserving of re-election.

3. No incompetent official is deserving of re-election.
   Mr. X is an incompetent official.
   SUPPRESSED CONCLUSION

For purposes of convenience, syllogisms with a *suppressed major, minor,* or *conclusion* are designated as enthymemes of the *first, second,* or *third* order, respectively.

PRACTICAL SUGGESTIONS

The immediate difficulty experienced by the student at this point is the problem of how to go about supplying the missing part of an argument. In this connection we must recall the importance of knowing, in the first place, precisely *what the argument is intended to prove.* The first thing to do, therefore, is to *set forth the conclusion.*

If the conclusion is given, there is very little difficulty in locating it, since it is usually preceded by such words or phrases as "hence," "therefore," "consequently," "as a result," "it follows that," and so on. Even if the conclusion is suppressed (third order enthymeme), one can readily supply it by simply determining the *point* of the argument in question. Recall again that the premises are only the means for *pointing to* the conclusion—the conclusion being the end or reason for which anything else appears in an argument. A casual inspection of the following premises should be enough to convince the student of the comparative ease of dealing with *third-order* enthymemes:

> No poorly written work is easy to read.
> Some term papers, however, are poorly written.
> Ergo?

> No first-rate newspaper is biased in its editorial opinions.
> Our local newspaper is notorious for its editorial bias.
> Ergo?

> An excessive fee is an unjust fee.
> Some doctors' fees are outrageous (that is, excessive).
> Ergo?

In supplying the conclusions to the above enthymemes the student will, no doubt, be led to question the common assumption that it is a mark of intelligence for one to "draw his own conclusions."

The difficulty that ordinarily presents itself is that of supplying a missing major or minor premise. Given one of the premises and the conclusion, the student may have the double difficulty of determining which of the premises is understood (major or minor) and what the wording of the missing statement should be.

With a view toward the solution of these difficulties, the following hints should prove of considerable help. Let us begin with the following example:

> Mere memorization of subject matter is no guarantee of one's having learned it. *For this reason,* one can't be sure, when cramming for an examination, of learning the subject matter.

The first step, of course, is to set forth the conclusion in clear, explicit terms, preferably in impersonal language. Thus, the *point* of the above enthymeme is as follows:

S	c	*P*
"Cramming" for an examination	is not	a guarantee of one's having learned his subject matter.

Since this is the *conclusion* of the argument, we immediately know the minor (*S*) and major (*P*) terms of the syllogism. A casual inspection of the remaining part of the enthymeme (as stated above) makes it quite clear that this is the *major premise* of the syllogism for the simple reason that it contains the *major term* (as already identified in the conclusion).

M		*P*
Mere memorization of the subject matter	is not	*a guarantee of one's having learned it* (subject matter).

In supplying the missing minor premise all that we need do now is identify the subject of the conclusion (*S*) with the middle term (*M*) of the major premise:

S	*c*	*M*
"Cramming" for an examination	is	merely to memorize (mere memorization of) the subject matter.

Accordingly, the syllogism, fully expressed, should read as follows:

MAJOR:

M		*P*
Mere memorization of the subject matter	is not	a guarantee of one's having learned it.

MINOR:

S		*M*
"Cramming" for an examination	is	merely to memorize the subject matter.

CONCLUSION:

S		*P*
"Cramming" for an examination	is not	a guarantee of one's having learned one's subject matter.

The example just given was an enthymeme of the *second order*. Of more frequent occurrence is the *first-order enthymeme*—the one in which the major premise is implied. Thus:

Because some men are truly virtuous, they are genuinely happy.

Because of the simplicity of the terms, there is little difficulty here in setting forth the conclusion:

S	*c*	*P*
They (that is, *some men*)	are	genuinely happy.

The appearance of the *S* term "some men" in the first part of the statement above ("because *some men* are truly virtuous") is an immediate indication that this is the *minor* premise of the syllogism. All that remains, then, is to identify the middle term (*M*) of the minor premise ("truly virtuous") with the predicate term (*P*) of the conclusion ("genuinely happy"). Yet, there is the difficulty here of deciding which of the two following statements should serve as major premise:

M		*P*
All *truly virtuous men*	are	*genuinely happy.*

Or

P		*M*
All *genuinely happy men*	are	*truly virtuous.*

If we select the first statement above, the form of our syllogism will be as follows:

MAJOR:	*A*	*Mu—Pp*
MINOR:	*I*	*Sp—Mp*
CONCLUSION:	*I*	*Sp—Pp*

This syllogism is cast in Figure 1, and it is *valid.* If we select the second statement, the syllogism will read thus:

MAJOR:	*A*	*Pu—Mp*
MINOR:	*I*	*Sp—Mp*
CONCLUSION:	*I*	*Sp—Pp*

This syllogism is cast in Figure 2, and it is *invalid* (undistributed middle).

How, then, shall we cast the syllogism? The following practical rule should be of considerable help in making a choice: If it is possible to construct a *valid* syllogism, this should be done, *provided that in so doing we do not commit ourselves to the statement of a major premise that is false.* Since the first major premise above is an evident statement of truth, we should accordingly select it as the major premise of our syllogism:

MAJOR:	All truly virtuous men	are genuinely happy.
MINOR:	Some men	are truly virtuous.
CONCLUSION:	Some men	are genuinely happy.

The importance of knowing how to handle enthymemes (especially those of the first order) is attested by the fact that sometimes the reasoning involved is based upon an assumption (that is, a premise) that is either *questionable* or downright *false.* Indeed, in the analysis of an abbreviated syllogism, it is of supreme practical importance for the student to *know how to make explicit the hidden premise.* The reason for doing this is to enable us either to examine the premise for its truth value or to examine it for the purpose of deciding whether the argument is valid or invalid. Consider the following piece of "reasoning":

Because Mr. X is a professor, he must be an eccentric person.

A brief analysis of this enthymeme would allow any of the following possibilities:

All professors are eccentric.
Mr. X is a professor.
Mr. X is eccentric.

This syllogism is *valid,* but the major premise is untrue

All eccentric people are professors.
Mr. X is a professor.
Mr. X is eccentric.

Here the major premise is again *untrue,* and the syllogism (in Figure 2) is *invalid* (undistributed middle).

Some professors are eccentric.
Mr. X is a professor.
Mr. X is eccentric.

Major premise as stated here may be taken as *true,* but the syllogism is *invalid* (undistributed middle).

Some eccentric people are professors.
Mr. X is a professor.
Mr. X is eccentric.

Major premise as stated may again be taken as *true,* but again the syllogism is *invalid* (undistributed middle).

Thus, however we try to handle this enthymeme, we find ourselves confronted with a false major premise, an invalid syllogism, or both.

To consider one more example of a first-order enthymeme, take the following:

Because this substance is hard, it must be made of steel.

The only way to *validate* this enthymeme is to supply as its major premise a proposition in which the middle-term is distributed:

	Mu	*Pp*
MAJOR:	*Every hard substance*	is *made of steel.*
	Su	*Mp*
MINOR:	This substance	is hard.
	Su	*Pp*
CONCLUSION:	This substance	is made of steel.

The syllogism as it now stands is valid but only at the expense of our having stated a major proposition that is *false*. It is advisable, therefore, to reconstruct it according to Figure 2, in which, although the major premise is true, there is a fallacy of an *undistributed middle*:

	Pu	*Mp*
MAJOR:	*Whatever is made of steel*	is *hard.*
	Su	*Mp*
MINOR:	This substance	is hard.
	Su	*Pp*
CONCLUSION:	This substance	is made of steel.

In argumentative discourse a speaker naturally has a choice of the means he may employ in refuting an argument of this kind. Since most people, however, are unacquainted with the names of logical fallacies, it would be of little advantage to tell a person, for instance, that he has an "undistributed middle." This remark might be taken as uncomplimentary, although not in the sense intended. Usually the most effective way to expose the invalidity of an argument is in some way or another to *manifest the absurdities* to which it might lead.[2] Most often this can be done *by the mere substitution of one of the terms of the argument as it was originally given.* For example:

[2] As a general method of refutaton this means of approach is sometimes called a *reductio ad absurdum.*

I grant that anything made of steel is hard. But so are my teeth. Should I conclude, then, that they too are made of steel?

This, we say, is perhaps the most effective *practical* way of refuting an invalid argument. But it is a method that should be employed with a proper degree of restraint, that is, without undue sarcasm.

FURTHER CONSIDERATIONS

In addition to knowing what an enthymeme is and how to handle it, the student should realize that a great deal of what appears in an ordinary piece of argumentative discourse is usually of a narrative, descriptive, or expository nature. Examine, for instance, the following paragraph:

> An economy that is based on excessive taxation is *fundamentally* an unsound economy. Every government has, of course, the right to tax both individuals and corporations, inasmuch as taxation is the only means that a government has of maintaining itself in existence. When, however, the costs of taxation are so high that they are prejudicial to a *free* economy, a situation has developed in which the government is no longer serving the interests of the citizenry at large. Is there any doubt about the fact that the economy of our government (based as it is on a system of excessive taxation) is *fundamentally* an unsound economy?

In studying an argument of this sort, the student will do well before examining any of its expository details to set forth its *leading major and minor premises* as well as its *leading conclusion.* What is the main point of the argument in question? Clearly, that

> The economy of our government is fundamentally an unsound economy.

The fact that the conclusion of the original statement is set forth in the form of a rhetorical question should in no way mislead the person who reads it into thinking that it is not a vital part of the argument. What reason, then, is given in support of this proposition arrived at by way of conclusion? It is the assertion (parenthetically stated!) that

> The economy of our government is one that is based on excessive taxation.

Syllogistically stated, then, the above argument should read as follows:

MAJOR:

> Any economy that is based on excessive taxation is fundamentally an unsound economy.

MINOR:

> The economy of our government is one that is based on excessive taxation.

CONCLUSION:

> The economy of our government is fundamentally an unsound economy.

Now that we have stated our argument in this form, we are in a far better position to examine it from the standpoint of both its logical structure and the truth value of its premises. We can also see that the part of the original paragraph that was not expressly set forth in our syllogism is given merely in support of the major premise.

An even more careful analysis of the example we have given above reveals that the major premise is supported by an argument of its own, that is, by an argument with respect to which the major itself might be regarded as a conclusion. This type of argument is most often referred to by logicians as an *epicheirema.*

Thus, an epicheirema is an argument that consists of *one basic syllogism*—with a leading major and minor premise—and a leading conclusion. What characterizes it, however, as a special form of argument is the fact that a *reason* is attached to one or both of its premises. The following example is a clear-cut illustration of this type of syllogism:

MAJOR:

Every realistic system of education is based on the needs of the student,

because the failure to cope with these needs defeats the very purpose for which education is intended.

MINOR:

Some systems of education, however, are not based on the needs of the student,

because they do not include adequate programs for vocational guidance, which, clearly, is one of the student's most basic needs.

CONCLUSION:

Some systems of education are not realistic.

There are, of course, various ways in which a *series* of syllogisms might be employed as part of the general fabric of an argumentative piece of discourse. However, the resolution of an argument into every *single* syllogism that is contained in it would prove not only tedious but in many respects impractical. It is suggested accordingly that in analyzing an argument the student devote the major share of his attention (initially at least) to an examination of the leading points of the argument.

From the standpoint of *argument construction,* too, the student will do well to set forth the *outlines* of the argument itself before presenting his "bill of details." In order to do this he should construct some *leading* syllogism around which everything else will converge as a subordinate part. Suppose we wish to *prove* the contention that

The United States can no longer afford the risk of an isolationist policy.

Having determined the *point* of the argument, we must now advance a fundamental reason for maintaining it. In short, what we need is a middle term. Let us say, that the basis for our contention is rooted in the conviction that

> No major government can any longer afford the risk of an isolationist policy.

Accordingly, the syllogistic outline of the argument that we shall use is established:

MAJOR:

> No major government can any longer afford the risk of an isolationist policy.

MINOR:

> The United States is a major government.

CONCLUSION:

> The United States can no longer afford the risk of an isolationist policy.

Knowing what we intend to prove and how we intend to prove it, we are free now to "build up" our argument in any way that we see fit. Nor is there any strict need for presenting it in precisely the order of major, minor, and conclusion. Note that in the following statement we give the conclusion in the very first line of the paragraph:

> The United States can no longer afford the risk of an isolationist policy. There was a time in the history of our country when, in the struggle for independence, it was neither desirable nor possible for the government of the United States to involve itself in either European or Asiatic affairs. Today, however, the situation is immensely changed. The present international situation is such that no major government can afford to close its eyes to the world-wide threat of Communism. That is to say, no major government can any longer afford the risk of an isolationist policy. Who can deny the fact that the United States, with its natural resources, industrial potential, and capacity for world-wide leadership is a major government?

CONCLUDING REMARKS. To prevent any misunderstanding that may arise from our application in this chapter of the theory of the syllogism to argumentative discourse, the student should note first that the scope of this chapter has been limited to the practical applications of the *categorical* syllogism. He should bear in mind that the other types of syllogistic reasoning, which will be studied in the next chapter, play an equally important role in our everyday reasoning. But since there is less difficulty in identifying the forms of *hypothetical* reasoning as they appear in everyday usage, there is no need for a special treatment of this subject. At any rate, it should be clear that besides the categorical syllogism, these others too are of great practical significance.

Further, there are many arguments that are employed in everyday thinking that are not simply reducible to a syllogism. In other words, *not all argumentative discourse is syllogistic.* Arguments of this sort, to mention only a few, are those involving an *appeal to belief,* the *employment of statistics, circumstantial evidence,* and the *use of analogy.*

Finally, the student must understand that it is neither possible nor desirable in an elementary textbook of logic to work out all the various ramifications of syllogistic reasoning, at least as it is found in everyday discourse. The most important forms, however, have been set forth in the hope that the student will apply for himself—both critically and constructively—his knowledge of the theory of the syllogism to its everyday, practical use.[3]

EXERCISES

Part I

1. What is the difference between a probable and a demonstrative argument?
2. Give your own example of each of these types.
3. Refute the following statement: "Because probable rea-

[3] At this point too the student is invited to consult any good text on argumentation and debate. *Argumentation and Debate,* edited by David Potter and published by Dryden Press, 1954, is recommended.

soning is of a nonscientific nature, it is, for all practical intents, of comparatively little value."

4. What is the meaning of the term *enthymeme* as originally understood by Aristotle? Discuss the *argument from a sign.*

5. Define *enthymeme* according to its modern signification.

6. Comment on the following statement: "The enthymeme is the syllogism as found in its common, everyday use."

7. What is the difference between enthymemes of the first, second, and third order?

8. If an enthymeme contains its conclusion, it usually expresses a word or phrase indicative of the conclusion. Draw up a list of five such words or phrases other than those given in the text.

9. In dealing with enthymemes explain the importance of deciding first on the conclusion. In the absence of some such words as "therefore," "hence," and similar ones, how do we determine the conclusion of an enthymeme?

10. In dealing with enthymemes of the first or second order, how do we determine whether it is the *major* or the *minor* premise that is understood?

11. What is the difficulty that ordinarily presents itself in stating the major premise of a first-order enthymeme? What practical considerations should be taken into account in the solution of this difficulty? Illustrate by means of your own example.

12. Draw up a list of practical suggestions for the handling of a syllogistic argument as it appears in an ordinary form of discourse.

13. Within the course of most arguments, assumptions are made that are only implicitly contained in the argument itself. Explain the importance of knowing how to make these assumptions explicit.

14. Suppose you are asked to engage in a debate in which you are to take the *negative* side of the following question: "A system of price controls should be a permanent institution in our government economy." How would you go about the task of proving *your* side of the question?

15. What is meant by an epicheirema? Give an example.

Part II

State in the form of a syllogism each of the following enthymemes. Decide in each case whether the syllogism is *valid* or *invalid.* In supplying the major premise of first-order enthymemes, avoid (if possible) giving a proposition that is patently false. As in the example given below, it is not necessary to match up the terms of the syllogism *word for word,* assuming, of course, that their meaning is the same:

EXAMPLE ONE: Because this child does not know how to spell, that is no reason for thinking that he is unintelligent.

IMPLIED MAJOR: Inability to spell is not a necessary indication of unintelligence.
MINOR: This child is unable to spell.
CONCLUSION: This child is not necessarily unintelligent.
Valid

EXAMPLE TWO: All doctors are well-trained men and so too (?) are mechanics. Draw your own conclusion.

MAJOR: All doctors are well-trained men.
MINOR: All (?) mechanics are well-trained men.
INTENDED CONCLUSION: All (?) mechanics are doctors.
Invalid: undistributed middle

1. A person who does not know how to study will not get the full benefit of his courses. Is it any wonder that your roommate is complaining about not getting what he should out of his courses?

2. JIM: I can't understand why I didn't get good grades this semester. You know how hard I studied.
ED: Yes, I know, Jim, but aren't you laboring under an assumption that is not necessarily true?

3. There are many arguments in which the key term of the argument is used in more than one sense. As I recall from my logic, this is enough to make an argument invalid.

4. No influence that is a threat to the morals of the com-

munity should be tolerated. Therefore, big-time gambling should not be tolerated.

5. "Filtered cigarettes are better for your health." Brand X filters its cigarettes. (Does the conclusion follow? Also discuss any ambiguity in the word "better." Does "better" at least imply "good"?)

6. Some people who smoke pipes occasionally smoke cigars. So I would not be surprised to find out that your dad smokes a cigar now and then. (Does this example have a connection with the argument from a sign?)

7. John is not a very cultured person. No one who fails to appreciate the musical masterpieces is a really cultured person.

8. Most arguments that have the appearance of being reasonable are persuasive. That's why (?) fallacious arguments are persuasive.

9. No one who is unprepared for the serious financial responsibilities of marital life should even think about getting married. John (whose wedding date is set for next month) doesn't even have a job.

10. All human beings do not enjoy the right to vote. Clearly, people living under a dictatorial rule are human beings. But does the conclusion follow?

11. Since an alien is not legally classified as a citizen, he is not allowed to vote.

12. Not every nation is free. Yet the United States is a nation. So?

13. It is evident that you are questioning the facts in this case. Anyone who questions a fact is being quite unreasonable. (Does the student recognize this example?)

14. All noise is distracting. But good music is not noise.

15. Some of the worst bores I have met are good-natured individuals; some comedians are extremely good-natured.

16. All the citizens of Nevada are Westerners. So, Californians are not Westerners.

17. "I see that the nutrition experts have found that folks who start the day with a good breakfast feel better and do better

work. That makes sense. And eggs make a good breakfast."—Advertisement found in an egg carton. (If you can't work out this example, don't give up on the others.)

18. A juvenile delinquent is not to be treated as a criminal, because he is too young to be a criminal.

19. Virtue is better than knowledge, and justice is a virtue.

20. No violent form of exercise which causes injury to the body is really a sport. For this reason, I cannot see why football should be considered a sport.

21. A well-trained child is one that has good manners. This child's manners are abominable.

22. I'm sure you find your new job pleasant because it affords you the opportunity of getting to know people from all walks of life.

23. Not every borrower is a good risk. But you are a good risk.

24. A healthy person is a wealthy person, and a wealthy person is one who has money.

25. A pen is a writing instrument, but a writing instrument cannot think for itself.

26. Many intoxicated persons cannot walk properly, because their sense of balance is impaired.

27. Any kind of work requires the use of the proper instruments, and so does eating.

28. Being a barber, you are no doubt a good conversationalist.

29. Not everything that is owned is earned. But I did earn this paycheck.

30. Anyone who is truly educated is a lover of great literature. But no illiterate person is truly educated.

31. Not every person who operates a car is a good driver. A good driver is an accurate judge of distance.

32. Certain people do not know how to think. But logicians are certain people.

33. He who knows everything knows nothing. But nobody knows everything.

34. Some rules admit of exceptions. Rules of this sort, therefore, are not principles.

35. Some entertainment is educational. Yet my own experience tells me that sitting through a class in geometry is anything but entertaining. The conclusion is obvious. (Is it?)

36. Evil as such is undesirable. But nothing that is truly good is an evil as such.

37. Money is not the measure of one's intrinsic worth, because money is purely an external good.

38. Fun is something you enjoy, and it's no fun studying for logic.

39. Today the temperature was in the mid-forties. Spring can't be far off. (Argument from a sign?)

40. People, they say, are funny. But most of the people I know are not funny.

41. You didn't find your purse, because you did not look for it.

42. Free enterprise, I say, is good for the country. That's why (?) the government should keep its hands out of private business. (Room here for ambiguity?)

43. People who live right feel well. But I do not feel well. Can it be . . .?

44. Life, they say, is what you make it. But no man "makes life."

45. All hot weather is disagreeable for study. But it never gets hot in St. Paul.

Part III

The following examples are anything but masterpieces of English composition. They are intended primarily to be informal expressions of ordinary argumentative discourse. It is possible to construct more than one syllogism from each of these examples, but the following steps are required:

a. Set forth (in its simplest possible form) what you consider to be the *leading* major, minor, and conclusion of each argument.

b. If one of the premises or the conclusion is missing, supply it.

c. Determine whether the syllogism (as restated) is valid or invalid.

1. Writing a term paper is no easy task. It's difficult enough to write a good English composition. But ordinarily it isn't necessary in writing a composition to do research. Writing a term paper, however, is a task that involves plenty of research work. This means going to the library to find the books you need, locating the passages that relate to your topic, and knowing how to interpret them. If you ever have had the experience of writing a term paper, I'm sure you've found out for yourself that term paper writing is no easy task. Nothing which involves research is easy.

2. There was a time when I used to enjoy shopping for groceries, but not any more. Shopping for basic grocery items in a modern supermart is a distressing experience because it gets a person all confused. Suppose you want to buy a carton of cottage cheese—just plain cottage cheese. What you find is cottage cheese mixed with all sorts of flavorings from pineapple to chives. Suppose, too, you want to buy some cereal—for humans, I mean. What you find is an infinite variety of foods for dogs, cats, and canaries! This, I say, is a distressing experience, because it gets you all confused.

3. I can't think of anything more futile than worrying about the past. Did you ever meet anybody who could change the course of past events? Of course not; past events are entirely outside of human control. Think of all the people who continually worry about their past lives, as if worrying made a difference. I'm sure that if these people would devote as much time and energy to present opportunities as they spend mulling over the past, they would be far better off. I repeat, it's futile to worry about the past, because the past is something that can't be controlled.

Part IV

State the *leading* major, minor, and conclusion of the following argument:

Any government which, to maintain itself in existence, habitually violates the rights of its individual citizens—any such form of government is inconsistent with the basic precepts of sound morality. This is a principle that scarcely needs proving. Yet, if anyone asks why, we need only point out that moral precepts are little more than an expression of what reason itself demands in the conduct of human affairs. To be moral is to act in a manner in which reason prescribes us to act. What is it, then, that reason demands in the matter of individual rights? Clearly, that they should at all costs be respected. Indeed, the very concept of right is destroyed if you remove from it the element of respect. Any government, then, that fails to respect individual rights or, what is worse, positively violates them is acting contrary to reason and hence immorally.

The question may now be asked whether the government of Germany under Hitler's rule was one that respected individual rights. The answer to that question is not hard to find. There is an abundance of evidence to show that under Hitler the rights of individual citizens were forfeited to the purposes of his dictatorial rule. Here we need but mention the widespread persecution of Jews simply because they were Jews and not members of a pure Aryan race; the control which Hitler's government exercised over the minds of German youth and that in spite of the protests of many conscientious parents; the curtailment of religious practices; and the liquidation of a free press. In the light of these facts, one cannot but conclude that the government of Germany under the Nazi regime of Hitler was fundamentally an immoral government.

Part V

In your study of the following dialogue answer these questions:

a. What is "Bill" trying to prove?

b. What are his basic premises?

c. What means does he employ in order to establish his premises?

d. Do you consider the argument as a whole satisfactory?

MIKE: Bill, I simply can't agree with you when you tell me that rights are not relinquishable. As far as I can see, any right that I have is *mine.* Grant you, I don't have any business interfering with the rights of others. Yet, if you speak of my having this right or that (say the right to private property), surely I can forego that right, if I want to.

BILL: Wait a minute, Mike. In the first place you're wrong in supposing that if something belongs to you, you are automatically in a position to give it up. For instance, you have relatives—they are *your* relatives. You can, if you want to, disown them, but they're still your relatives. When it comes to the question of rights I want to make sure you understand me. I allow that there are some rights you can forego. You have a right to the hat you are wearing, and you also have the right to use it. If you give me your hat, obviously you are giving up your right to own and to use it. The point of my argument is that not all rights are relinquishable. There are some rights you can't get rid of.

MIKE: Prove it.

BILL: Well, do you agree that you have some rights which you didn't really acquire—natural rights?

MIKE: I'm not so sure.

BILL: What about your right to live? How did you get it?

MIKE: Just by being born, I suppose.

BILL: In other words, it's part of your nature. It belongs to you as a human being.

MIKE: All right, I'll grant you that. There are some rights that I have which are part of my nature. They belong to me as a human being. But this doesn't prove that I can't give them up. What about a fellow who commits suicide? Doesn't he give up his right to live?

BILL: I suppose I'd have to admit that in a way he does. Certainly, he gives up the *use* of that right—something which in this case he has no business doing. But the right itself—I don't think he's really giving that up.

MIKE: It's a little hard for me to see the difference between a right and the use of a right. Aren't they really the same thing?

BILL: No, they are not. You have many rights that you don't

necessarily use. You have the right to move to another city, if you wish. But supposing you stay here, does that mean that you don't have the right?

MIKE: That makes your distinction a little more plausible.

BILL: O.K., then, besides agreeing that you have certain natural (let's say inborn) rights, do you also agree that you can't give them up, even though you sometimes forego their use?

MIKE: Admitting your distinction between *having* a right and *using* it, I have no choice but to agree.

BILL: Then what I said in the first place is true: some rights, that is, *natural* rights, are not relinquishable.

13

Hypothetical Syllogisms

INTRODUCTORY REMARKS. When a logician speaks of *the* syllogism—that is, without specifying the type of syllogism to which he is referring—what he usually has in mind is the categorical syllogism. It must not be thought, however, that this is the sole type, the one to which all others are reducible. Much of our reasoning is of a *hypothetical* nature, involving as it does the use of conditional suppositions and alternatives.

The purpose of this chapter is to set forth some of the fundamental types of hypothetical inference. At the outset we must emphasize the point that hypothetical syllogisms operate according to their own set of rules. Accordingly, what was set forth in the preceding chapters on the moods, figures, and rules of the categorical syllogism simply does not apply to the types of inference to be dealt with in the pages that follow.

THE CONDITIONAL SYLLOGISM

The fundamental type of hypothetical inference is the conditional syllogism, the major premise of which is always a *conditional* proposition. Here a word is in order by way of review of the nature of a conditional proposition. For example:

If a person is nearsighted, he needs glasses.

As in the example given here, the condition, or *antecedent,* of any conditional proposition is usually set forth in the form of an *if* clause. What is asserted to follow (necessarily) upon fulfillment of the condition is the *consequent.* If the consequent follows necessarily from the given antecedent, the proposition is true.

The following is an example of a conditional syllogism in its simplest form:

MAJOR:	If a person is nearsighted, he needs glasses.
MINOR:	John *is* nearsighted.
CONCLUSION:	John *does* need glasses.

Structurally a conditional syllogism is one in which the major premise is a conditional proposition and the minor and conclusion are categoricals.[1]

Before we explain the rules of the conditional syllogism, it is necessary first to distinguish its *moods.* In the example above the minor premise restates (categorically) the antecedent of the major; the conclusion restates the consequent. The example in question is a conditional syllogism in the *positing mood.* Here the student must

note that to *posit* an antecedent or a consequent means *to take it over as it is given:* if it is affirmative, *keep it affirmative;* if it is negative, *keep it negative.*

[1] Authors often refer to this type as a *mixed* conditional, that is, as opposed to a *pure* conditional, in which each proposition (major, minor, and conclusion) is conditional. Because this latter type is rare, we have omitted it.

Thus, in the example above the antecedent and the consequent of the major premise are affirmative enunciations. Accordingly, in *positing* the antecedent the minor premise posits it affirmatively ("John *is* nearsighted"); the conclusion affirmatively posits the consequent ("John *does* need glasses").

Using the same major premise as in the example above, it is possible also to construct a syllogism in the *sublating mood:*

MAJOR: If a person is nearsighted, he needs glasses.
MINOR: Tom does *not* need glasses.
CONCLUSION: Tom is *not* nearsighted.

In connection with this example, note well the meaning of the term "sublate": To *sublate* an enunciation is to *contradict* it. Thus, to sublate an *affirmative* enunciation (antecedent or consequent) is to make it *negative;* to sublate a *negative* enunciation is to make it *affirmative.* Observe that in the example given the minor premise *sublates*—that is, *contradicts*—the consequent; and the conclusion sublates or contradicts the antecedent. The syllogism, accordingly, is in the *sublating mood.*

The rules, then, for the conditional syllogism are the essence of simplicity itself:

1. ***Positing mood***
   a. ***Minor posits antecedent***
   b. ***Conclusion posits consequent***
2. ***Sublating mood***
   a. ***Minor sublates consequent***
   b. ***Conclusion sublates antecedent***

Thus, for each of the two moods of the conditional there is one right way of constructing a syllogism and one way that is wrong.

1. For the *positing* mood it is *incorrect* to posit the consequent in the minor and the antecedent in the conclusion. Thus:

MAJOR: If you do not eat, you will get a headache.
MINOR: You have a headache.
CONCLUSION: So you did not eat.

Invalid: fallacy of positing the consequent
(that is, in the minor)

To validate the above syllogism, we must make the minor and conclusion read thus:

MINOR: You are *not* eating.
CONCLUSION: So you *will* get a headache.

The conclusion as it is now stated *logically* follows from what is given. It assumes, of course, that the major premise is true: namely, that there is a connection between "not eating" and "getting a headache."

2. For the *sublating* mood it is *incorrect* to sublate the antecedent in the minor and the consequent in the conclusion.

MAJOR: If you work hard, you will be tired.
MINOR: You did not work hard.
CONCLUSION: You are not tired.

Invalid: fallacy of sublating the antecedent
(that is, in the minor)

In order to validate this syllogism, that is, for the sublating mood, we should make the minor and conclusion read as follows:

MINOR: You are *not* tired.
CONCLUSION: So you did *not* work hard.

The conclusion as thus stated *logically* follows from the premises. The *truth* of the conclusion, however, is dependent upon the truth of the connection stated in the major between "working" and "getting tired."

In order that the student may acquire a firm grasp of the rules stated above, he should first understand thoroughly *the theory that is the basis of these rules.* For the *positing* mood, then, we must ask the question: Why is it right to proceed from the truth of the antecedent (in the minor) to the truth of the consequent (in the conclusion) and not conversely? To answer this question we must further examine the nature of a conditional proposition.

The distinguishing feature of most conditional propositions

is that it is possible for any number of conditions to lead to a given consequent. Thus, if we suppose as a consequent the enunciation "I shall be late for class," there are any number of conditions that may guarantee its fulfillment.

If I oversleep, If I read the morning newspaper, If I miss the bus, If I get involved in an accident, If I go to the wrong building, Etc.	*I shall be late for class.*

If we *posit* any one of the above antecedents, we are correct in positing also the consequent "I shall be late for class." Suppose, however, that "I AM late for class." In that case we may not infer conversely the fulfillment of any one of the *specific* antecedents above, for the simple reason that the mere positing of the consequent leaves *indefinite* the question as to *which* of the antecedents has been fulfilled.

Occasionally it happens that the antecedent and consequent of a conditional proposition are mutually interchangeable. For example:

If the will is free, it is not determined.
If the will is not determined, it is free.

The interchange of the enunciations in this example is possible by reason of the matter or content expressed. Although this type of proposition is rare, it is materially correct on the basis of such a proposition to infer the truth of the antecedent from the truth of the consequent.

If the will is free, it is not determined.
The will is not determined.
The will is free.

In all other types of conditionals, however, there is no logical assurance that, given a consequent, a certain *definite* antecedent has been fulfilled.

With respect to the *sublating* mood of the conditional syllogism, we may now ask the question: Why is it necessary to sublate the consequent in the minor and the antecedent in the conclusion? Note that we are correct in making the following inference:

MAJOR: If I oversleep, I shall be late for class.
MINOR: But I was *not* late for class.
CONCLUSION: So I did *not* oversleep.

Here the *nonfulfillment* of the consequent justifies our inference of the nonfulfillment of any one or all of its possible antecedents. Since the consequent itself did *not* eventuate, *none* of the conditions that *might have* induced it were fulfilled. Since "I was not late for class," *none* of the conditions that might have caused me to be late were fulfilled.

I did not oversleep.
I did not read the newspaper.
I did not miss the bus.
I did not get involved in an accident.
I did not go to the wrong building.

Conversely, it would be *wrong* to suppose from the nonfulfillment of a *specific* antecedent that the consequent itself did *not* take place. For example:

If I oversleep, I shall be late for class.
I did *not* oversleep.
I was *not* late for class.

According to the example given "I may be late for class, even though I did not oversleep," that is, because of the possible fulfillment of one or more of the other conditions. Accordingly, the mere fact that *one* of the conditions did not take place is no guarantee that *none* of the others took place. If, as a matter of fact, only *one* of the other conditions had been fulfilled, then the consequent would have been realized.

PRACTICAL OBSERVATIONS

Here we should note first the possible confusion that may arise in the positing and sublating of certain types of conditionals. In this connection it is well to observe that the conditional proposition usually takes one of the four following forms:

1. *Both enunciations affirmative:*
If a is b, then a is c.
If this flower grows, it will bloom.

2. *Negative antecedent, positive consequent:*
If a is *not* b, then a is c.
If a child is *not* sick, it will play.

3. *Positive antecedent, negative consequent:*
If a is b, then a is *not* c.
If a nation is prosperous, it does *not* need financial aid.

4. *Both enunciations negative:*
If a is *not* b, then a is *not* c.
If you do *not* eat, you will *not* recover.

In view of these possibilities, when we are constructing a syllogism in the *positing* mood, we should be careful to restate an enunciation *as given in its original quality*. Thus, to exemplify form 3 above:

If a nation *is* prosperous, it does *not* need financial aid.
This nation *is* prosperous.
It does *not* need financial aid.

In the *sublating* mood, let us *contradict* an enunciation in the manner we have already explained:

If a nation *is* prosperous, it does *not* need financial aid.
This nation *does* need financial aid.
It is *not* prosperous.

In the practical application of this type of syllogism, it is also necessary to be able to identify a conditional proposition in the absence of the familiar "if" form. Thus, each of the following are conditionals:

> Had you not been at home, you would not have received my call.
>
> Unless (that is, if—not) you know how to study, you will not learn.
>
> Provided that she knows how to cook, she'll be a good wife.

Frequently, too, an inverted word order is encountered in which the consequent is given first:

> You cannot study if you do not know how to read.

Suppose that we construct from this last statement a conditional syllogism in the *sublating* mood. The minor and conclusion would have to appear thus:

MINOR: You can study.
CONCLUSION: You do know how to read.

It is entirely possible that a conditional syllogism or, for that matter, any other type of hypothetical syllogism will take the form of an enthymeme. For example:

FIRST ORDER

MAJOR: SUPPRESSED
MINOR: This child is singing.
CONCLUSION: It must be happy.

SECOND ORDER

MAJOR: If a child sings, it is happy.
MINOR: SUPPRESSED
CONCLUSION: So this child must be happy.

THIRD ORDER

MAJOR: If a child sings, it is happy.
MINOR: But this child is singing.
CONCLUSION: SUPPRESSED

With respect to the first-order enthymeme above, note that, given the minor and the conclusion, we have a choice of reconstructing it either as a categorical or as a conditional syllogism:

Categorical	*Conditional*
Any child that sings is happy.	If a child sings, it is happy.
This child is singing.	This child is singing.
This child is happy.	This child is happy.

However we choose to reconstruct an enthymeme of this type, care must be taken to ensure the truth of the major premise.

THE DISJUNCTIVE SYLLOGISM

As we shall see in a moment, every disjunctive syllogism has as its major premise a disjunctive proposition. Since the very nature of this type of reasoning depends totally on the type of proposition that it employs as its major, the student will do well to pause and review the following points:

1. There are two basic types of disjunctive propositions—the *proper* and the *improper* disjunctive.
2. Both of these types are signified by the words "either—or."
3. In order that a proper disjunctive may be true, its parts must be *complete* and *mutually exclusive.*
4. In order that an improper disjunctive may be true, it *need only be true in one of its parts,* though not necessarily false in the rest.
5. Whether a given statement is properly or improperly disjunctive must be decided most often by its *context.*

The bearing that these points have on the theory of the disjunctive syllogism will be brought out in the discussion which follows.

In its simplest form a disjunctive syllogism is one that employs as its major premise a proper disjunctive that contains *two* enunciations which are complete and mutually exclusive. For example:

One is either a born or a naturalized citizen.

To construct a disjunctive syllogism from the above proposition is a relatively easy matter, although here too we must distinguish between the *positing* and the *sublating* moods. The procedure for this type of syllogism is as follows:

1. ***Positing mood***[2]
   a. ***Posit one alternative in the minor.***
   b. ***Sublate the other in the conclusion.***

For example:

MAJOR:	One is either a born or a naturalized citizen.
MINOR:	Murphy *was* born in this country.
CONCLUSION:	He is *not* a naturalized citizen.

2. ***Sublating mood***
   a. ***Sublate one alternative in the minor.***
   b. ***Posit the other in the conclusion.***

For example:

MAJOR:	One is either a born or a naturalized citizen.
MINOR:	Schulz was *not* born in this country.
CONCLUSION:	He *is* a naturalized citizen.

The intent of the major premise in the examples given is that with respect to the two alternatives *one must be true and the other false.* Consequently, if one of the alternatives is *specified as true* in the minor, it is correct to designate the other as *false* in the conclusion. Likewise, from the *falsity* of one alternative in the minor one may adjudge the other to be *true* in the conclusion.

Note: The following forms are further illustrations of how this type of syllogism is employed in both of its moods. Each proposition is to be taken in the order given as major, minor, and

[2] Whether any disjunctive syllogism is valid in the positing mood is dependent in each case on the "disjunctive" character of its major premise. *Only if the major premise is strictly and properly disjunctive is it permissible to employ a disjunctive syllogism in the positing mood.* The possibility of doing this is clearly dependent on the *matter* of the proposition expressed, that is, since the copula "either—or" leaves it open to question whether any given proposition is properly or improperly disjunctive.

conclusion. In reviewing these examples keep in mind the meaning of the terms "posit" and "sublate."

1. *Positing mood*

a. a is either b or c.
   a *is* b.
   a is *not* c.

b. a is either b or non-b.
   a *is* b.
   a is *not* non-b.

c. a is either b or non-b.
   a *is* non-b.
   a is *not* b.

d. a is either non-b or non-c.
   a *is* non-b.
   a is *not* non-c.

In each of these forms the minor *posits* one of the alternatives, and the conclusion *sublates* the other.

2. *Sublating mood*

a. a is either b or c.
   a is *not* b.
   a *is* c.

b. a is either b or non-b.
   a is *not* b.
   a *is* non-b.

c. a is either b or non-b.
   a is *not* non-b.
   a *is* b.

d. a is either non-b or non-c.
   a is *not* non-b.
   a *is* non-c.

In each of these forms the minor *sublates* one alternative, and the conclusion *posits* the other.

Once we know how to posit and sublate correctly, the theory of the disjunctive syllogism in any of its above forms is relatively easy to apply. *From the standpoint of form alone* the only mistake that we might make would be either to posit or to sublate both of the given alternatives. The example below makes the mistake of sublating both alternatives:

Either you are nonrational or you are a human being.
You are rational.
So you are not a human being.

Since the minor of the above example *sublates* (contradicts) the first alternative, the conclusion should *posit* the other thus: "You *are* a human being."

Here we must take special note of the fact that a disjunctive syllogism frequently has as its major premise a proposition that contains *more than two enunciations.* If the intent of the major as a *proper* disjunctive is to give enunciations that are *complete and mutually exclusive,* then the procedure suggested by the following examples should be employed:

1. Positing mood

MAJOR: You are in either grade school, high school, or college.
MINOR: You *are* in high school.
CONCLUSION: You are in *neither* grade school *nor* college.

Minor posits one of the members; conclusion sublates, or removes, the others.

2. Sublating mood

MAJOR: You are in either grade school, high school, or college.
MINOR: You are in *neither* grade school *nor* college.
CONCLUSION: You *are* in high school.

Minor sublates (or removes) all of the members except one; conclusion posits the remaining member.

Up to this point we have restricted our attention to the disjunctive syllogism that has as its major premise a proposition that is *properly* and *strictly* disjunctive. Such a syllogism is, as we have seen, valid in both of its moods. The question of the function (in this type of reasoning) of an *improper* or *imperfect* disjunctive must now be raised. Can such a proposition be employed as the basis of a disjunctive argument, that is, in such a way that it leads to a *necessary* conclusion? If so, can it be employed in both of the moods?

The importance of the above questions arises from the fact that there is a great deal of disjunctive reasoning which, though apparently sound, frequently proves misleading. Take the following as an example:

Either you do not know how to study, or you do not care, or you do not know how to concentrate.
But you do not know how to study and you do not care.
So you *do* know how to concentrate.

It will be noted that this argument posits two of the members in the minor and sublates the remaining part in the conclusion. To do this is in effect to state: "Since two parts of the original statement are true, the remaining part of the original is false; it is necessary, therefore, by way of conclusion to set forth its contradictory." In judging the soundness of this argument it is to be noted first that the major premise is an *improper* disjunctive. What, then, is the meaning of an improper disjunctive? Only this: At least one of its parts is true, *there being no implication as to the truth or falsity of the remaining parts.*

A careful examination of this last consideration should point to the fact that the conclusion of the above argument does not really follow from what is laid down. Thus, *given as true* "You do not know how to study and you do not care," the remaining part of the major *may be* true or it *may be* false. Since there is no *necessary* implication one way or the other, it would be wrong to think that the third part of the original statement is false. From the above it should be clear that any disjunctive syllogism that employs as its major premise an *improper* disjunctive is invalid in the positing mood.

To determine now whether an improper disjunctive can be set up in the sublating mood, note again the sense of this type of statement: "At least one member is true." Clearly, then, if we sublate all the members in the minor *except one,* we are pointing out that all of these members are *false.* In this case, we would be justified in positing as *true* the remaining member in the conclusion.

Your sickness was caused either by overwork, too little sleep, or an improper diet.
But you have not been overworking, and you have been getting enough sleep.

Therefore, your sickness must have been caused by an improper diet.

Assuming the original proposition to be true, the conclusion of the above argument *necessarily* follows from its premises.

CONJUNCTIVE SYLLOGISM

A conjunctive proposition (it will be recalled) is negative in form. For example:

You cannot at one and the same time love God and hate your neighbor.

The question here is not one of a complete disjunction, which involves the necessity of one of the alternatives being true and the other false. All that the proposition states is that *both cannot be true.* A *conjunctive syllogism* is one whose major premise is of this sort.

For a conjunctive syllogism to be valid it is necessary to *posit* one of the alternatives in the minor and to *sublate* the other in the conclusion. For example:

MAJOR: You cannot love God and hate your neighbor.
MINOR: But you do love God.
CONCLUSION: You do *not* hate your neighbor.

Because of the nature of a conjunctive proposition, it would be *invalid* to place a conjunctive syllogism in the *sublating* mood, as in the following:

You cannot be both an American and a European.
You are not a European.
You are an American.

As a matter of fact, you may be an Asiatic. The above syllogism is invalid for the simple reason that the nontruth of one alternative does not necessarily imply the truth of the other. Both alternatives of the major premise might conceivably be false.

THE DILEMMA

The dilemma is a hybrid type of syllogism which combines the use of both conditional and disjunctive propositions. It is a type of argument that, if well constructed, can prove highly effective; yet, as we shall see, it is one that is also subject to serious abuse.

Since a dilemma in the sublating mood is of very infrequent occurrence, we shall restrict our attention here to the two most common varieties, both of which are in the positing mood.

Simple Constructive Dilemma

Every dilemma has as its major premise *two* conditional propositions. The major premise of a simple constructive dilemma is one having *two different antecedents,* both leading to the *same consequent.* For example:

MAJOR: If this thief attempts a getaway, *he will be caught.*
If he remains at the scene of his crime, *he will be caught.*

The *minor* premise of this type of dilemma *disjunctively posits* the two antecedents of the major. Thus:

MINOR: This thief will either attempt a getaway or he will remain at the scene of his crime.

The conclusion *categorically posits* the single consequent of the major:

CONCLUSION: He will be caught.

Here it is worth noting that the major premise of this type of dilemma is frequently expressed in the form of a single statement thus:

> Whether this thief attempts a getaway or whether he remains at the scene of the crime, he will be caught.

A glance at this example shows that the dilemma follows the same pattern as the rules for the conditional syllogism, already given in this chapter:

> Minor posits antecedents.
> Conclusion posits consequent.

Complex Constructive Dilemma

This type of dilemma differs from the one above in that the two antecedents of the major premise lead to *two* different consequents:

MAJOR: If a politician votes according to his conscience, he will lose the support of his constituents.

If he votes according to the desires of his constituents, he violates his conscience.

Here *the minor disjunctively posits the antecedents of the major:*

MINOR: This politician will vote either according to his conscience or according to the desires of his constituents.

Since the major premise has two different consequents, it is necessary to posit both of them *disjunctively* in the conclusion:

CONCLUSION: He will either lose the support of his constituents or violate his conscience.

It would be a formal violation of the rules of the constructive dilemma to posit the consequent(s) in the minor and the antecedents in the conclusion (*fallacy of positing the consequent*).

In criticizing a dilemma on *material* grounds, it is necessary to examine carefully the *truth* of the major and minor premises.

Major Premise

Since the major is *conditional* in form, you deny its truth by pointing out that an alleged consequent does not follow from its given antecedent. To do this is to "take the dilemma by the horns."

Minor Premise

Deny the minor premise, which is *disjunctive,* by showing that the alternatives given are either incomplete or not mutually exclusive. This procedure is more commonly known as "escaping between the horns of a dilemma."

EXAMPLE OF A FAMOUS DILEMMA

Protagoras the Sophist agreed to teach Eualthus the art of pleading, on the condition that Eualthus pay him one half of the fee upon completion of his course and the other half after he had won his first case in court. Because of Eualthus' failure, upon completion of the course, to practice law, Protagoras decided in order to collect the other half of the fee to initiate a court action against Eualthus. The substance of his appeal to the court was as follows:

> If I win this case, Eualthus must pay by order of the court; if I lose, he must pay me by the terms of our contract. I shall either win the case or lose it. In either event Eualthus must pay the fee.

The following was Eualthus' rebuttal:

> If I win this case, I shall not have to pay by reason of the court's decision. If I lose this case, I shall not have to pay by reason of the terms of the contract. I shall either win or lose. In either event I shall not have to pay.

Since the appeal of both of these men is directed to the court, neither of them is consistent in his appeal to the terms of the contract (that is, *against* the order of the court). Accordingly, if Protagoras loses the case, he has no right (against the decision of the court) to collect his fee, that is, by the original terms of the contract. He might, of course, initiate another court action, but under the circumstances that is beside the point. Likewise, if Eualthus loses, the decision of the court would again be binding *against* the terms of the contract. Neither Protagoras nor Eualthus can "have it both ways."

CONCLUDING REMARK. A good deal of our everyday reasoning is hypothetical in form; that is, it is reasoning of the sort that involves the use of conditions and alternatives as a practical means of resolving doubts. A mother concerned with the whereabouts of her child might reason to herself thus:

> Either Jimmy went with his father to the grocery store or he is romping about somewhere in the neighborhood. But he can't be [that is, is likely not] with his father—because his father was in a hurry [it being assumed that he never takes the child when pressed for time]. So I'll see if I can locate him at the Smith's [the most likely neighborhood hangout].

This example is a typical illustration of the role that hypothetical inference plays in the *problem-solving techniques* that we employ in our everyday lives. Indeed, the success of these techniques is very largely dependent on our ability to "size up" likely alternatives (as inductive hypotheses) which *in relation to a given set of circumstances* are complete and mutually exclusive. Their periodic failure, on the other hand, is most often characterized by the omission of some alternative which, though obvious enough in itself, for one reason or another is overlooked. It is thus that the dramatic success of many a mystery story hinges on the reader's failure to take into account some one alternative (hypothesis) that he should have been considering "all along."

The chart that appears on the facing page is a summary of the different types of hypothetical syllogisms.

EXERCISES

Part I

1. Explain what is meant by the *positing* and *sublating* moods of the conditional syllogism. Give an example of each type.
2. What do you understand by the fallacy (a) of positing the consequent? (b) of sublating the antecedent?
3. Explain the theory (using your own example) behind the positing mood of the conditional syllogism.

Type of Syllogism	*Structure*		*Positing Mood*		*Sublating Mood*	
Conditional	*Major:*	Conditional				
	Minor:	Categorical	Posits antecedent		Sublates consequent	
	Conclusion:	Categorical	Posits consequent		Sublates antecedent	
Disjunctive	*Major:*	Disjunctive	Proper	Improper	Proper	Improper
	Minor:	Categorical	Posits one alternative	*Invalid*	Sublates alternative (s)	Same as for proper
	Conclusion:	Categorical	Sublates remaining alternative (s)	*Invalid*	Posits remaining alternative	Same as for proper
Conjunctive	*Major:*	Conjunctive			*Invalid*	
	Minor:	Categorical	Posits one alternative			
	Conclusion:	Categorical	Sublates the other alternative			
Dilemma			*Simple*	*Complex*	*Simple**	*Complex**
	Major:	Two conditionals	Different antecedents Same consequent	Different antecedents Different consequents	Same antecedent Different consequents	Different antecedents Different consequents
	Minor:	Disjunctive	Disjunctively posits antecedents	Disjunctively posits antecedents	Disjunctively sublates consequents	Disjunctively sublates consequents
	Conclusion:	Disjunctive (or categorical)	Categorically posits consequent	Disjunctively posits consequents	Categorically sublates antecedent	Disjunctively sublates antecedents

* Rare

4. Explain the theory (using your own example) behind the sublating mood of the conditional syllogism.

5. Give five examples of conditional propositions whose antecedent is not expressed by the conjunction "if." From these examples construct five conditional syllogisms in the positing mood and five in the sublating mood.

6. Give examples of conditional syllogisms that are enthymemes of the first, second, and third order.

7. Explain why the matter of a *proper* disjunctive provides a suitable basis for a syllogism in the *positing* mood. Exemplify.

8. What logical procedures are to be followed in the positing and sublating moods of a disjunctive syllogism?

9. What are the dangers of disjunctive reasoning? Show why an *improper* disjunctive is not a suitable basis for a syllogism in the *positing* mood. Exemplify.

10. May an improper disjunctive be employed as the basis of a disjunctive syllogism in the sublating mood? Explain and exemplify.

11. Give an example of your own of a valid conjunctive syllogism.

12. Explain why a conjunctive syllogism is invalid in the sublating mood.

13. What is the difference between a simple and a complex dilemma? Give your own example of each type.

14. What is meant by "taking a dilemma by the horns"?

15. What is meant by "escaping between the horns of a dilemma"?

Part II

Identify the type of syllogism employed in each of the following examples, and evaluate each syllogism both on the grounds of its matter and on the grounds of its form.

1. If you fall, you will get hurt. But you are hurt, so you must have fallen.

2. Provided that you look for a bargain, you will find one. You did not find any bargains, so you could not have looked.

3. If a person works hard, the time passes quickly. The time is passing quickly, so I must be working hard.

4. One cannot be a good student without reading books. But I am reading plenty of books. So I must be a good student.

5. You will not have any friends unless you are kind to people. But you do have friends.

6. If Smith sues Jones and loses the case, he has nothing to gain. If he sues Jones and wins, the money will go to his lawyer. In either case he has nothing to gain.

7. If this operation is not performed, the patient will die. The patient died, so the operation was not performed.

8. If you are interested in helping your constituents (and I know that you are), you will oppose any further tax increase.

9. Mary will not go to the dance unless she has a partner. But she does have a partner, so she will go.

10. Either you eat or you starve. Since you are not eating, you are starving. (Define the word "eat.")

11. If a boat sinks, it is no longer seaworthy. This submarine is sinking. (Any ambiguity?)

12. This tooth should either be extracted or filled. But it is useless to fill it.

13. If a dog barks, it will not bite. This dog does not bark; so it will bite.

14. If you wear a hat, you will not catch cold. But you did not wear your hat, so you did catch cold.

15. You will pass if you know how to study. But you failed your course. Therefore, you do not know how to study.

16. If you do not study, you will not pass. But you do study, so you will pass.

17. If a worker is discontented with his pay, he will be inefficient. But most workers are efficient.

18. If you are consistent, you are logical. If you are inconsistent, you are human. Therefore, you are either a logician or a human being.

19. If a government economizes on its military expenditures, it weakens its defense. If it does not, it must maintain a high scale

of taxes. Our government then must either weaken its defense or maintain a high scale of taxes.

20. If a speech is effective, the audience will respond. But the audience is not responding. Draw your own conclusion.

21. If a person is a miser, he will not be a generous contributor. But Bill is a generous contributor.

22. If the patient refuses to obey his doctor's orders, he will suffer a relapse. But he has suffered a relapse.

23. If men are not virtuous, they are unhappy. Some men are miserable. Therefore, they are not virtuous.

24. If wages go up, prices do too. Lately there have not been any price increases.

25. If a contract is binding in law, it is binding in conscience. This contract is not binding in law.

26. Men become wise if they learn from experience. Some people, however, never learn from experience.

27. "If there is no payoff, there is no gambling," said the Chief of Police. "It is as simple as all that. In Des Moines there is no payoff. In Chicago there is gambling. Draw your own conclusion."

28. Recently, a friend of mine (a business executive) told me that most fortunes are made, not found. In other words, if you want to get ahead in the business world, you have to work at it and not trust to luck. Now, I know a number of people who, after spending years in their respective fields of business, ended up complete failures. It must be that they did not try hard enough.

29. If you are in love, you will find it hard to study. But you told me yourself that you are not in love. So you should not have any trouble studying.

30. The accused is either lying or he is ignorant of the law. In any event, he can be prosecuted.

31. A country cannot enjoy peace and wage war at the same time. Since our country is not waging war, it is enjoying peace.

32. Provided that an intelligent student applies himself, he will pass his courses. There is no doubting the fact that John has intelligence. Yet, there were some of his courses that he failed.

33. You should get a job. If you are poor, you *have* to work. It is not a question of choice. Even if you have money, you should work in order to keep yourself occupied.

34. You cannot be at home and at school at the same time. Since you were not at school yesterday, you must have stayed home.

35. You cannot at one and the same time live in California and miss the enjoyments of nature. There are many people, however, who do miss the enjoyments of nature. It must be that these people do not live in California.

36. Either the baby is asleep or he is "awfully quiet." But the baby is asleep. So he's not "awfully quiet."

37. Either this man does not know what he is talking about, or he is not telling the truth. But he does know what he is talking about, so he is not telling the truth.

38. If you are in St. Louis, you are not at home. But you are in St. Louis.

39. It is ridiculous for anyone to read Mortimer Adler's *How to Read a Book.* If you know how to read, you do not need to read it; if you do not know how to read, there is no point in trying.

40. Money is useless: the poor cannot get it and the rich do not need it.

41. If men do not have rights, then birds do not have feathers. But men do have rights.

42. Either you study what you know or you do not know what you are studying. Either way, there is no advantage to studying.

43. If reason is infallible, error is impossible. But error is possible.

44. Most people are never satisfied with life: if they do not have what they need, they will do anything they can to get it; if they get it, they will do anything they can to get more.

45. A person will either profit by his mistakes or fail to correct them. Unfortunately, most people do not profit by their mistakes.

46. *Scene:* Student taking an examination in logic.

Question: True or false: a syllogism is an act of inference.

Student's Reasoning: The answer to this question must be "false." If the answer were "true," the instructor would be asking too easy a question; no instructor of logic asks easy questions.

47. If you think about what you are writing, you cannot think about your writing; if you think about your writing, you cannot write about what you are thinking. Now, either you think about what you are writing, or you think about your writing. Draw your own conclusion.

48. Socrates to Meno: See what a tiresome dispute you are introducing. You argue that a man cannot inquire either about that which he knows, or about that which he does not know; for if he knows, he has no need to inquire; and if not, he cannot; for he does not know the very subject about which he is to inquire. —*Meno,* 80.

49. Happiness is not something that can be bought, because if it could be bought, the rich would certainly buy it.

50. Education is not something to be measured in terms of dollars and cents. If the only criterion of a good education were its capacity for increasing one's earning power, then I should have to admit that most education is useless.

14

Fallacies

Linguistic Fallacies
Nonlinguistic Fallacies

INTRODUCTORY REMARKS. The term "fallacy" as it appears in ordinary usage has a meaning so broad that it defies definition. What the "man in the street" understands by "fallacy" is any kind of error, prejudice, mistaken impression, or illusion. In its more restricted logical meaning a fallacy is generally taken to be an *argument which, although having some semblance of validity, is actually inconclusive.* Accordingly, a fallacy is not primarily a mistake in judgment, but a mistake in reasoning. It is a mistake in reasoning which most often *leads to* a false judgment.

It is generally maintained that a *fallacy,* as opposed to a sophism, is an *unintentional mistake* in reasoning, whereas a *sophism* is a mis-reasoning *deliberately calculated* to deceive. Whatever the merits of this distinction from a psychological point of view, it is preferable from the standpoint of logic to include under the term "fallacy" any mistake—unintentional or deliberate—in reasoning.

The purpose of this chapter is not to draw up a complete

catalogue of fallacies. In view of the many strange twists and turns that the human mind can take in an argument, such a feat would be impossible. Rather, the purpose is to examine a select list of some of the more common fallacies in the hope that the student will be on his guard against them and other related types.

Indeed, the study of fallacies is not, at this point, something altogether new to the student. The import of the preceding chapters has been (from a negative point of view) to explain the most common sources of invalidity with respect mainly to the *form* of an argument. The student's familiarity with the leading types of *formal fallacies*—for example, the undistributed middle, illicit minor, illicit major, fallacy of positing the consequent, and so on—is taken for granted. Accordingly, our objective here is to analyze other kinds of fallacies which arise from various sorts of *linguistic ambiguities* or from sources other than linguistic, namely, those which are consequent upon a defect in the *matter* of a given argument.

LINGUISTIC FALLACIES

The generally accepted list of linguistic fallacies embraces the following five:

1. Equivocation
2. Amphiboly
3. Composition and division
4. Accent
5. Parallel word construction

Equivocation

We need not dwell at any length on the *fallacy of equivocation* for the simple reason that it has, in effect, been covered in our treatment of the fallacy of the ambiguous middle. This fallacy consists in the assignment of more than one meaning to the same word within the course of an argument. The term "equivocation" here is taken in a broad sense as referring both to the analogous and to the equivocal use of terms in a syllogism.

It is highly unlikely that anyone would be "taken in" by an argument that employs terms whose meanings are completely unrelated ("equivocal" in the strict sense). The danger lies, rather, in the use of terms that are likely to take on an analogous signification—terms, chiefly, whose meanings are but vaguely defined, as, for example, democracy, progress, religion. The remedy, of course, in guarding against the type of argument in which the meaning of a term changes (however slightly) is to ask the one using it to *define* his terms. A rather patent example of the fallacy of equivocation is the following:

Every philosopher is a scientist.
Every man is a philosopher.
Every man is a scientist.

Amphiboly

The *fallacy of amphiboly* is one that arises from a defect in grammatical construction. Any English instructor who is involved in the work of correcting first-year composition papers has an adequate storehouse of examples leading to this type of fallacy. It is most often caused by dangling participles, misplaced adverbial and prepositional phrases, and misplaced relative clauses. For example:

While standing on his hind legs, the master played with his dog.

As the fisherman landed his muskie, he fell into the water.

Frequently, too, persons employ words or phrases that they do not actually intend to use and thus say things that they do not mean or fail to say what they actually do mean. During a recent political campaign a congressman was accused by a television news commentator of having accepted a bribe. The accusation was refuted, and the following apology was made:

I apologize for the misstatement I made concerning the fact that Congressman X was guilty of accepting a bribe.

From the context of the statement it seemed reasonably clear that the news commentator was in good faith about retracting his original accusation. An analysis of the wording of the statement, however, reveals that this is a dubious apology indeed.

Fallacy of Composition and Division

This type of fallacy was treated in Chapter 12 as a special instance of the *ambiguous middle.* The *fallacy of composition and division* occurs when, in the course of a single argument, a term is taken divisively in one proposition and collectively in another, or vice versa.

A person is guilty of this fallacy if he reasons, for example, as follows:

> Because there are many *wealthy* capitalists living in the United States, the United States itself is a *wealthy* nation.

Clearly, the mere fact that the term "wealthy" is predicable divisively of one or more individuals is not *of itself* a sufficient reason for applying this same term collectively to some organization or group to which these individuals belong.

Let us consider an example which works in the opposite direction from that of the example just given:

> A student thinks himself to be *intelligent* because, according to the testimony of his instructor, the class to which he belongs is *intelligent.*

The mere fact that the term "intelligent" is predicable collectively of a group as such is no guarantee that this term may be predicated divisively of every member of that group.

Accent

In its most restricted meaning, the *fallacy of accent* is one that gives rise to a difference of interpretation through misplaced emphasis upon a syllable, word, or phrase in a sentence. Anyone who is familiar with the various techniques of speech—inflection, pause, emphasis—is in a position to know how readily the meaning of a statement can be changed by the manner in which it is uttered by the speaker. Note how the meaning of the following sentence changes in accordance with the way it is spoken or, as here, *italicized*:

> *You* may think as you please.
> [But others may not]
>
> You *may* think as you please.
> [It is permissible, but . . .]
>
> You may *think* as you please.
> [But you may not *act* as you please]

To misplace the emphasis upon a syllable, word, or phrase in a sentence is, in effect, to take that syllable, word, or phrase *out of context,* that is, out of proper relation with the rest of the sentence. *By extension* the fallacy of accent may be made to apply also to *anything* taken out of context, that is, not only words or phrases, but entire sentences, paragraphs, or even speeches.

There is, perhaps, no more common (and we might add *justifiable*) complaint than that of either being misquoted or quoted out of context. Thus, a newspaper quotes excerpts from a Senator's speech that he made five years ago in order to "prove" that the views that he expressed at that time concerning military defense are inconsistent with the ones that he now holds. In the earlier speech the Senator was opposed to a military build-up, whereas now he advocates just such a measure. But does this "prove" anything? It might only prove that at the time the Senator made his earlier speech the need for a military build-up did not exist, whereas now it does.

Some of the most striking examples of the *indeliberate* appearance of this fallacy (misquoting or quoting out of context) can often be found in the "notes" that a student takes from his instructor.

Parallel Word Construction

Whenever a person reasons that because two words are similar in their structure, they are *in that respect* similar also in meaning, he is guilty of the *fallacy of parallel word construction.* The commonest instance of this fallacy lies in thinking that because two words have the same prefix or suffix, they are *in that respect* the same in their meaning. Thus, "immortal" means "not mortal," but it is not correct to think on that account that "immemorable" means "not memorable." [1] Likewise, it would be wrong to reason that because "audible" means "what can be heard" and "visible" means "what can be seen," therefore, "desirable" means "what can be desired." The simple fact of the matter is that "desirable" means "worthy of desire."

NONLINGUISTIC FALLACIES

Those fallacies which arise from a source other than a mere ambiguity of language are generally listed as follows:

1. Accident
2. Special case
3. Ignoring the issue
4. Begging the question
5. False cause
6. Complex question

Accident

There is a considerable amount of disagreement among logicians as to the precise nature of the *fallacy of accident.* In the cause of simplicity we may consider this fallacy, according to its modern interpretation, as one that rests on the assumption that a general rule is rigidly applicable to every seeming instance that falls under its extension. For example:

[1] See Obversion, Chap. 8.

Circumstances alter cases.
Rules have their exceptions.
Youth is inexperienced.

These propositions, although true for the most part or as a general rule, are not always true under all circumstances, without exception, or in every respect. Failure to make allowance for exceptions to these general rules (so-called *moral universals*) produces the fallacy of accident as described above. Thus, to infer that because youth is inexperienced, therefore, Mr. X, who is a youth, is inexperienced is (to say the least) to reason on very tenuous grounds. Mr. X may very well be more experienced than many of his elders.

Special Case

This fallacy, which is the reverse of the one just described, consists in arguing that what is true of one or more special cases is true of all cases without exception. Thus, it is assumed that because in some cases the use of alcoholic liquor leads to ruin, therefore *all* use of alcoholic liquor is wrong (that is, *for everybody*); that because in some instances almsgiving is conducive to indolence, therefore almsgiving should in all instances be discouraged; that because in some cases this medicine prevents patients from coughing, therefore it should be prescribed for all patients, regardless of the nature or cause of their cough.

In general, any unwarranted "leap" from the truth of the particular to the supposed truth of the universal is an instance of the fallacy of special case. Two of the commonest forms of this fallacy are (1) concluding from the abuse of a thing in a few particular cases to its complete abolition, and (2) concluding from the effectiveness of a certain remedy in a few special cases to its effectiveness for all similar cases without exception.

With respect to the second form it may very well be true that "what is good for the goose is good for the gander"; yet it is fallacious to think that what is good for one "goose" or "gander" is good for all. In any event, the *fallacy of special case* can claim as an ever present victim anyone who naïvely puts his confidence in panaceas.

Ignoring the Issue

This fallacy consists in either disproving what has not been asserted or proving a point other than the one at issue. In the absence of any solid proof in defense of his own position, a person engaged in a discussion or debate will frequently employ all sorts of distracting techniques as a means of evading the issue, not the least of which is the technique of setting up a "straw man." The straw-man type of argument consists essentially in refuting an opponent by making him responsible, not for something that he actually said or, for that matter, implied, but for some proposition that is allegedly connected with his original statement—one which the opponent himself repudiates. Listen sometime to a political broadcast over television or radio. The following remarks are typical of what you are most likely to hear:

SENATOR A: I cannot agree with you, Senator B, in your claim that all of the Republican senators are opposed to administration policy.

SENATOR B: Sir, that is not what I said. What I *did* say was that some Republican senators are opposed to the policies of the present administration.

SENATOR A: I don't care what you said, because by your previous statement you *implied* that no honest Republican could (in accordance with his principles) support the policies of this administration.

SENATOR B: Yes, I did say that, Senator, but I didn't imply, as you claim I do, that all Republicans are *actually* opposed to administration policy. To say that none of them (as Republicans) should support the administration is not to imply that all of them are really opposed to it.

An analysis of the above dialogue should be a reminder to the student, not only of the prevalence of the fallacy we are examining, but of the importance as well of knowing how to distinguish one type of proposition from another (Chapter 6) and of making proper implications (Chapters 7 and 8).

Under the general heading of the *fallacy of ignoring the issue,* the following various appeals, all of which involve the employment of (unfair) diversionary tactics, are customarily included:

APPEAL TO THE MAN (*argumentum ad hominem*). This line of attack is based on appeal to the person and is an attempt to discredit an opponent's argument *by discrediting the opponent himself.* Frequently it takes the form of mere name-calling. Sometimes, too, it involves a pernicious attempt to destroy an opponent's reputation.

There are circumstances, of course, in which it is perfectly legitimate to attack the person, as, for example, in disqualifying an unsuitable court witness or exposing a mere pretender. In circumstances of this sort it is very much to the point to "consider the source." For instance, it is perfectly justifiable to question the "authority" of a news commentator who, without the proper background and experience, sets himself up as some sort of expert in the field of education.

APPEAL TO THE POPULACE (*argumentum ad populum*). This is a familiar type of rhetorical appeal. It is based on an attempt by the speaker to "sell" his cause to the people by addressing himself to their prejudices, their emotions, their own characteristic local interests, and by similar appeals. It is most often in dictatorial countries that one finds a rabble-rousing leader playing up to the instincts of the mob by the employment of the "principles" of mass psychology. This type of appeal, however, is not altogether absent in democratic countries, especially at election time.

APPEAL TO PHYSICAL FORCE (*argumentum ad baculum*). By the use of threats, loud demonstrations, or violence an attempt is sometimes made *to win by demand through fear* some cause that cannot be won by rational persuasion.

APPEAL TO PITY (*argumentum ad misericordiam*). As a means of disguising the guilt of a court defendant, for instance, a lawyer will frequently resort to all sorts of sentimentalist appeals in the hope of winning a favorable verdict from the jury. The appeal to pity is merely one more instance of substituting emotional appeal for rational argument.

APPEAL TO REVERENCE (*argumentum ad verecundiam*). The irrelevancy of this type of appeal is manifest when someone, instead of weighing a question on its intrinsic merits, attempts to awe his listeners by invoking the authority of tradition or of those upholding it. This is, of course, a perfectly legitimate type of appeal, but one easily subject to abuse.

APPEAL TO IGNORANCE (*argumentum ad ignorantiam*). In common parlance this sort of appeal is often referred to as a "snow-job." It is typified by a speaker who, taking advantage of a lack of knowledge among his hearers, attempts to impress his point upon them by confusing them with all sorts of statistics which they are not in a position to analyze or check. Many of our present-day advertisements, too, are striking examples of the so-called "appeal to ignorance." Many a product is sold on the basis of the unchecked (and in many cases *uncheckable*) claim that it contains some new chemical formula hitherto unknown to science.

Begging the Question

By "question" here is meant the proposition to be proved. By "begging the question" is meant assuming, in one way or another, as proved the very point that is to be established. This can happen in a number of ways: for example, by the employment of merely synonymous terms:

> The color of your eyes is an hereditary factor because it is a characteristic which is handed down to you by your parents.

The question still remains: What *proof* is there for the assertion that is made?

A common form of this fallacy is the familiar *vicious circle.* A circular argument takes place when a person (1) gives a reason for some proposition that he maintains (his conclusion) and (2) proceeds forthwith (as a means of defending the reason he has invoked) to "prove" it *by means of the conclusion.* Note the following example:

All radicals should be deported from our country, *because* they are a constant menace to good government.

(1)

These men are a constant menace to good government, *because* they are radicals (!)

(2)

Also to be classed under the fallacy of begging the question is the *question-begging epithet.* This is defined as one that very compactly either commends its object to the listener (or reader) or equally compactly condemns it. For example:

the fair-play amendment
the people's candidate
the favorite of millions
the century of enlightenment
the dark ages
a do-nothing Congress

Little need be said of this type of device except that it has, when uttered with sufficient repetition and emphasis, a remarkable way of making a permanent impression upon an unreflecting mind.

False Cause

The *fallacy of false cause* is usually interpreted in two different ways. According to its traditional interpretation it involves an attempt to draw from the conclusion of an adversary's argument an absurd or untrue consequent that does not necessarily follow from it.

In this connection it must be noted that one of the legitimate types of demonstration is the method of *indirect proof,* which, if *improperly* used, results in the fallacy of false cause. The object of this method of proof, that is, as a means of refutation, is to demonstrate indirectly the falsity of one proposition by pointing out the falsity of a second proposition that logically follows from it. Let us suppose, for instance, that someone maintains the following proposition:

> The individual citizen living in a democracy does not actually enjoy political freedom.

In order to show *indirectly* that this proposition is false, we must draw from it a consequent that the opponent himself will have to admit as false. For example:

> In that case, the individual citizen (living in a democracy) is not allowed to vote.

In admitting the falsity of this second proposition, the opponent would also have to admit as false, or at least qualify, his original statement.

This, we say, is a legitimate type of proof, *provided that the second proposition truly follows from the first.* Otherwise, it is the fallacy of false cause, as below:

BILL: I maintain that the government should increase its welfare benefits.

TOM: On your own recommendation, then, the country might just as well go communist.

Under the fallacy of false cause, according to its modern interpretation, it is customary to include the *inductive* fallacy known as *post hoc, ergo propter hoc* (literally, "after this, therefore on account of this"). This fallacy is rooted in the assumption that two events which are circumstantially related to each other in the order of time or place are related also as cause and effect. Some examples are:

> Because Smith was standing next to me when I first noted the disappearance of my wallet, I accuse him of having stolen it.
>
> Because I observed that my instructor was looking at me during the examination period, I assume that his reason for doing so was that he suspected me of cheating.

All superstitious practices are, in effect, instances of this fallacy, assuming as they do a causal relation between mere chance events.

It is a point worth noting that a person guilty of this fallacy may nevertheless *happen* to be right in his supposition. The fallacy itself lies in the *premature* supposition of a causal connection, that is, a causal connection assumed to exist prior to an examination of the evidence.

Complex Question

A question may be so worded that the person answering it by a simple "yes" or "no" unsuspectingly "incriminates" himself. For example:

> When did you decide in favor of this nonsense of going to college?
>
> How long have you been stealing your neighbor's apples?

Of course, the answer to a "loaded" question of this sort lies in a denial of the double supposition upon which it rests. Suppose, for instance, that some "high-pressure" salesman asks the following question:

> Have you placed an order yet for your new refrigerator?

I might promptly reply that I neither placed an order for *a* refrigerator nor do I consider it *mine* until I buy it (unless, of course, he chooses to give it away!).

CONCLUDING REMARKS. As part of the business of critical thinking, it is suggested to the student that he draw up his own list of fallacies, relating them as carefully as he can to the ones we have treated in the text. We have, for instance, treated the *fallacy of accent,* which *by extension* involves the overemphatic assertion of an incidental point in an argument. Does it not appear that the reverse of this fallacy is that of the *euphemistic understatement* whereby one attempts to "play down" some relevant point of an argument? Again, we have treated the *fallacy of equivocation,* which involves the use of the same word or phrase in more than one meaning. Is it not equally fallacious to pretend that words or phrases having the *same meaning* stand for two different things?

Frequently by the employment of the *merely verbal distinction* a person will unfairly attempt to disguise a situation whose evidence he refuses to accept. Although the following example may seem ludicrous, it is not too far removed from more serious attempts at making a "distinction without a difference":

> Don't say that I exaggerated what you said; say, rather, that I gave it a little more emphasis than it deserved.

The attempt by the mere employment of words to make a "distinction without a difference" is perhaps a far less commendable practice than the failure to make a distinction that is necessary.

The above examples are sufficient at least to indicate the fact that our list of fallacies is far from complete; that there are many other fallacies, which, though unnamed, are part and parcel of the misreasoning common to everyday life.

EXERCISES

Part I

1. Comment on the statement: "A fallacy is not primarily a mistake in judgment, but a mistake in reasoning."

2. What is a sophism? Is a sophism really distinct from a fallacy?

3. What is the basis for the division according to which fallacies were treated in this chapter?

4. Does the fallacy of equivocation apply only to an argument in which terms are used equivocally?

5. Give three examples of sentences that are likely to give rise to a false interpretation by reason of their defective grammatical construction. What is the name of the fallacy to which examples of this sort give rise?

6. Give two examples of the *fallacy of composition and division,* paralleling those in the text.

7. Explain the *fallacy of accent* as taken in its more restricted meaning.

8. Discuss the practice of quoting out of context. Explain why this practice may *by extension* be considered the fallacy of accent.

9. What is the assumption underlying the *fallacy of parallel word construction?* Exemplify this fallacy.

10. Give three examples of maxims that are generally taken to be true and show how their rigid application to a specific instance is in each case fallacious.

11. Define the *fallacy of special case.* What are two of the commonest instances of this fallacy? Exemplify.

12. What is the ordinary procedure involved in setting up a "straw man"? Give an example of this technique.

13. Give your own explanation of each of the following: (a) attack upon the person; (b) appeal to the populace; (c) appeal to physical force; (d) appeal to pity; (e) appeal to reverence; (f) appeal to ignorance.

14. Exemplify the *fallacy of begging the question* as taking place through the employment of (a) synonymous terms; (b) the question-begging epithet; (c) the vicious circle.

15. What do you understand by the *method of indirect proof? proof?*

16. Give an illustration of the perverted use of this method (*false cause*).

17. Explain what is meant by the inductive fallacy *post hoc, ergo propter hoc.* Give an example.

18. Explain and illustrate the *fallacy of the complex question.*

19. Discuss the "fallacies" mentioned in the concluding remarks to this chapter.

20. Can you specify any types of fallacies not treated in this chapter?

Part II

Some of the examples below are clear-cut reproductions of the fallacies discussed in this chapter; others are not. Assign the proper name to the fallacies below and give your reason. If you are not sure as to the precise nature of the fallacy, analyze the example for any unsupported assumptions that underlie it.

1. All's fair in love and war. So you cannot really blame anyone for breaking off an engagement.

2. Because it is wrong to use swear words, it is wrong to take an oath in court.

3. Your father must be an educated man: he reads the newspaper editorials.

4. Pipe smoking, they say, is an aid to concentration. Most scientists, I notice, are pipe smokers.

5. The accused is insane, because he lacks sufficient mentality to be guilty of crime.

6. Only one person will win the prize. Since I am only one person, I shall win the prize.

7. The doctor says I have ulcers. This confirms my conviction that my wife never was a good cook.

8. This man is a skeptic. He does not agree with any of my arguments.

9. There is too close a tie-up between gambling and politics. For that reason all gambling should be abolished and so too should politics.

10. You poor child! Did your mother spank you again? How can a woman be so cruel as to torture her own flesh and blood?

11. A little knowledge is a dangerous thing. As an undergraduate student of logic, I have only a little knowledge of it. So what I know about logic must be dangerous. (Discuss meaning of word "little" in this argument.)

12. This person is near-sighted because he has myopia.

13. Lincoln, who was born in a log cabin, became president. Why can't you?

14. Don't you ever tire of repeating that nonsense?

15. Women are better drivers than men, because statistics prove that women have fewer accidents than men.

16. How long have you been nursing along your imaginary ailments?

17. An hour ago, when I said, "It is five o'clock," my statement was true. If I say that it is five o'clock now, my statement is false. This proves that any statement you make is true at one time and false at another, so that all truth is relative.

18. Marks are no necessary sign of a student's intelligence. Then, why not do away with the whole system of the assignment of grades?

19. Psychiatrists are very presumptuous people to think that they can read a person's mind.

20. There is nothing more certain than the fact that nothing can be known with certainty. (Is this self-contradictory?)

21. Einstein's theory of relativity does not make much sense. After all, there are very few people who claim to understand it.

22. According to the Scriptures it is wrong for a man to judge his fellow men. Should we not, then, do away with the practice of judging a fellow man in court?

23. There is only one way to convince a reactionary; send him to a concentration camp.

24. There is no more effective method of punishing crime than the death sentence. Sentence every criminal to death, and crime will soon disappear.

25. Most of the time spent in reading books is wasted because a person forgets more of what he reads than he remembers.

26. Religion is merely a form of hypocrisy. I know many people who are regular church-goers, but their lives are anything but models of good conduct.

27. Having completed four years of college, you must have a thorough knowledge of the classics.

28. Haste makes waste. Since efficiency experts encourage haste, they encourage waste.

29. Wife to husband: "Dear, you can't imagine how much money I saved for you this week. I've been out shopping for bargains."

30. The best things in life are free. Since going to school takes money, education is not one of the best things in life.

15

Induction

Ways of Knowing and the Need for Induction

Point of Departure; Fundamental Goal

Notes to Chapter on Induction

INTRODUCTORY REMARKS. To undertake an exhaustive analysis of the various methods of scientific induction is a task that would carry us beyond the scope, not only of elementary logic, but of logic itself. Indeed, the use of inductive method, as found in the specialized departments of scientific inquiry, is so varied and complex as to require a considerable knowledge of the subject matter of the science in which the method is employed. Moreover, there is a fair amount of controversy among scientists themselves both as to the relative importance of the various phases of inductive procedure and as to the means of adapting these procedures to their specialized fields of research. (1)* Hence, it is important to realize that in its scientific phases induction is a highly complex process that is applicable in an indefinite number of ways to the various problems of scientific research. *There is no such thing as a single method of induction to which all others are reducible.*

* Notes corresponding to parenthetical reference numbers in the text appear at the end of this chapter. First read the chapter without the notes. Then study it in conjunction with the notes.

In spite of the above-mentioned facts it is possible to examine some of the fundamental features of induction as it is applied, not only to problems of science, but, even more fundamentally, to the problems of everyday life. Even such an examination as this, however, would require (at the very least) another one-semester course in logic, one that would go beyond the matter treated in the present text. Accordingly, the purpose of the remarks that follow is not in any way to present a kind of summary of the *logic of induction* (2), but merely to indicate in a very general sort of way the need for induction as a method of inquiry distinct in its nature from any of the forms of inference dealt with in the preceding chapters.

WAYS OF KNOWING AND THE NEED FOR INDUCTION

Much of what we know to be true we know as a matter of *belief*. In general, to *believe* that a certain proposition is true is to give our assent to that proposition on the grounds that someone whom we consider to be a reliable witness has said so. Suppose, for instance, that you want to find out the score of last night's basketball game. To do this you consult your morning newspaper, and, unless you have some reason for suspecting that the report is unreliable (for example, a misprint), you *know* as a matter of belief what the score of the game really is.

Apart from what we know to be true by way of belief (3), however, there are, generally speaking, three different ways whereby we come to find out for ourselves that a certain proposition is probably or certainly true. In one way we come to know the truth of a proposition by a mere inspection of the meaning of the terms which it contains. To know something in this way is to know it as *self-evident*. Consider the following proposition:

The whole is equivalent to the sum total of its parts.

Once we have a proper understanding of the terms that it embodies, we immediately give our assent to the above proposition as being *certainly* and *self-evidently* true. As we have noted in Chapter 9, first principles are known to be true in this way. Consequently, it is neither necessary nor possible to demonstrate the truth of first principles. In the order of self-evident truths, that is, those to which the mind *immediately* gives its assent, are to be included also those truths that we know by our sense experience. Thus, we know as an immediate observation of sense that *this is a sunshiny day.*

Since it is a simple fact that not all truths are known as self-evident, it is necessary, then, to come to know them in other ways, on the basis, that is, of the truths we already know. Now the next best way of coming to know some truth is *to know it by a direct act of inference.* (4) Suppose, for example, that we know as a *universal* truth the following proposition:

Every agent acts for an end.

Suppose, further, that we know man to be an agent, that is, a being who exercises his capacities for performing various types of activity; it is, then, a simple matter to conclude (infer, deduce) *with certainty* in the light of these two known propositions that

Man is a being who acts for an end.

The truth of the proposition just stated is such that there is *no need* to establish it in any other way, for it follows as a matter of *logical necessity* from the two other previously known truths. Consequently, it would be utterly pointless *as a method of proof* for us to conduct some sort of experiment in which we would examine the behavior of all different types of men to determine whether or not their actions are (in each case) purposeful. If, of course, we should prefer to examine our conclusion with a view toward corroborating it in various individual cases, we are perfectly free to do so. The point, however, is that there is no need to *verify* the above proposition. It has already been adequately verified in the relation that is seen to exist between it and its premises.

This way of coming to know something as true is, we say, "second best," which means second only to the way in which we know something as self-evidently true. Indeed, if everything could be known as self-evident, there would be no need for deduction. Further, if every other truth not known as self-evident could be known by deduction alone, *then that would be the proper method to use, to the exclusion of all other methods.*

The reason for this should be clear: what we know by inference alone we know in a way that is far more *simple, direct,* and *productive of certainty* than anything we know by induction.(5) Unfortunately, however, there are many truths which in the way that we come to know them are *neither self-evident nor inferential.* These are the truths which, in a word, must be *discovered* by the use of *induction.* The *need* for induction—and hence also its importance—is evidenced not only by the peculiar nature of the problems of positive science(6), but by the nature of most problems that confront us in our everyday experience, such as,

why some of the more intelligent students in the class are receiving below average marks in their examinations;
why the house, after having been painted only a year ago, needs to be painted again;
why business production has fallen off in the last three months;
how to locate some missing article.

With respect to problems of this sort the *practical truth* that we want to discover is the one that satisfactorily answers the question: What is the unknown cause (or combination of causes) that adequately accounts for the "phenomenon" under investigation? Now, the very first step toward the inductive solution of any problem of this kind is a precise determination of the problem itself. This, we say, is the first step in the inductive process, a step that *directly* calls for the use, not of inference, but of careful, painstaking *observation.* It is a step that involves the gathering of all sorts of data relevant to the phenomenon whose cause we are seeking to explain.(7)

Next, assuming that a careful analysis of the relevant data has been made, it is necessary forthwith to begin constructing a series of tentative *hypotheses,* one of which might in the end prove to be the final solution to the problem at hand. Now, an "hypothesis" is nothing more than a likely supposition as to what might be the cause or combination of causes of the effect that is being considered. In the normal course of inductive procedure a number of hypotheses are constructed, one after another, each of which is found wanting as the true explanation of the phenomenon under investigation. If the procedure is successful, we finally "hit upon" some hypothesis that survives each test that is made as a means of determining that this hypothesis (and no other) is the true cause of the effect for which one is trying to account.(8)

Whatever the methods of induction and the means of putting them to use, it should be clear above all else that induction is not a simple matter of inference. Suppose, for example, that the motor of your automobile is not running as smoothly as it should, and we are interested in finding out why. Although the "phenomenon" in question is perfectly evident to us through sense observation, the reason why this is so is far from evident. Further, the nature of the problem itself is such that the cause of the "phenomenon" cannot be discovered by an unaided act of inference. Under what conceivable combination of circumstances would it be possible to *deduce,* or *infer,* the cause of a poorly running motor? In the presence of any number of possibilities that *might* be the cause of our motor trouble, the first thing to do is clearly, not just to "sit down and figure it out," but to lift up the hood of the car. To say nothing of the problems of science(9), there are, then, many problems (familiar to everyone) that cannot be solved by inference alone—problems that call for the use of induction, if only on a most elementary plane.

Before we conclude our brief analysis of induction from the standpoint of the needs that govern it, a few words are in order here as to what constitutes the *starting point* of all inductive procedure and its *fundamental goal.*

INDUCTION: ITS POINT OF DEPARTURE; ITS FUNDAMENTAL GOAL

All new knowledge has as its point of departure certain truths already known, whether as self-evident or as the result of some previous demonstration. The evident truth or truths that constitute the starting point of the inductive process are specific facts, data, or phenomena that are furnished to us through the medium of our sensible experience.(10) These are the kind of truths that are knowable only as the result of direct observation. For example:

This food has a strong odor.
These children have soft teeth.
This monkey is covered with fleas.

It is truths of this sort, that is, truths relating to the singular objects of sensible experience, that furnish the mind with the problems that the inductive process is intended to solve and from which it takes its lead.

Given, then, as the starting point of inductive inquiry a certain phenomenon sensibly observed, the *goal* of induction, expressed in very general terms, is to discover by various means the cause or causes of the phenomenon under observation. This, we say, is not a simple matter of inference, and in order to understand *why*, it may be helpful at this point to recall a few basic considerations set forth in Chapter 13.

In Chapter 13 we explained why, in the construction of a conditional syllogism in the positing mood, it is necessary to posit the antecedent in the minor and the consequent in the conclusion. Thus, given a conditional proposition as true and given as categorically true the enunciation expressed in its antecedent, we know *by a simple act of inference* the categorical truth of the consequent:

If the patient has tuberculosis, he will have a serious cough.
This patient has tuberculosis.
He has a serious cough.

Suppose, however, that the only thing that is known to be true *categorically* is the truth of the consequent:

This patient has a serious cough.

Even assuming our knowledge of the conditional proposition above, *there is no possibility here of inferring that the patient has tuberculosis,* for the simple reason that tuberculosis is only *one* of an indefinite number of possibilities that *may* be the reason why "this patient" has a serious cough. Hence, in the construction of a conditional syllogism it is wrong to posit the consequent in the minor and the antecedent in the conclusion.

The considerations set forth in the preceding paragraph should be of no small help toward an authentic understanding of the fundamental goal or purpose of all inductive procedure. From a negative point of view, it is the purpose of induction to accomplish *by other means* (observation, hypothesis, experiment) what cannot be accomplished by inference alone. From a positive point of view, it is the business of induction to account for a certain effect in terms of the real cause or causes that produced it. Regarding this latter point, it should be noted that it is the peculiar nature of the problems of induction that what is antecedent in the real order of events is consequent in the order of knowledge; conversely, what is antecedent in the order of our knowledge is consequent in the order of events. Thus, the *starting point* of our knowledge in any inductive problem is some *real* consequent (effect, datum, phenomenon); the *goal* of induction is to trace this real consequent to its *real* antecedent (cause or combination of causes).

CONCLUDING REMARK: We have stated in very general terms the goal of *all* inductive procedure, scientific and nonscientific alike. By way of conclusion, a word must be said as to the nature and characteristic goal of *scientific* induction. In this connection it should be pointed out that a scientist as such is never concerned with the singular objects of experience *in their purely isolated status as singulars.* Science, as it is so often said, is of the universal, and by "the universal" is meant primarily the *universal law.* Accordingly, whether the method of a science be primarily deductive or inductive, it is always with regard to the universal law that the method is put to use.

Now, a science that is primarily deductive in its method is interested in the universal law with a view to its *application* to the specific instances falling under its extension. On the other hand, any science that is intrinsically dependent in its nature upon the use of induction has as its immediate objective, not the application, but the *discovery* of those universal laws that are the explanatory cause of the phenomena of sensible experience. Herein, then, lies the significance of induction: that it *is an indispensable means for the discovery of those laws of nature which would otherwise be hidden from the eye of our human intelligence.* Whereas it is the purpose of *all* induction to explain effects in terms of their respective causes, it is the peculiar nature of scientific induction to examine a *typical* group of particular effects with a view toward establishing not only the cause of these particulars *but of all like instances of the phenomena that they represent.* Such, then, is the goal of scientific induction, namely, to advance from the truth of the observable "some" to the truth of the nonobservable "all," and this we insist is not a mere matter of inference.

Seen in its proper light, scientific *induction is essentially a process whereby we judge that what is true of a sufficient number of singular instances of a given phenomenon is true of all without exception.* To know *how* this comes about, it is necessary to familiarize oneself with the various phases and techniques of scientific method; to know *why* it is possible for the scientist to form *universal* judgments about the limited objects of his experience, it is necessary to understand the foundations upon which induction rests: the law of causality and the law of the uniformity of nature. Finally, a careful inspection of the above definition should lead to the conviction that induction, as an over-all process, is more closely bound up with *abstraction* than with any one form of inference.

EXERCISES

1. Comment on the statement: If all truth were self-evident, there would be no need for inference.

2. What is the value of inference as a means of arriving at *certain* knowledge?

3. Draw up a list of problems which in your opinion cannot be solved by inference alone.

4. Do you agree with the statement that induction is not a simple matter of inference? Explain and illustrate your answer.

5. What is the general goal of induction? The goal of scientific induction? Explain.

NOTES TO CHAPTER ON INDUCTION

1. In addition, the fact is that most scientists are so busily engaged in the *subject* of their inquiries that they have little occasion to *reflect* on the specific nature of the methods they actually use.

2. It is important to note that the logic of induction is "logic" in a sense only analogous to the meaning of that term as applied to the different types of (formal) inference. Thus, in spite of the fact that there are certain basic "canons" of induction (for example, of the sort set forth by John Stuart Mill), induction itself is not per se a formalized method of procedure. Accordingly, the methods of induction are not such that they can be determined and regulated by a *formal* set of rules the mere application of which would infallibly lead to the attainment of certain definite results.

Indeed, the success of inductive procedure depends very largely upon such nonstandardized factors as a precise determination of the circumstances relevant to the phenomenon at hand, the setting up of "working" hypotheses, and the testing of these hypotheses by the use of different types of experiment. *Now none of these procedures is such that it can be prescribed by logical rule,* as one would prescribe, for example, the rules of the syllogism with a view toward correct inference. As a result of all this, the success of the inductionist is as much dependent upon his powers of observation, his familiarity with the subject matter that he is investigating, his ability to construct creatively certain fruitful hypotheses and by the use of experiment to verify them, as it is dependent upon his "powers of reasoning."

3. The point concerning the importance of belief as a genuine source of knowledge must be stressed here.

4. The student should again be reminded that we are limiting the present discussion to knowledge that we acquire for ourselves, that is, independently of what we *believe* to be true.

5. In any contrast that is drawn between the methods of deduction and the methods of induction one should always keep in mind the fact that in their actual use there is a constant interplay of *both* methods. Thus it is that (scientific) induction most often supplies us with premises from which we reason deductively. A

scientist, for instance, by applying an inductive principle (a true universal) can often predict *deductively* the occurrence of a future event—for example, an eclipse. On the other hand, *deduction plays a vital role as part of the general process of inductive inquiry, and that very largely in the elimination of nonsuccessful hypotheses.* Here we might note that the rejection of a nonexplanatory hypothesis takes the form of a conditional syllogism in the sublating mood:

> If hypothesis *A* is the cause of the phenomenon *P,* then it must satisfactorily account for circumstances *a, b, c, d,* and *e* of *P.*
>
> But hypothesis *A* does not satisfactorily account for circumstances *a* and *c.* Ergo.

6. The term "positive science" includes both the physical and the so-called social sciences.

7. The term "observation" as applied to inductive procedure is, to a very large extent, misleading. For purposes of induction to "observe" means a great deal more than "sitting back" to see how the object will "strike" one's senses. What observation primarily connotes is an active "hunting out" of all the relevant data. Moreover, since the problem of induction is to give an accurate account of the cause or causes that constitute the true explanation of the phenomenon under "observation," it is only reasonable to expect that before we even begin to seek the cause we have a well-rounded view of the effect we are considering. This means, of course, more than a mere vague, general, offhand acquaintance, that is, of the sort gained by mere passive observation. Indeed, even the ordinary problems of induction are seldom so simple as initially they may appear to be.

Let us take what might be considered a very "crude" problem of induction. Suppose that our car is using more gas than we suspect it should be using. The problem as thus visualized is too general. Accordingly, with a view toward a more accurate determination of the "phenomenon," we must begin *actively* to seek answers to questions of the following sort: Have we been doing more city driving than usual? Has our car over the period of the last month been consistently using more gas than in the month previous? If the gas consumption is erratic, *how much more* gas does the car consume during certain definite periods than it does at certain other definite periods? A careful analysis of these pertinent data may lead to a speedy solution: for example, that the periods of excessive gas consumption corresponded exactly with those periods immediately after the car had been refilled with gas, the cause of the phenomenon being a leak near the upper part of the gas tank.

8. Suppose, however, that upon elimination of a series of nonexplanatory hypotheses, there remain two hypotheses, each of which seems to account satisfactorily for all of the circumstances attendant upon the phenomenon being investigated. In this case it would be necessary to recheck the data to determine some relevant circumstance that apparently was not taken into account. Doing this would call for more extensive observation (and experiment) than was made prior to the construction of hypotheses. The periodic need for rechecking the data and thus re-examining one's original observations is a clear-cut indication of the fact that, although observation and hypothesis are two distinct phases of inductive inquiry, they are seldom so neatly set apart in their actual use.

9. Scientific induction, it is true, is a process infinitely more refined, critical, and exacting than any of the methods of induction which we use as a means of solving "practical" problems. Thus, to study induction from the standpoint of its "ordinary" use is, to a very large extent, to leave unexplained the various methods of scientific procedure. However, in view of the basic continuity between the methods of inquiry at the "common-sense" level and the methods of inquiry utilized in the various sciences, the study of induction in its "ordinary" use should be of no small help toward gaining a basic understanding of the methods of science itself.

10. Whether *macroscopically,* as when we observe something by the *mere* use of the senses, or *microscopically,* as when we make use of scientific instruments. Here it should be noted that the purpose of most scientific instruments is to augment our powers of sense perception in a way that allows for *accurate* observation of phenomena.

Glossary

All of the following terms appear in the text. Some of the definitions are worded differently from the way they are in the text; a comparison of the two may prove helpful to the student.

accent, fallacy of. A difference of interpretation through misplaced emphasis upon a syllable, word, or phrase in a sentence.

accident. As a predicable, the reference that a predicate may have to a subject but without having any bearing on the essence of that subject or the species to which it belongs.

accident, fallacy of. In its modern sense, the assumption that a general rule is rigidly applicable to every seeming instance that falls under its extension.

accidental description. A means of marking off one individual from all others by giving a sufficient number of accidental characteristics, such as size, shape, time, place.

accidental division. A division that has as its basis a consideration of a thing with respect to one of its nonessential characteristics.

accidents. As categories, a list of universal terms (or concepts) that refer to the various ways in which a substance can be modified or determined.

action. As a category, a universal term that characterizes one substance as producing a certain effect upon another.

added determinants, method of. A method of attaching to each of the terms of a proposition some modifying word or phrase that is the same in meaning for both.

adversative proposition. A multiple proposition in which one enunciation is set up in opposition to another by the use of such words as "although," "despite."

alternatives. The parts or enunciations given in a disjunctive proposition.

ambiguous middle, fallacy of. A special instance of the fallacy of four terms in which the middle term of a syllogism is employed in two different meanings.

analogous use of terms. The application of a term to two or more objects in such a way that the term has different, though not unrelated, meanings.

analogy, argument from. An argument in which, on the basis of literal points of resemblance found to exist between two objects or classes of objects, an attempt is made to establish further points of resemblance.

antecedent. The conditional or *if* clause of a conditional proposition; in another context, the premises of a syllogism.

apprehension. *See* simple apprehension.

basis of a division. The guiding principle underlying the division, that is, the reason for the making of it.

begging the question, fallacy of. The assumption that the very point to be established has been proved.

belief. Assent to a proposition on the grounds that it has been proposed by one who is considered a reliable witness or authority.

categorical judgment. An act or operation by means of which the intellect asserts one object of thought to be identical or nonidentical with another.

categorical proposition. A proposition that asserts as a matter of fact that a given predicate does or does not belong to a given subject.

categorical syllogism. An argumentation in which two terms, by virtue of their identity or nonidentity with a common third, are declared to be identical or nonidentical with each other.

categories. A group of universal terms or concepts so general in their signification that they cannot be included within any genus higher than themselves.

causal proposition. A multiple proposition in which one enunciation is given as the reason for the other and is signified by such words as "because," "since."

central sense. A faculty or power of internal sensation that differentiates the data of the external senses and unifies them into a single sense image called a *phantasm.*

certainty. With respect to a given judgment, a state of mind that precludes fear of error or contradiction; sometimes used by analogy as synonymous with "fact."

circular argument. A special instance of the fallacy of begging the question; it occurs when a person in giving a reason for an intended conclusion attempts to "prove" the reason itself by the conclusion he hopes to establish.

circular definition. An attempt at real definition mainly by the use of synonyms.

class. A term used to indicate the species to which many individuals of the same essence belong.

codivision. The employment of more than one division, each according to a different basis, of one and the same logical unit.

collective use of terms. A manner of assigning a predicate to a subject in such a way that the predicate applies to the subject considered only as a group or a unit.

common sense. A term that has various meanings, of which the following are the most important in this text: (1) ability to confront and solve practical problems without undue deliberation, that is, ability to form sound probable judgments in relation to a given set of circumstances; (2) fundamental knowledge that is or should be obvious to everyone, such as first principles; (3) sometimes taken in technical sense as referring to the internal faculty of sensation which is also called central or synthetic sense.

complex conception, method of. A method of adding a new word or phrase to a given proposition in such a way that the new word or phrase becomes the leading part of each term of the second proposition, while the original terms are retained only as modifiers.

complex term. A term that comprises several words but signifies a single object of thought.

complex question, fallacy of. The phrasing of a question in such a way that the person who answers it by a simple "yes" or "no" yields to an admission that he would not otherwise make.

composition and division, fallacy of. The result of taking a term divisively in one proposition and collectively in another, or vice versa, in the course of a single argument.

comprehension. That aspect or property of a concept or a term that has reference to its meaning or content; hence, the embodiment of its essential notes; *synonyms*: intension, connotation.

concept. A nonsensuous, intellectual medium of representation whereby something is actually understood.

conception. *See* simple apprehension.

conclusion. The propositon that any given argument is intended to prove.

conditional proposition. A proposition that explicitly asserts that, given the fulfillment of a certain specified condition or antecedent, a given consequent must follow.

conditional syllogism. A syllogism that employs a conditional proposition as its major premise.

conjunctive proposition. A proposition that states the impossibility of two or more enunciations being true at the same time and in the same respect.

conjunctive syllogism. A syllogism that employs a conjunctive proposition as its major premise.

contradictory opposition. The opposition that exists between two propositions of which one is the simple denial of the other; with reference to single categoricals, the relationship between two propositions which have the same subject and predicate but differ both in quantity and in quality.

contrary opposition. In general, the opposition that exists between two proposiitons of which one not only denies the other but makes an assertion in the line of the other extreme; with reference to single categoricals, the opposition that exists between two universal propositions (of the same subject and predicate) which differ in their quality.

conventional sign. A sign the meaning or significance of which is determined by usage or agreement.

conversion. A process of interchanging the subject and predicate terms of a given proposition in such a way that the derived proposition (the converse) is consistent with the meaning of the original.

copula. A word or words used to assert the connection that exists between the parts of a given proposition.

copulative proposition. A multiple proposition that unites or disunites its enunciations on a purely coordinate basis by the use of such words as "and," "both—and," "neither—nor."

cross-division. A division in which the parts or dividing members do not mutually exclude each other.

deduction. A method of reasoning in which on the basis of certain truths already known the reasoner infers another truth that is logically related to the others.

dichotomous division. The division of a genus by means of formal contradictories, such as the division of "book" into "bound" and "*un*bound."

difference. As a predicable, the reference that a predicate may have to that part of the essence of the subject which distinguishes the subject from other species of the same genus.

dilemma. A type of hypothetical argument that employs two conditional propositions as its major premise and a disjunctive proposition as its minor.

disguised multiple. *See* exponible proposition.

disjunctive proposition. A proposition that alernatively combines two or more enunciations in a manner which states indeterminately that one of these enunciations is true.

disjunctive syllogism. A syllogism that employs a disjunctive proposition as its major premise.

distinctive definition. The definition of an object with respect to one or more of its properties.

distributed term. *See* universal term.

division. In general, the resolution or analysis of a given whole into its constituent parts.

divisive use of terms. The assignment of a predicate to a subject in such a way that the predicate applies to each member falling under the extension of the subject.

eduction. A process of making explicit in a second proposition a meaning that is virtually contained in the original from which it is derived.

efficient cause, definition by. The definition of an object with respect to its productive agent or agents.

enumeration. A listing of individuals that belong to a given whole or unit.

enunciation. A term that may generally be taken with reference to any of the component parts of a multiple or a hypothetical proposition.

enthymeme. In its original Aristotelian use, a type of probable argument, such as the argument from a sign; in modern use, any abbreviated syllogism that implies one or the other of its premises or its conclusion.

epicheirema. A syllogism that contains a subordinate proof in defense of one or both of its premises.

equivocal use of terms. The application of a term to two or more objects with meanings that are totally unrelated to each other.

equivocation, fallacy of. The assignment of more than one meaning to the same word or phrase within the course of a single argument.

essence. That by reason of which a thing is what it is, that is, by reason of which it belongs to one class or species of objects rather than another.

essential definition. The definition of an object with respect to its proximate genus and its essential difference.

euphemistic understatement, fallacy of. An attempt to diminish the importance of some relevant point of an argument.

evident multiple. *See* overt multiple.

exceptive proposition. A multiple proposition in which a predicate is assigned to a subject to the exclusion of one or more members which fall under the subject's extension; identified by such words as "except," "save."

exclusive proposition. A multiple proposition in which a predicate is assigned to a subject to the exclusion of all other subjects, or vice versa; identified by such words as "only," "alone."

exponible proposition. A multiple proposition which has the appearance of a single proposition.

extension. That aspect or property of a concept or a term that has reference to the things to which that concept or term applies; *synonym*: denotation.

fallacy. An argument that is actually inconclusive although it has some semblance of validity.

false cause, fallacy of. Traditionally, an attempt to draw from the conclusion of an adversary's argument an absurd or untrue consequent that does not necessarily follow from it; in its modern meaning, the inductive fallacy of thinking that events that are circumstantially related to each other in the order of time or place are related also as cause and effect.

falsity. The nonconformity of a judgment or a proposition with a state of affairs as it exists outside the mind.

figure of a syllogism. The position of the middle term as it appears in both premises of a syllogism.

final cause, definition by. The definition of an object with respect to its end, purpose, or use.

first principles. Self-evident truths that underlie all human judgments and reasonings.

form of a syllogism. The logical structure of a syllogism with respect to its figure and its mood.

foundation of a division. *See* basis of a division.

four terms, fallacy of. The use of four different meanings within a single syllogism.

genus. As a predicable, the reference that a predicate may have to that part of the essence of the subject that the subject has in common with other species.

habitus. As a category, a universal term that characterizes a substance with respect to apparel, costume, or physical equipment.

half-truth. In its strictly logical meaning, a multiple proposition that is partly true and partly false.

hypothesis. A likely supposition as to the cause or combination of causes of a given phenomenon.

hypothetical proposition. A generic term used to designate a conditional, disjunctive, or conjunctive proposition.

hypothetical syllogism. A generic term indicating any type of syllogism that employs as its major premise a conditional, disjunctive, or conjunctive proposition.

idea. *See* concept.

ignoring the issue, fallacy of. The attempt either to disprove what has not been asserted or to prove something other than the issue at hand.

illicit major, fallacy of. The overextension in the conclusion of the predicate term of a syllogism.

illicit minor, fallacy of. The overextension in the conclusion of the subject term of a syllogism.

implication. A meaning that is not explicitly expressed in a given proposition but is nevertheless consistent with the original meaning and derivable from it.

improper disjunctive. A disjunctive proposition that states indeterminately that at least one of its enunciations is true, there being no implication as to the truth or falsity of the other(s).

indesignate proposition. A proposition that has no explicit sign of quantity.

indirect proof, method of. As a means of refutation, an attempt to demonstrate the falsity of one proposition by pointing out the falsity of a second proposition which logically follows from it.

induction. A process of coming to know a certain truth or law by the use of such procedures as observation, hypothesis, and experiment; further, a process which, although it involves reasoning, is not reducible to any specific form of reasoning and is more closely related in its fundamental nature to abstraction.

inference. *See* deduction.

intuitive knowledge. In general, any kind of knowledge in which something is known immediately and as self-evidently true.

invalid. A term used with reference to arguments that are unsound or incorrect.

judgment. *See* categorical judgment.

logic. The science that directs our mental operations in such a way that they may proceed with order, facility, and consistency toward the attainment of truth.

logical division. The resolution of a genus into its species or of a species into its subspecies.

logical form. The expression of a proposition in such a way as to clarify its basic logical structure and meaning.

logical supposition. The use of a term in a proposition in such a way that it "stands for" something as it exists only in the mind.

major premise. In a categorical syllogism, the premise that contains the predicate term of the conclusion.

major term of a syllogism. *See* predicate term.

material object. The subject matter that belongs to a given field of investigation, especially with reference to science.

material object of logic. The consideration of the three basic operations of the intellect (simple apprehension, judgment, and reasoning) and their corresponding means of expression (terms, propositions, and syllogisms).

matter of a syllogism. The propositions and terms contained in a syllogism.

meaning of a proposition. What a proposition is literally and explicitly intended to convey.

middle term of a syllogism. The common standard of reference that serves as a means of uniting or disuniting the two terms of the conclusion.

minor premise. In a categorical syllogism, the premise that contains the subject term of the conclusion.

minor term of a syllogism. *See* subject term.

modal proposition. A proposition that expresses a manner or mode of agreement or disagreement between two terms, of which there are four such modes: necessity, impossibility, possibility, and contingency.

mood of a syllogism. With reference to categorical syllogisms, the respective designation of the premises and conclusion as *A, E, I,* or *O* propositions.

multiple proposition. A proposition that expresses more than one object of agreement or disagreement and hence is resolvable into its single components.

natural sign. A sign which, as opposed to a conventional sign, is founded upon the order of things themselves and is not the result of an arbitrary determination.

nature. The essence of a thing considered as the source of activity; this term is often used synonymously with the term "essence."

nominal definition. An explanation of the meaning of a term.

nonsequitur. A Latin expression that means "it does not follow," and is very often applied to invalid conclusions.

norms. The principles or standards that serve to regulate thought, as in logic, or conduct, as in ethics.

object of thought. Anything that is known by means of abstraction.

obversion. A process of changing the quality of a proposition in a manner that is consistent with its original meaning.

omitted determinants, method of. A method of eliminating from one or both of the terms of a proposition a modifying word or phrase in a manner that is consistent with the meaning of the original term or terms.

opinion. A judgment based in some measure on evidence but made with some fear that the opposite (contradictory) may be true.

opposition. The relation that exists between propositions that have the same subject and predicate terms, but which differ in their quantity or quality or in both respects.

order. The proper disposition of parts in relation to a given whole.

outline. A means of dividing a given subject matter into its logical parts.

overt multiple. A proposition that is clearly multiple in form.

parallel-word construction, fallacy of. The assumption that, because two words are similar in structure, they are therefore similar in meaning.

particular term. As used in a proposition, a term that is applied to an indeterminate part of a given class.

passion. As a category, a universal term that characterizes one substance as receiving an effect from another.

phantasm. A unified sense image, which, as a product of central (synthetic) sense, represents an object in its concrete, singular notes.

phenomenon. Etymologically, "something that appears"; a fact or datum that is observed or observable by means of sense experience or the techniques of scientific inquiry.

physical division. The reduction of any natural or artificial unit into its actual, constituent parts.

place. As a category, a universal term that characterizes a substance with respect to other surrounding bodies.

posit, to. To reassert an enunciation as it is given in its original quality.

posture. As a category, a universal term that characterizes a substance with respect to the relative disposition of its parts in space.

practical knowledge. Knowing which of its nature is ordered to some end other than the end of knowing itself.

predicable. One of the five different modes of predication; that is, one of the five possible ways of saying something about a given subject.

predicate term. In a categorical or modal proposition the term that gives information about a subject; in a syllogism, the term that appears as the predicate of the conclusion.

predicate, to. To say something either affirmatively or negatively of a subject.

prejudice. A rash judgment; that is, one that is formed prior to a consideration of the evidence.

premise. A proposition that is used in an argument or a syllogism as a means of establishing a conclusion.

principle. Anything from which something further proceeds, as "principle of knowledge."

principle of noncontradiction. A first principle that forbids one to assign contradictory predicates to one and the same subject at the same time and from the same point of view.

proper disjunctive. A disjunctive proposition that employs alternatives that are complete and mutually exclusive.

property. As a predicable, the reference that a predicate may have to some quality or attribute of the subject, which, though no part of that subject's essence, belongs to the species as such.

proposition. A statement that expresses something that is true or false.

proximate genus. In relation to a given species, the genus that is immediately determined by the (essential) difference.

quality. As a category, a universal term, that characterizes a substance by its habits, capacities, figure, or shape.

quality of a proposition. That aspect of a proposition by virtue of which it is affirmative or negative.

quantity. As a category, a universal term that characterizes a material substance with respect to the extension of its parts.

quantity of a proposition. That aspect of a proposition by virtue of which it is universal, particular, or singular.

question-begging epithet. A special instance of the fallacy of begging the question; the use of a phrase that commends its object to the listener or places it in an unfavorable light.

rationalizing. The habit of thinking up reasons in support of a judgment or a course of conduct that, independently of these reasons, has already been decided upon or accomplished.

real definition. A definition of an object as distinguished from a nominal definition, which is merely the definition of a term.

real supposition. The quality that a term or concept has in a proposition of "standing for" individual things or some real nature found in individuals.

reasoning. In its strictest sense, an act by which the intellect unites two distinct judgments and in this very act knows some new truth as causally related to the others.

reductio ad absurdum. An attempt to expose the falsity of a proposition or the invalidity of an argument by manifesting the absurdities to which its acceptance would lead.

reduplicative proposition. A multiple proposition in which a predicate is assigned to a subject in a manner that formally signifies the reason for the predication made; this is done by the use of such words as "as," "as such."

relation. As category, a universal term that characterizes one substance in the reference that it bears to another.

relative proposition. A multiple proposition in which one enunciation is subordinated to another in the order of a time relationship by the use of such words as "before," "during," "after."

remote genus. The genus that is farthest removed from the essential difference of any given species; a category.

scientific induction. A process whereby one judges that what is true of a sufficient number of singular instances of a given phenomenon is true of all without exception.

scientific knowledge. Knowedge of things through their principles and causes.

sign. Anything that points to something beyond itself.

sign, argument from. An attempt on the basis of a given phenomenon to make an immediate supposition as to its cause or effect, that is, without further examination of the supposition that is made.

simple apprehension. An act whereby the intellect knows an object without, however, either affirming or denying anything about it.

simple term. A term composed of a word which by itself signifies an object of thought.

single proposition. A proposition that contains but one logical subject and predicate.

singular term. A term that applies to only one specified object, whether that object be a person, place, thing, or event.

skeptic. One who in varying degrees and for various reasons denies the capacity of the human mind to know truth.

sophist. In the generally accepted meaning, one who habitually resorts to fallacious types of argumentation, usually with a view to the advancement of one's own ends or goals.

special case, fallacy of. The assumption that what is true of one or more specific instances of a given phenomenon is true of all without exception.

species. As a predicable, the reference that a predicate may bear to the complete essence of the subject, that is, as expressing the class to which that subject belongs.

speculative knowledge. Knowledge for its own sake, or knowledge as an end in itself.

square of opposition. A diagram used to represent the four types of opposition: namely, contrary, subcontrary, subaltern, and contradictory opposition.

subaltern opposition. The relationship that exists between a universal and a particular proposition (of the same subject and predicate) which are the same in their quality.

subcontrary opposition. The relationship that exists between two particular propositions (of the same subject and predicate) which differ in their quality.

subdivision. The employment of another division which is subordinate to one of the leading, coordinate members of the original division.

subject term. In a categorical or modal proposition the term *about which* a certain predication is made; in a syllogism the term that appears as subject of the conclusion.

sublate, to. To contradict an enunciation.

substance. The most basic of the ten categories, which, as a universal term or concept, gives information about a thing as it is in itself and not as in another.

supposition. The manner in which a given term "stands for" its object in the context of a given proposition.

syllogism. A deductive argument that is reducible to some basic logical structure.

synthetic sense. *See* central sense.

term. A word or combination of words that conventionally signifies an object of thought.

thinking. A term that refers to any type of mental activity, although in its most proper sense it refers to reasoning.

time. As a category, a universal term that characterizes a substance with respect to the order of past, present, or future events.

truth. The known conformity that exists between our judgments about things and the things themselves.

undistributed middle, fallacy of. The failure to make the middle term universal in at least one of the premises of a syllogism.

undistributed term. *See* particular term.

universal. As an adjective, with reference to concepts, a manner of so representing an essence, or nature, that the essence, or nature, in question may be applied to all the members of a given class; as a noun, the term for the very concept itself.

universal term. As used in a proposition, a term that is applied, whether affirmatively or negatively, in its complete extension, that is, to all the members of a class.

univocal use of terms. The application of a term to two or more objects in a manner that is the same in meaning for both.

valid. A term used to designate the correctness of an act of reasoning with respect to the manner in which the conclusion logically follows from the premises.

verbal distinction, fallacy of. An attempt to establish a real difference or distinction on the basis of mere verbal dissimilarity.

wishful thinking. A kind of thinking that is determined, not by evidence, but by one's personal inclinations, feelings, emotions, or desires.

subject. [illegible] immediately [illegible]

synthetic sense. See second sense.

Index

Chpt. 13

Test. Wed

233766

W.S.C. - receipt #